MAD ABOUT
TRUMP

A BRILLIANT LOOK AT OUR BRAINLESS PRESIDENT

BY
"THE USUAL GANG OF IDIOTS"

MAD
BOOKS

CONTENTS

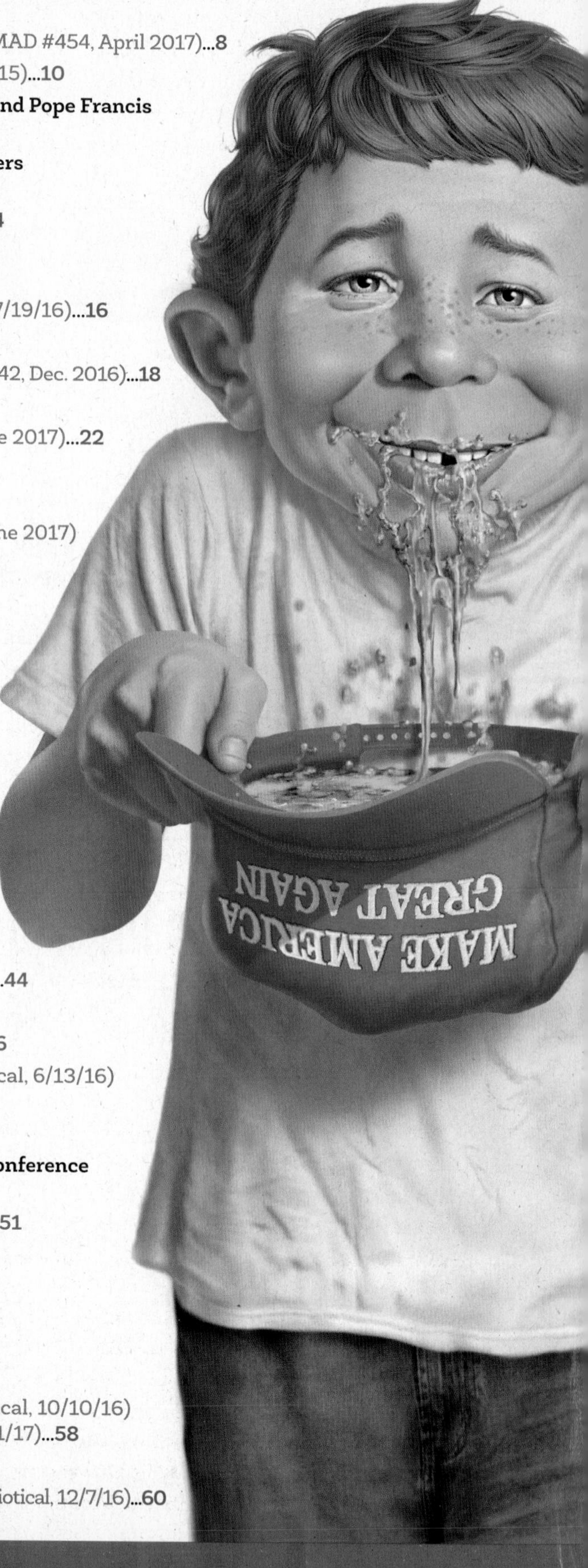

MAKE AMERICA
GREAT AGAIN

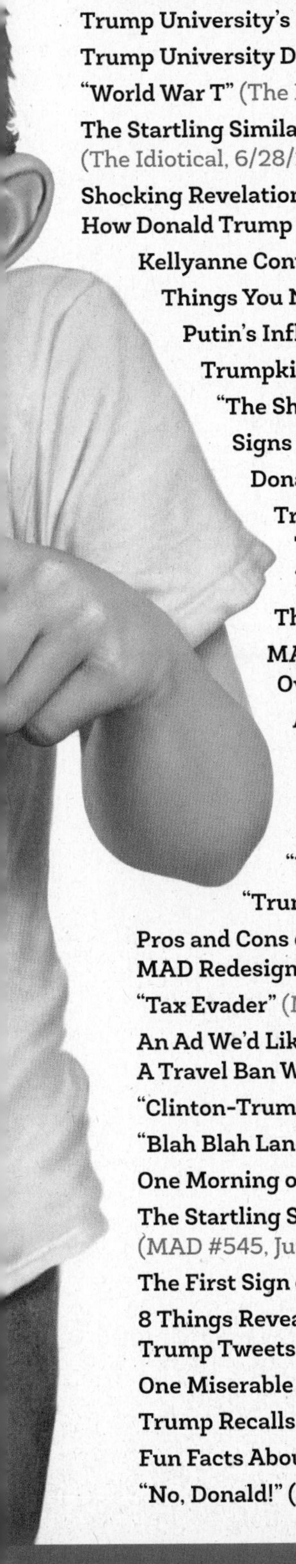

ARTIST:
MARK FREDRICKSON

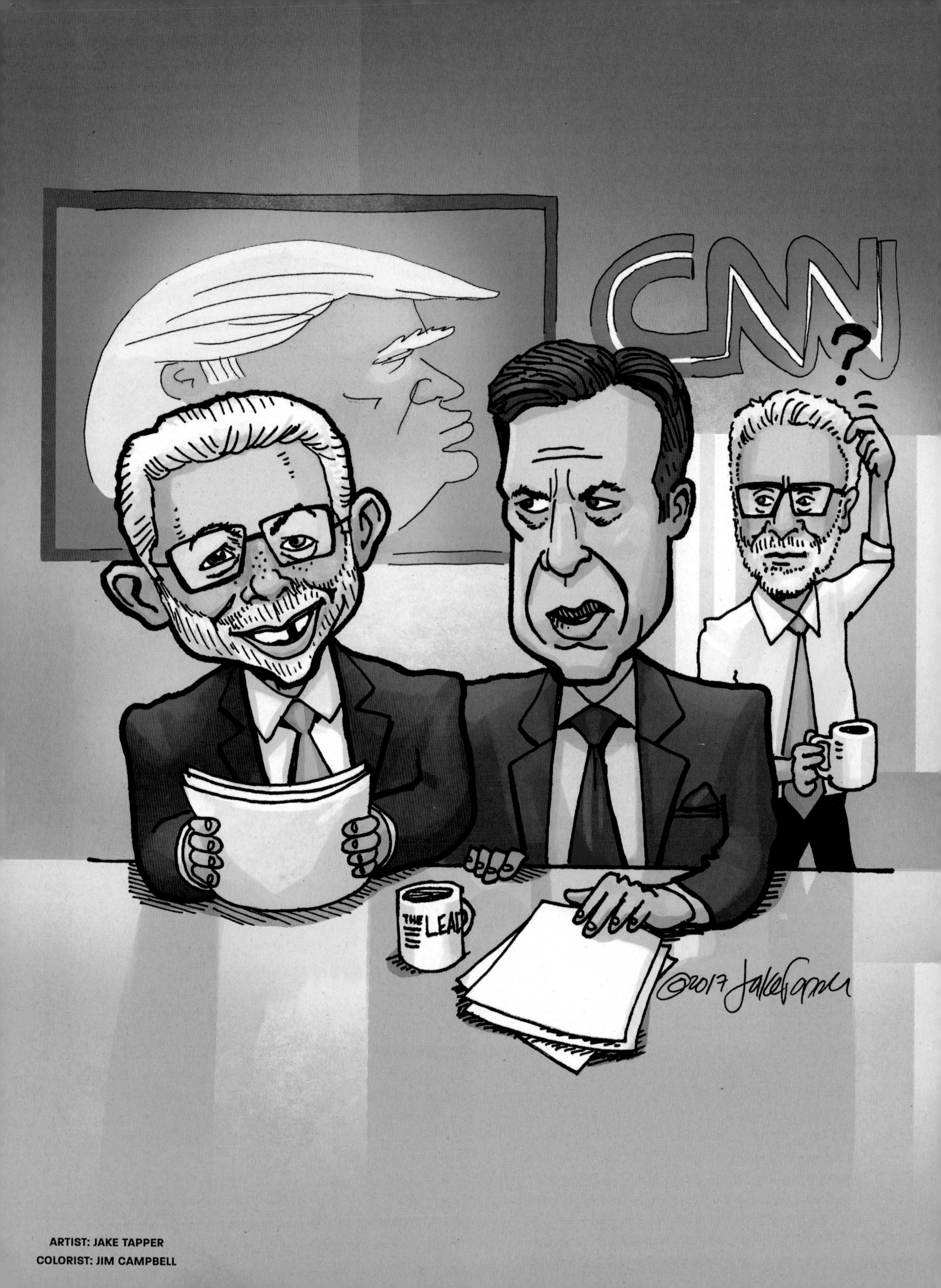
CNN
?
THE LEAD
©2017 JakeTapper

ARTIST: JAKE TAPPER
COLORIST: JIM CAMPBELL

FOREWORD BY
JAKE TAPPER

To whom it may concern:

The December 1976 issue of MAD magazine, with the Fonz on the cover, sprung out from the newsstand and enthralled a seven-year-old Jacob Tapper. A seduction of the innocent, as it were.

From that date through my adulthood, MAD magazine has been poisoning my mind with its rudeness, disrespect and unadulterated nonsense.

Throughout my childhood, I collected back issues (purchased at Fat Jack's Comics in Philly) and a library's worth of paperbacks — anachronistic material cynically re-packaged and inserted on supermarket shelves for gullible young children to sneak into the grocery cart. Not entirely unlike the volume you hold in your hands right now.

It is a sickness.

How am I supposed to explain to my classy and brilliant wife that one of my prized possessions is Mort Drucker's original art from issue #276, of President Reagan and Senator Gary Hart? What am I supposed to tell her about why I had it framed? Where on earth would you propose I hang it in my otherwise adult-themed house?

How do I explain the thrill when my friend Stephen Colbert emailed to tell me that Ward Sutton had caricatured me in issue #540, except to say that I mention it here so you now know that Stephen Colbert is my friend?

Since 1952, MAD has been corrupting the minds of impressionable youth with outrageous and often mean-spirited, puerile and occasionally libelous "satire."

I agreed to write this essay honoring this book not because I think it remotely appropriate that the commie offspring of MAD's forefathers are devoting an entire book to disrespecting the commander-in-chief — exploiting the fascination the public has with him while also trying to make a cheap buck from it (which honestly should only be allowed by cable news).

I write this not to celebrate that somehow you have all escaped committal to a hospital of the criminally unfunny.

No, I do it because I revere the First Amendment, and I recognize that it cloaks not only the important and worthwhile journalism I share with the world on a daily basis, but the likes of you as well. And the more you are permitted to be deranged, the more Stephen Bannon will focus on you and not me.

Hoping for the best and expecting the worst,

Jake

Dedicated to Hillary Clinton,
without whom this book would not be possible.

He was a moron
with a stupid haircut.
But he had a knack
for making
millions.

Forrest Trump

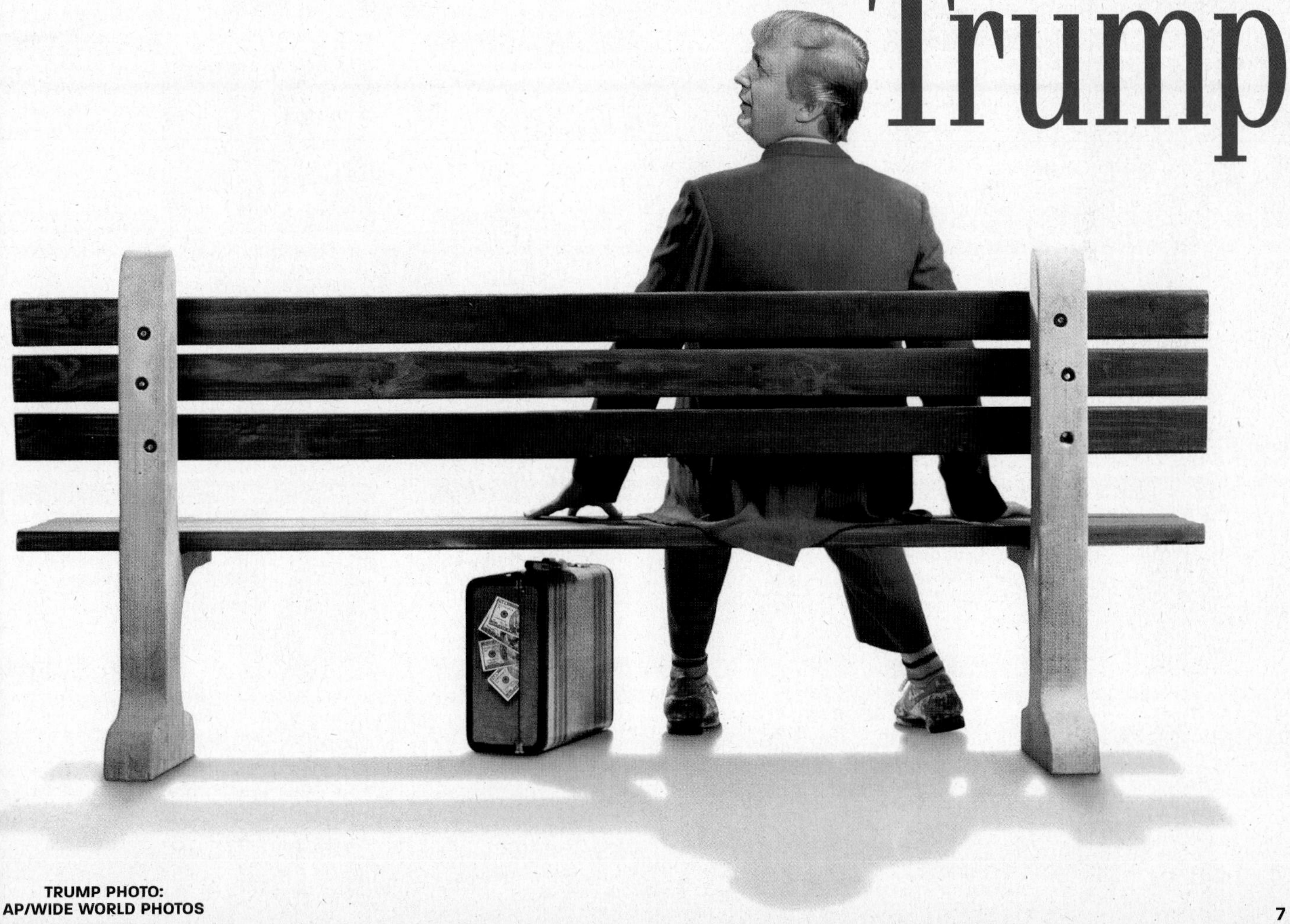

TRUMP PHOTO:
AP/WIDE WORLD PHOTOS

ASSAIL TO THE CHIEF DEPT.

Whether you love or hate Donald Trump, you have to admit one thing about him: he is the President! Seriously, you have to admit it — it's not healthy to keep living in denial! Once you've made peace with that (we'll wait), you can see how he compares to everyone else who's done the job!

HOW DONALD AGAINST THE OTHER 43 U.S

WRITER: JEFF KRUSE TRUMP PHOTOS: DREAMSTIME.COM

JOHN ADAMS

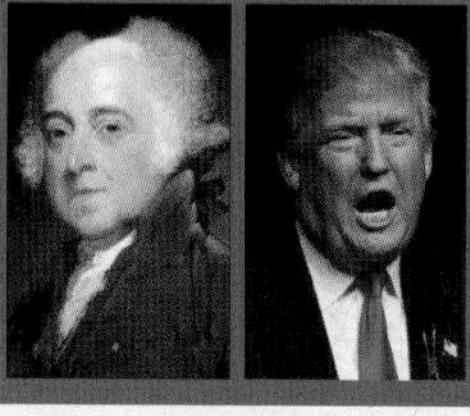

John Adams had his policies criticized by Alexander Hamilton. Trump had his Vice President criticized by the cast of *Hamilton*.

EDGE: **ADAMS**

THOMAS JEFFERSON

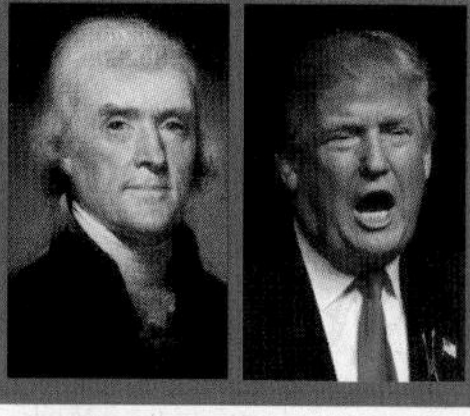

Thomas Jefferson founded the University of Virginia. Trump founded a website with the word "University" in it.

EDGE: **JEFFERSON**

JAMES MADISON

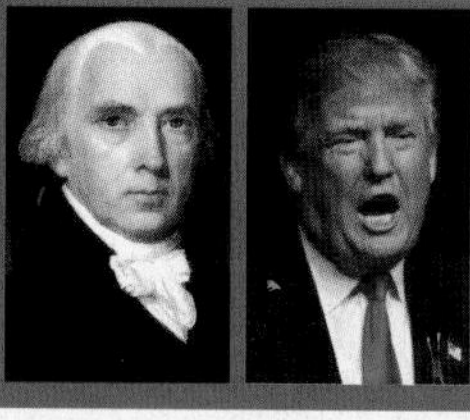

James Madison is "The Father of the Constitution."
Trump is the father of a woman he'd date if sh weren't his daughter.

EDGE: **MADISON**

MARTIN VAN BUREN

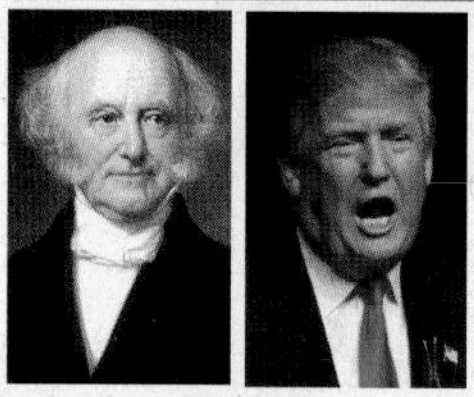

Martin Van Buren was blamed for the depression of 1837. Trump was blamed for the depression of half the country, plus another three million voters

EDGE: **VAN BUREN**

WILLIAM HENRY HARRISON

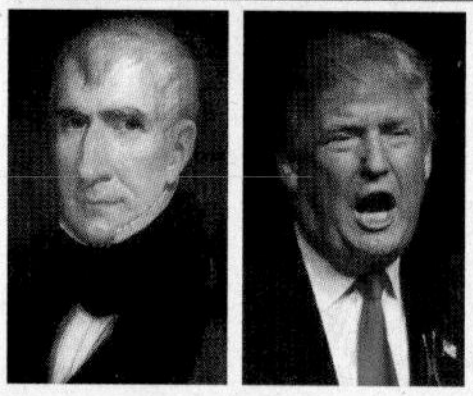

William Henry Harrison was President for just one month before he bit the dust. Trump was president-elect for just one week before many of his campaign promises bit the dust.

EDGE: **HARRISON**

JOHN TYLER

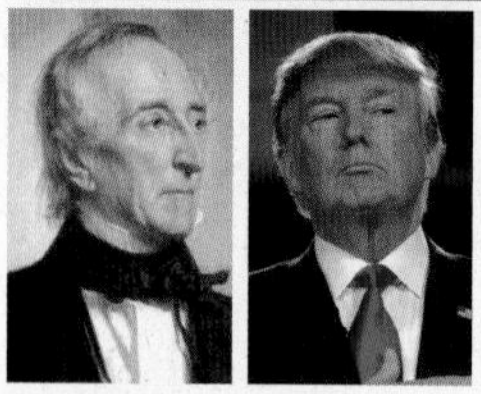

John Tyler owned many slaves. Trump didn't o any slaves, but he nev paid many of the peop who did work for him.

EDGE: **NEITHER**

FRANKLIN PIERCE

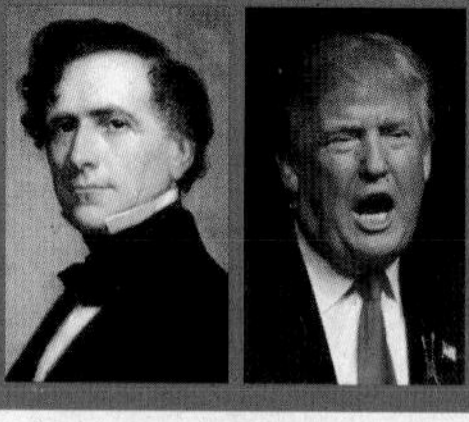

Franklin Pierce is usually ranked by historians as being amongst the worst U.S. Presidents. Trump won't be receiving that critique for at least another few weeks.

EDGE: **PIERCE**

JAMES BUCHANAN

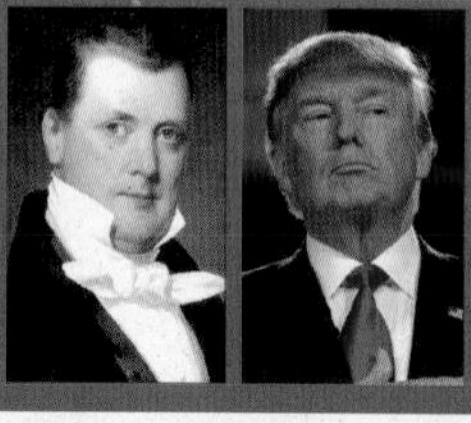

James Buchanan wrote the very first Presidential memoir, though it was not a big seller. *The Art of the Deal* was a huge seller, though Trump didn't actually write it.

EDGE: **EVEN**

ABRAHAM LINCOLN

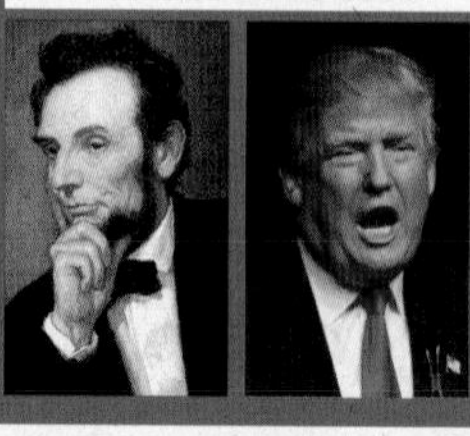

Abraham Lincoln belie in "malice toward none with charity for all." Trump...well, let's just he doesn't.

EDGE: **LINCOLN**

JAMES A. GARFIELD

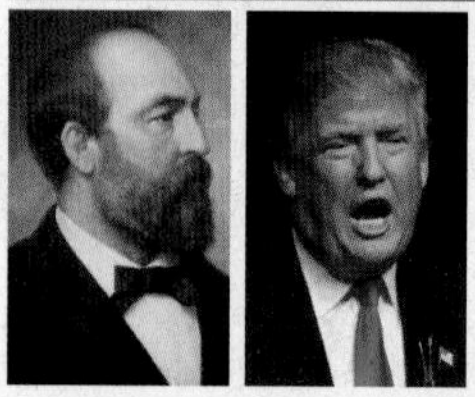

James A. Garfield managed a number of achievements despite being in office for just 200 days. Trump managed to piss off China, alienate the CIA and ally himself with Russia before even taking office.

EDGE: **GARFIELD**

CHESTER A. ARTHUR

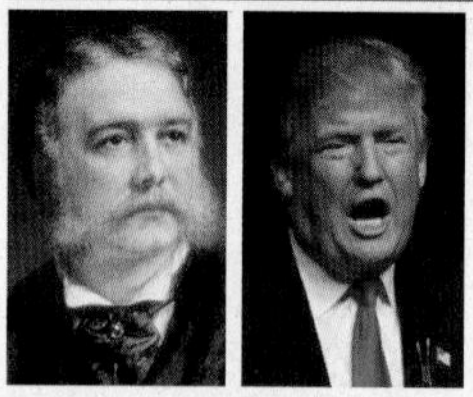

Chester A. Arthur changed suits several times a day. Trump seems to be settling suits every day.

EDGE: **ARTHUR**

GROVER CLEVELAND

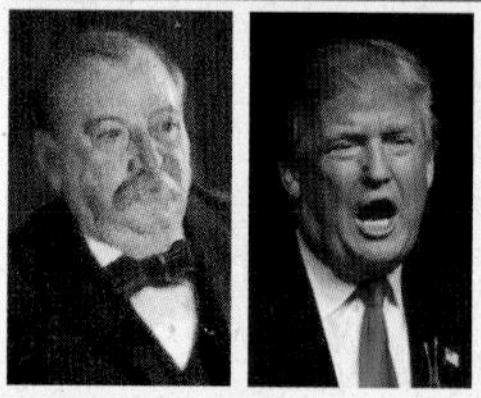

Grover Cleveland serve two non-consecutive terms as President. Tru will take a couple of ye off between seasons o hosting *The Celebrity Apprentice*.

EDGE: **CLEVELAND**

WILLIAM HOWARD TAFT

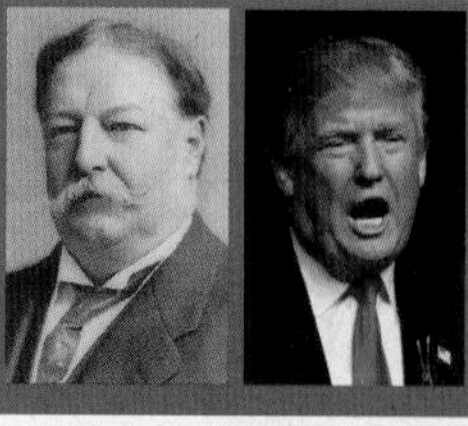

William Howard Taft was known for his massive girth. Donald Trump is known for his tiny hands.

EDGE: **TAFT**

WOODROW WILSON

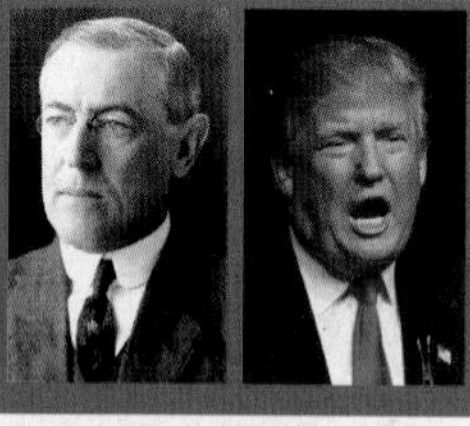

Woodrow Wilson negotiated a treaty with Germany that ended World War I. Donald Trump negotiated God-knows-what with Russia to end Hillary Clinton's political career.

EDGE: **WILSON** (ONLY SLIGHTLY)

WARREN HARDING

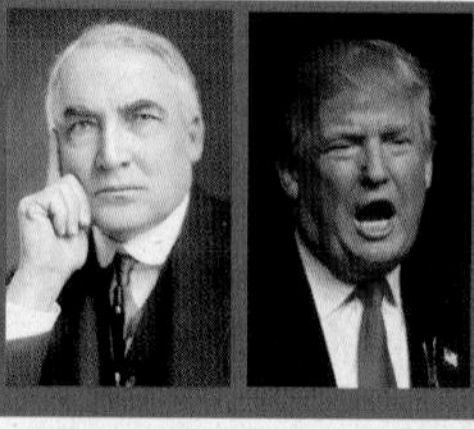

Warren G. Harding diec a cerebral hemorrhage Many have wondered i Trump suffers from bra damage.

EDGE: **HARDING**

HARRY TRUMAN

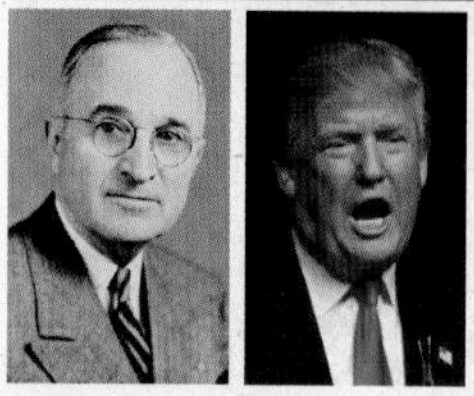

Harry S. Truman's middle initial didn't stand for anything. Other than a handful of pet issues, Trump doesn't stand for anything.

EDGE: **TRUMAN**

DWIGHT EISENHOWER

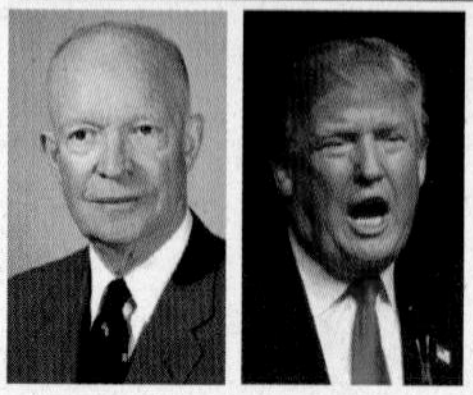

Dwight D. Eisenhower led attacks in North Africa and Europe. Trump leveled attacks at a P.O.W. and a Gold Star Family.

EDGE: **EISENHOWER**

JOHN F. KENNEDY

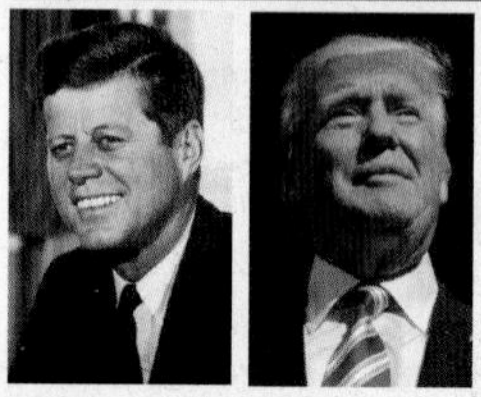

John F. Kennedy had a beautiful and glamoro wife. Trump has had th times that many.

EDGE: **TRUMP**

JIMMY CARTER

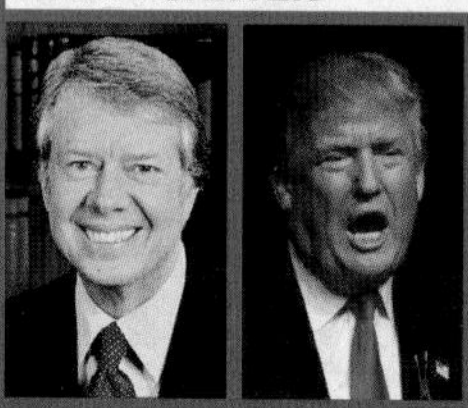

Jimmy Carter won a Nobel Peace Prize. Trump is still bent out of shape that *The Apprentice* didn't win an Emmy.

EDGE: **CARTER**

RONALD REAGAN

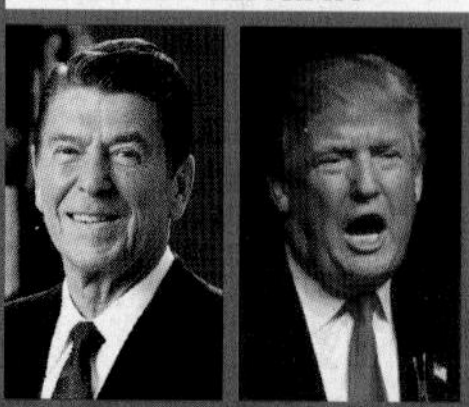

Ronald Reagan struck a blow for freedom when he declared, "Mr. Gorbachev, tear down this wall!" Trump struck a blow for xenophobia when he declared, "I will build a wall!"

EDGE: **REAGAN**

GEORGE H.W. BUSH

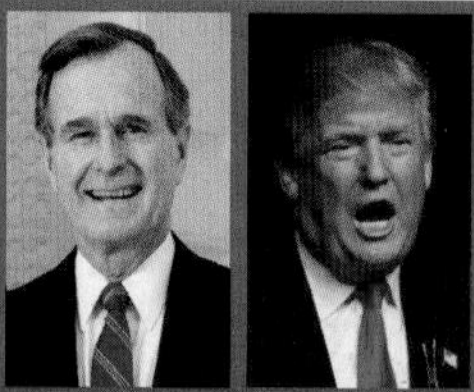

George H.W. Bush had fighter jet shot down in World War II. Trump wo probably prefer that gi right about now.

EDGE: **BUSH**

TRUMP STACKS UP PRESIDENTS

GEORGE WASHINGTON

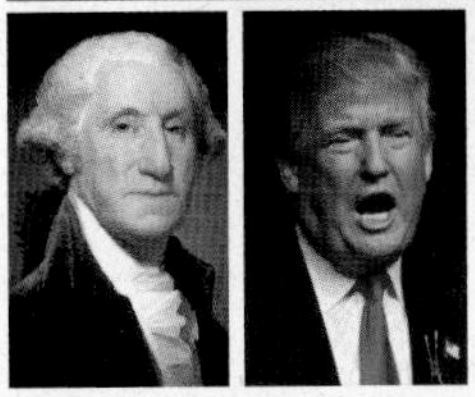

George Washington was a U.S. Army general. Trump owned the USFL's New Jersey Generals.

EDGE: WASHINGTON

JAMES MONROE

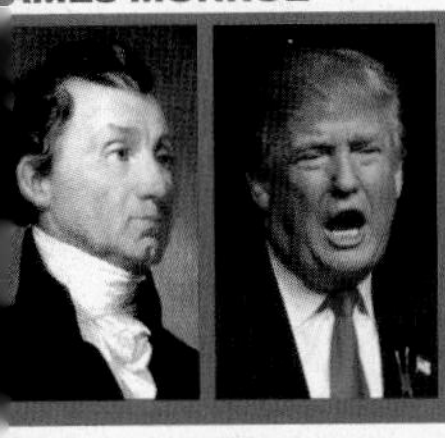

James Monroe presided over "The Era of Good Feelings." We're not sure what the Trump years will be nicknamed, but we'd bet anything it won't contain the word "good."

EDGE: MONROE

JOHN QUINCY ADAMS

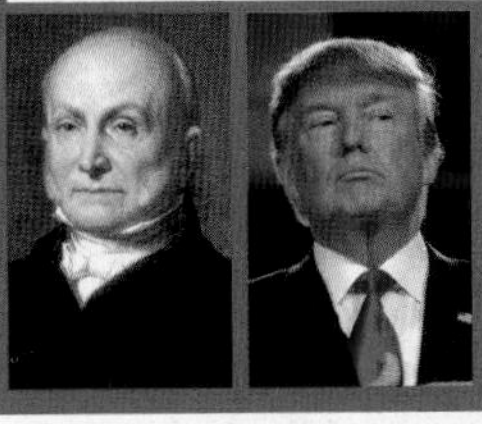

John Quincy Adams inherited a wealth of political knowledge from his father. Trump inherited wealth from his father.

EDGE: ROUGHLY EVEN

ANDREW JACKSON

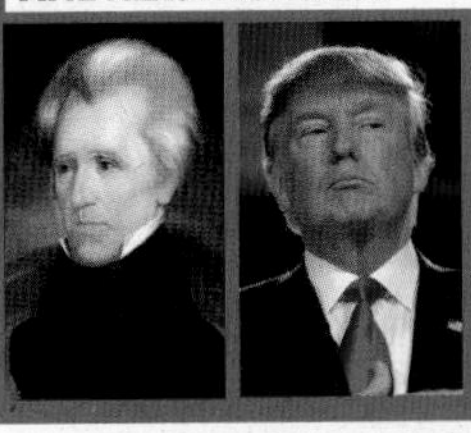

Andrew Jackson evicted more than 15,000 Cherokees from the Southeast. Trump evicted people of all races from his apartment complexes.

EDGE: NEITHER

JAMES POLK

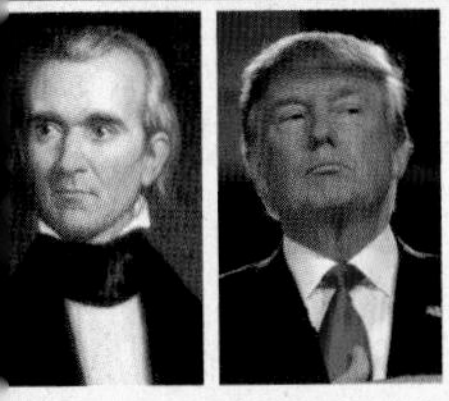

The Mexican-American War broke out during the James Polk years. Trump declared war on Mexico years before he ever became President.

EDGE: EVEN

ZACHARY TAYLOR

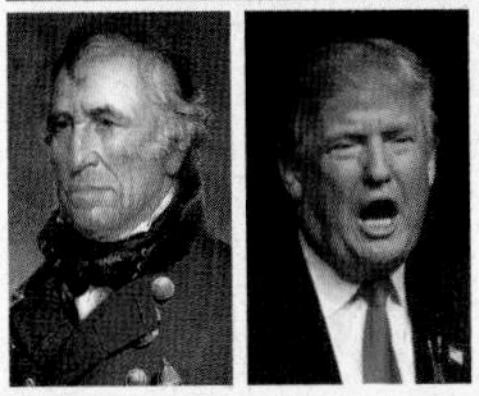

Zachary Taylor fought in four wars in three different decades. Trump fights that many Twitter wars in three days.

EDGE: TAYLOR

MILLARD FILLMORE

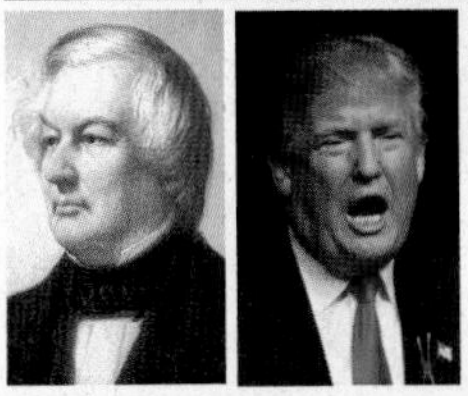

Millard Fillmore had no Vice President. Trump has Mike Pence.

EDGE: FILLMORE

ANDREW JOHNSON

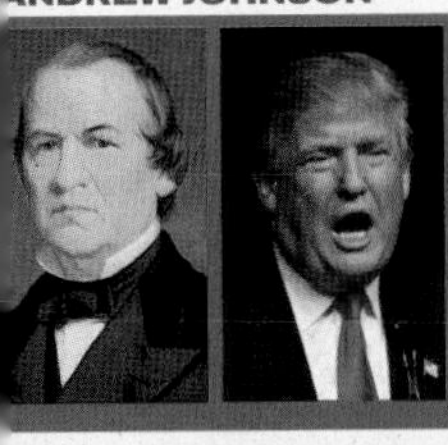

Andrew Johnson rose to the Presidency despite being born into poverty. Trump rose to the Presidency despite being morally bankrupt.

EDGE: JOHNSON

ULYSSES S. GRANT

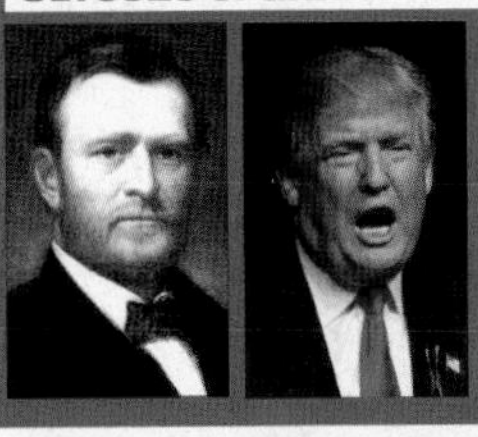

Ulysses S. Grant's tomb is the largest mausoleum in North America. Trump's ego is the largest in North America.

EDGE: GRANT

RUTHERFORD B. HAYES

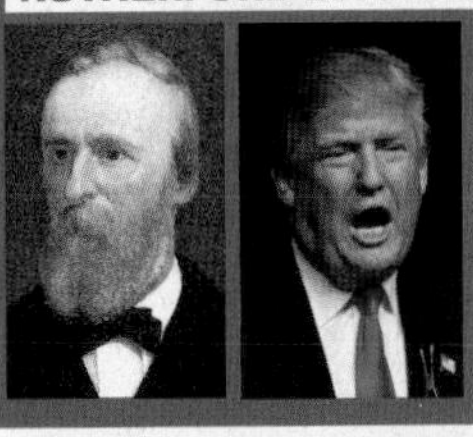

Rutherford B. Hayes thought it was essential to maintain the gold standard. For Trump, it's standard to cover everything he owns in gold.

EDGE: HAYES

BENJAMIN HARRISON

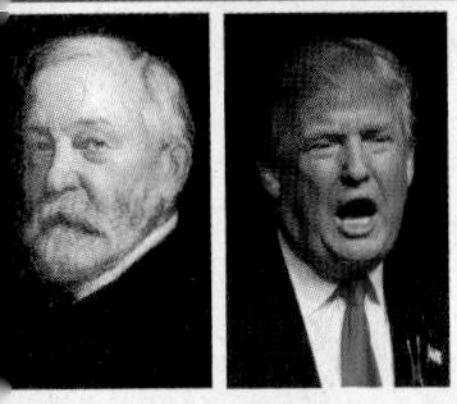

Benjamin Harrison was the last President to sport a full beard. Trump is the first President to sport a peach-tinted swoop-over.

EDGE: HARRISON

WILLIAM McKINLEY

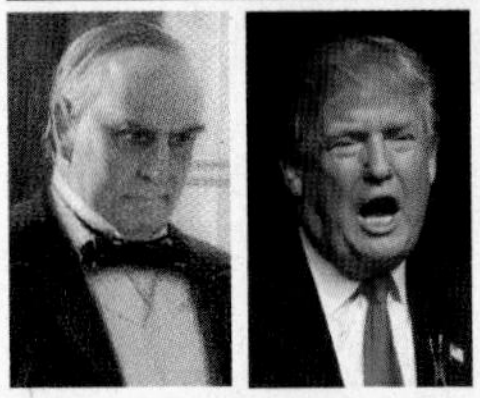

William McKinley was the last President to have served in the American Civil War. Trump may be the first President to serve during America's second Civil War.

EDGE: McKINLEY

THEODORE ROOSEVELT

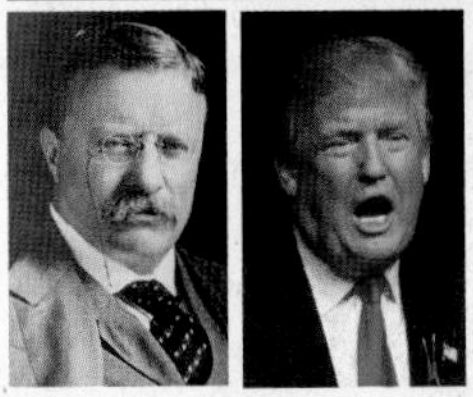

Theodore Roosevelt was a Rough Rider. Under Trump, the next four years are going to be a rough ride.

EDGE: ROOSEVELT

CALVIN COOLIDGE

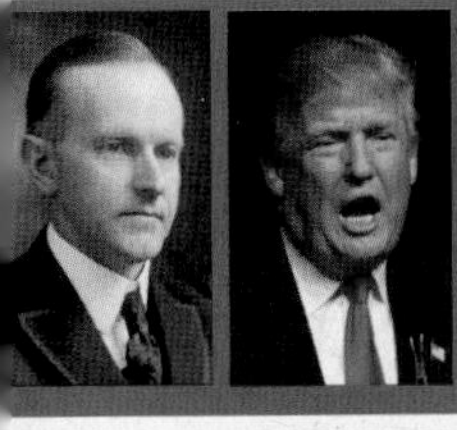

Calvin Coolidge was known for saying very little, though he was an articulate speaker. Trump is known for saying very little, though he almost never shuts up.

EDGE: COOLIDGE

HERBERT HOOVER

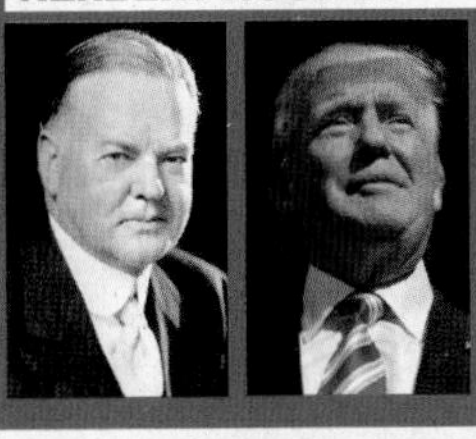

Many historians rank Herbert Hoover as the worst U.S. President ever. Trump ranks himself as the best U.S. President ever.

EDGE: TRUMP

FRANKLIN DELANO ROOSEVELT

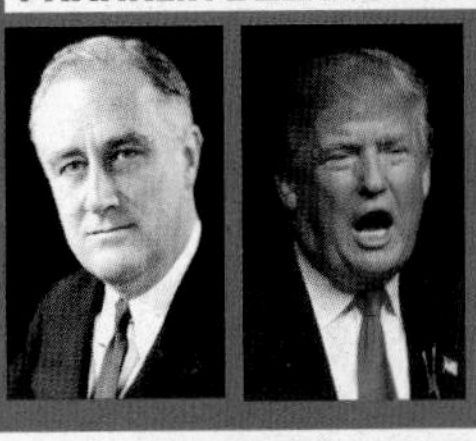

Franklin Roosevelt was famous for his fireside chats. Trump is famous for the phrase "You're fired!"

EDGE: ROOSEVELT

LYNDON B. JOHNSON

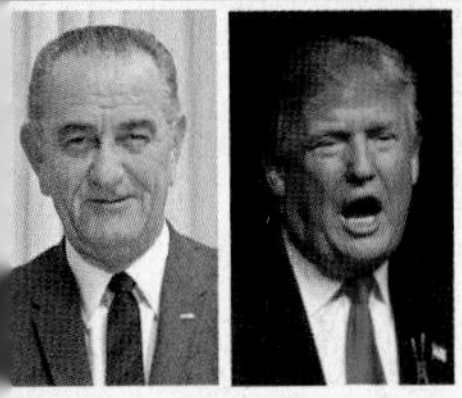

Lyndon B. Johnson had a space center named after him. Trump would never wait for someone to name something after him.

EDGE: JOHNSON

RICHARD NIXON

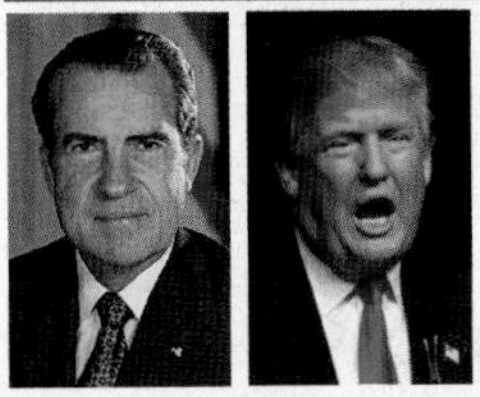

Richard Nixon famously said, "I am not a crook!" Trump has made no such denial.

EDGE: NIXON

GERALD FORD

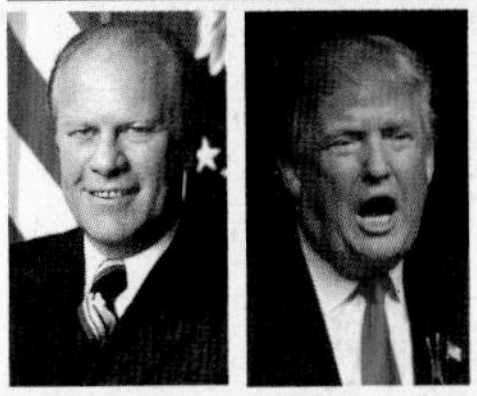

Gerald Ford pardoned Richard Nixon. Trump forgot all his promises to lock up "Crooked Hillary."

EDGE: FORD

BILL CLINTON

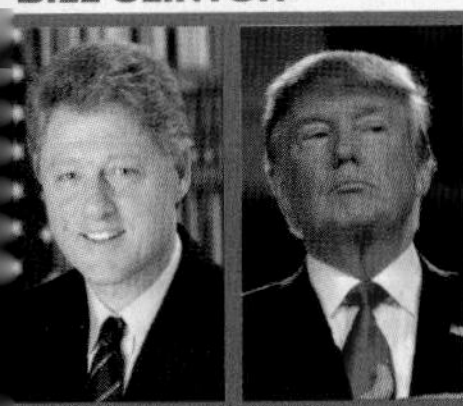

Despite allegations that he treated women horribly, Bill Clinton still got elected...no, wait, we're thinking of Trump... hold on, we were right the first time...wait, wait...

EDGE: NEITHER

GEORGE W. BUSH

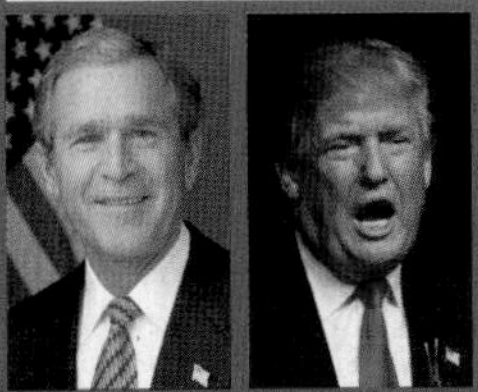

George W. Bush went to war in Iraq based on faulty intelligence. Donald Trump stakes out most of his positions based on faulty intelligence.

EDGE: BUSH

BARACK OBAMA

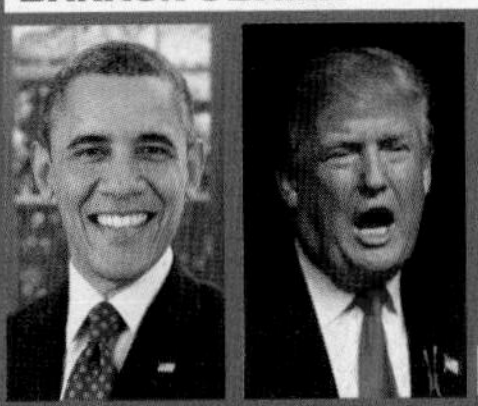

Barack Obama is credited with killing Osama Bin Laden. Trump is credited with killing American democracy.

EDGE: OBAMA

TONIGHT!

"THE BLOOD FEUD"

TALE OF THE TAPE

DONALD "KID LOUDMOUTH" TRUMP VS MEGYN "FOXY LADY" KELLY

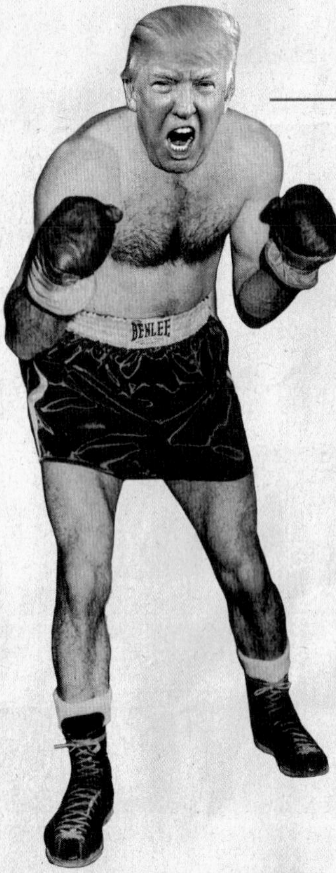

DONALD TRUMP June 14, 1946 Queens, NY		MEGYN KELLY November 18, 1970 Syracuse, NY
LOW BLOW	**SIGNATURE ATTACK**	GOTCHA QUESTION
CAN'T TAKE A PUNCH	**WEAKNESS**	EYE BLEEDING (APPARENTLY)
HIMSELF	**UNSCRUPULOUS PROMOTER**	HERSELF
FIVE	**HOURS SPENT ON HAIR, DAILY**	THREE
NO	**IS SEEN AS A SERIOUS POLITICAL THINKER**	NO
YES	**SOURCE OF RIGHT-WINGERS' FANTASIES**	YES
YES	**HAS MEAT LOAF IN HIS/HER CORNER**	NO

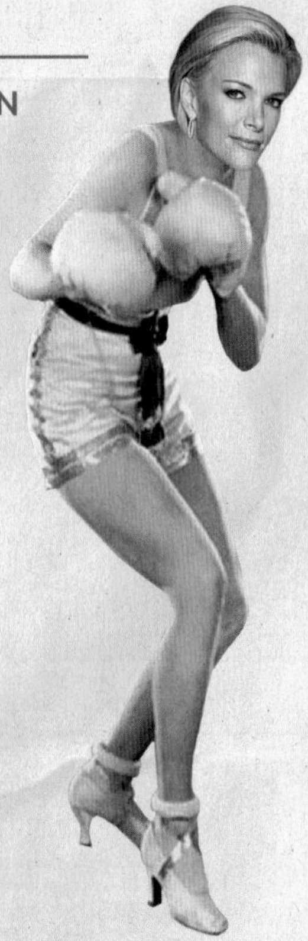

The Startling Similarities and Differences Between

DONALD TRUMP
and
POPE FRANCIS

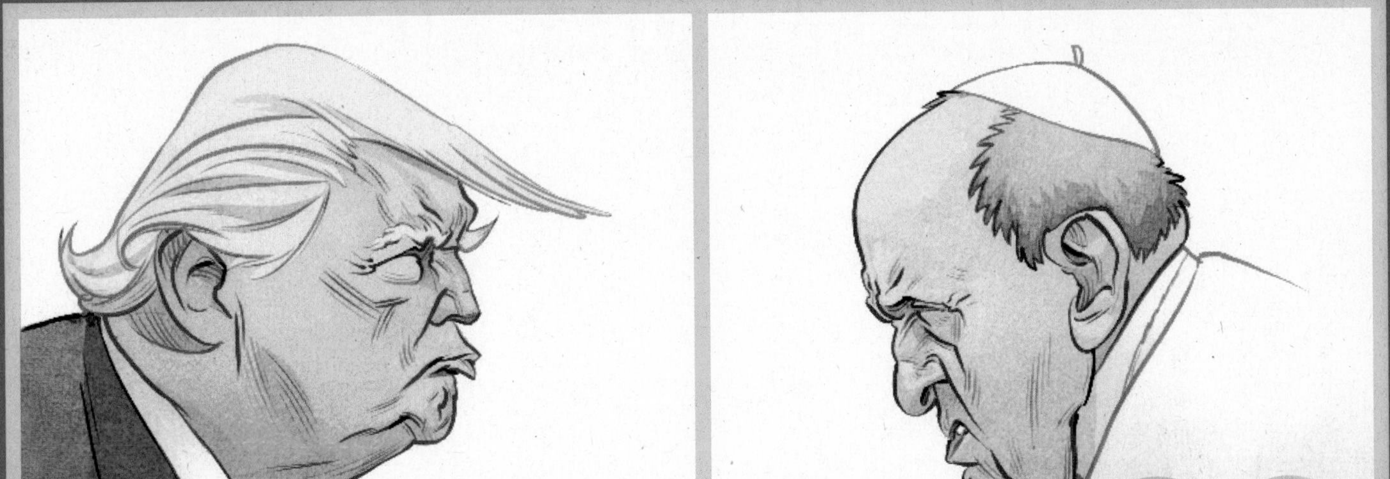

	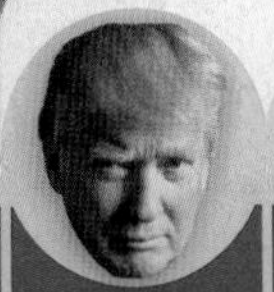	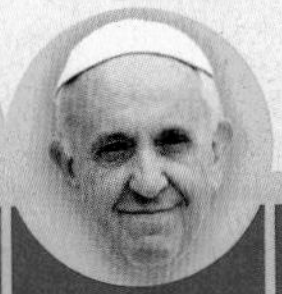
Lives an opulent lifestyle full of gold and private jets	✓	✓
Says a person who builds walls "isn't Christian"	—	✓
Lives in Vatican City, which is completely surrounded by walls	—	✓
Is a big fan of "Two Corinthians"	✓	✓
Wears about a foot of synthetic material atop his head	✓	✓
Is not accepting contributions from outsiders	✓	—
Leads an army of gullible believers	✓	✓

CHART FAILURE DEPT.

The 2016 election featured a mind-numbing stream of polls – and we're not talking about the ten-foot ones you wouldn't use to touch either historically unpopular candidate. Still, the question must be asked: who exactly voted for these morons? To combat the mainstream media's unenlightening analysis, we at MAD have put our middle school-level statistics skills to the test in order to provide…

MAD's Break

Donald Trump's Voters

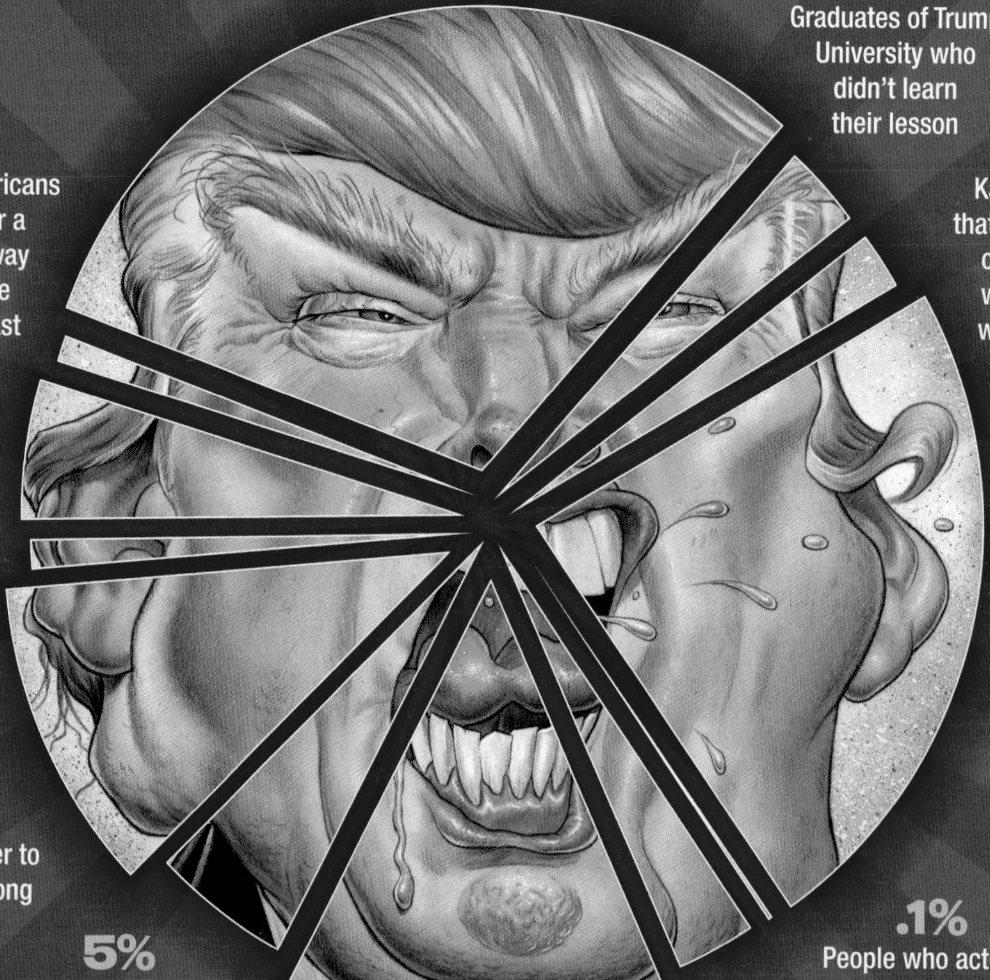
31%
Conservatives intent on voting against their own interests
3%
Graduates of Trump University who didn't learn their lesson
2%
Kansans hopeful that Trump's climate change denials will leave them with beachfront property
23.9%
The "poorly educated"
.1%
People who actually like Donald Trump
3%
Pervert fathers who also fantasize about "dating" their daughters
14%
Comb-over enthusiasts
5%
New Yorkers who just want Trump to get the hell out of town
11%
Evangelicals waiting for end-of-world prophecies, eager to nudge things along
1%
Orange-Americans
5%
Unemployed wall builders
1%
Muslim-Americans looking for a free one-way trip to the Middle East

down of
Hillary Clinton's Voters

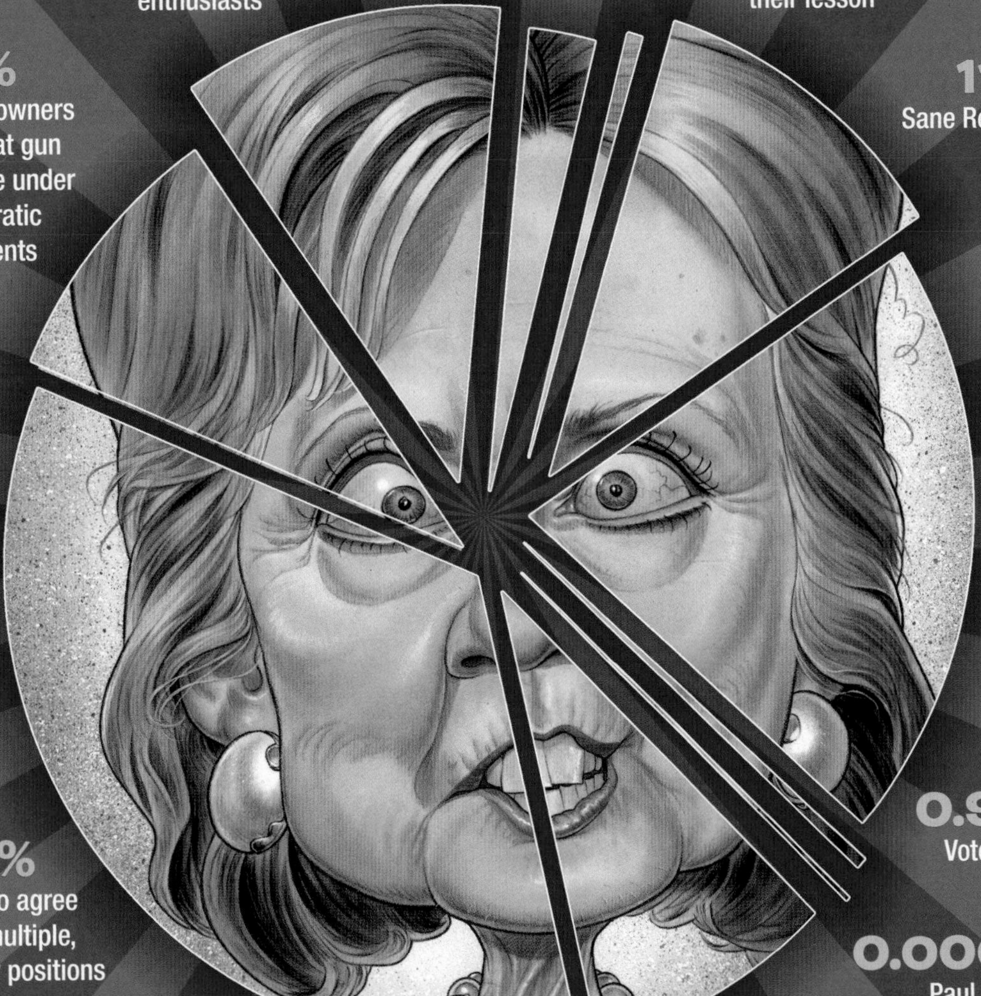

11%
Pantsuit enthusiasts
2.5%
Bored housewives who do whatever Oprahs tells them to
.5%
Graduates of Trump University who learned their lesson
9%
Gun store owners aware that gun sales spike under Democratic Presidents
11%
Sane Republicans
21%
Liberals intent on voting against their own interests
35%
People who agree with her multiple, contradictory positions on the issues
0.99999%
Voters who actually like Hillary
0.00001%
Paul Ryan
9%
Citizens who rate "Untrustworthiness" as the quality they most look for in a President

WRITER: STAN SINBERG ARTIST: SAM SISCO

Trump Criticizes Other AMERICAN HEROES

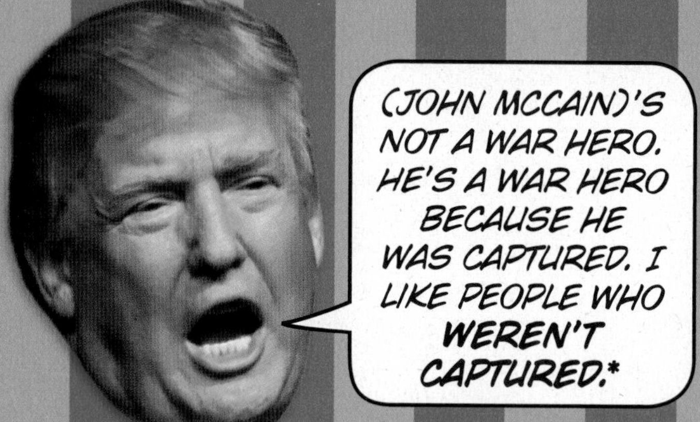
(JOHN MCCAIN)'S NOT A WAR HERO. HE'S A WAR HERO BECAUSE HE WAS CAPTURED. I LIKE PEOPLE WHO **WEREN'T CAPTURED.***

*actual quote from July 18, 2015

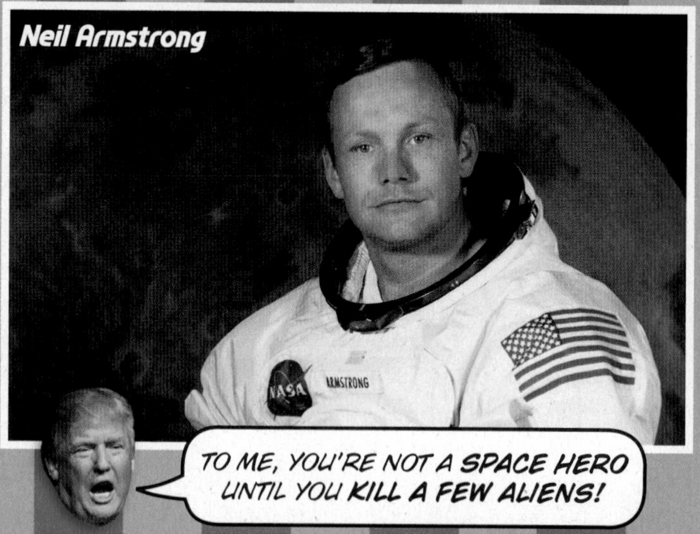
ARMSTRONG
TO ME, YOU'RE NOT A **SPACE HERO** UNTIL YOU **KILL A FEW ALIENS!**
Neil Armstrong

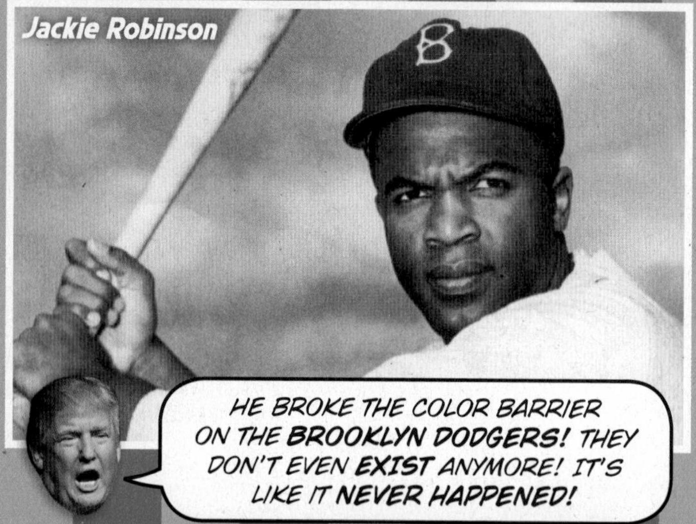
HE BROKE THE COLOR BARRIER ON THE **BROOKLYN DODGERS!** THEY DON'T EVEN **EXIST** ANYMORE! IT'S LIKE IT **NEVER HAPPENED!**
Jackie Robinson

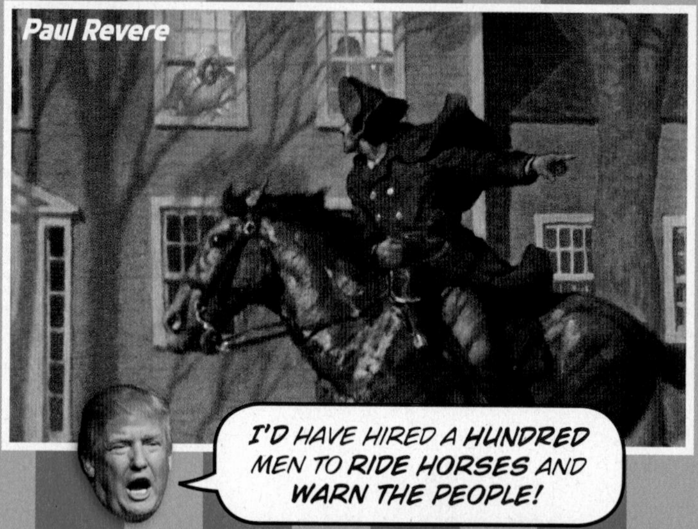
I'D HAVE HIRED A **HUNDRED** MEN TO **RIDE HORSES** AND **WARN THE PEOPLE!**
Paul Revere

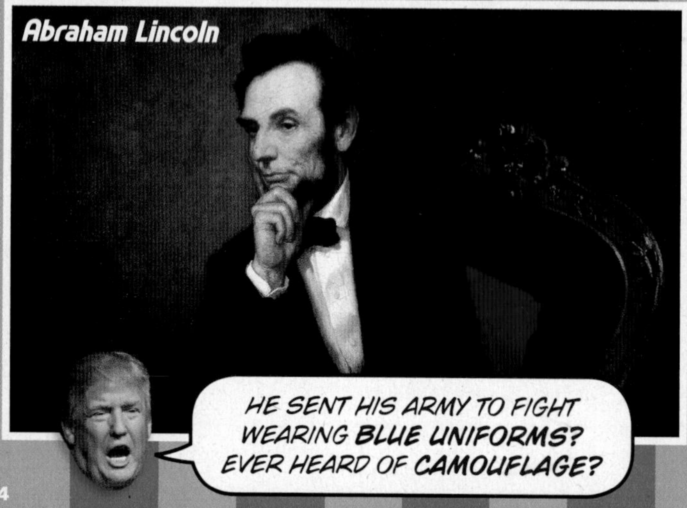
HE SENT HIS ARMY TO FIGHT WEARING **BLUE UNIFORMS?** EVER HEARD OF **CAMOUFLAGE?**
Abraham Lincoln

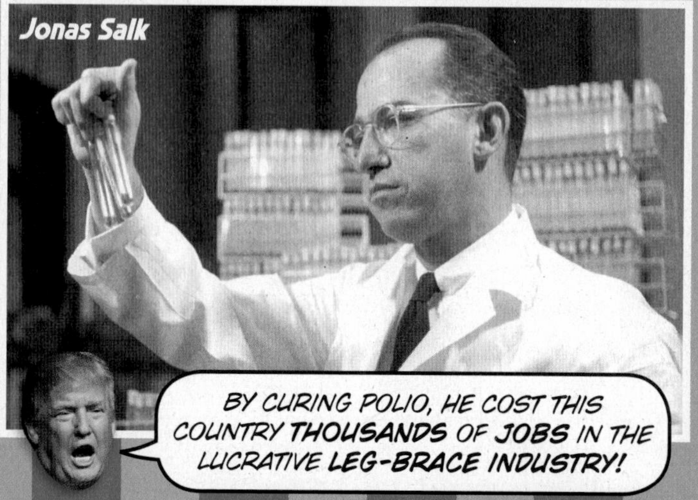
BY CURING POLIO, HE COST THIS COUNTRY **THOUSANDS** OF **JOBS** IN THE LUCRATIVE **LEG-BRACE INDUSTRY!**
Jonas Salk

Donald Trump was an obnoxiously rich reality-TV jackass until he became...

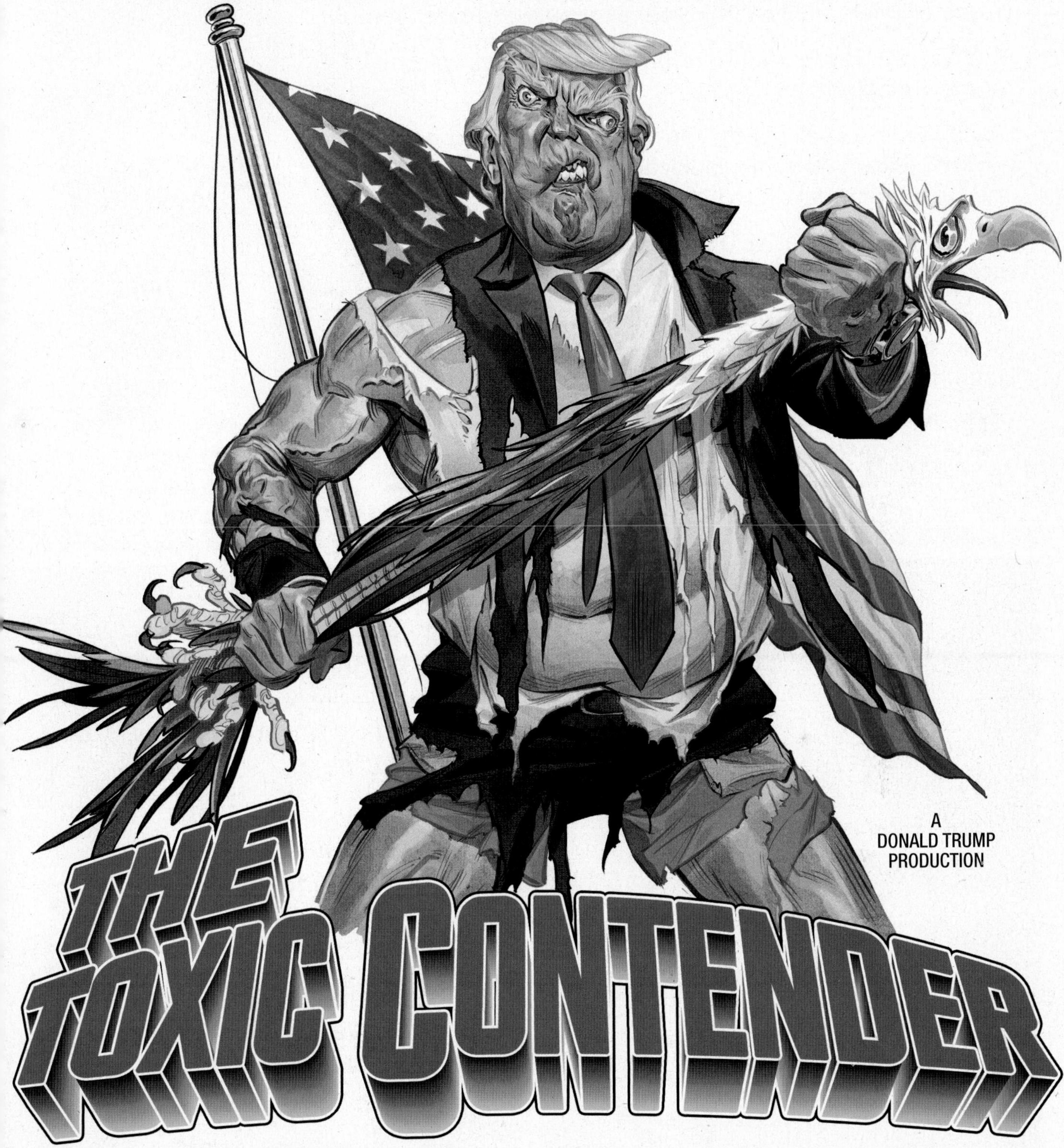
A
DONALD TRUMP
PRODUCTION
THE TOXIC CONTENDER

THE UNCHECKED EGO OF A SOCIOPATH IN ASSOCIATION WITH A DECADE OF THE GOP PANDERING TO ITS WORST FACTIONS PRESENTS THE TOXIC CONTENDER

STARRING MISOGYNY, XENOPHOBIA, RACISM AND FEAR-MONGERING AS "THE HORRIFYING PERSONALITY DISORDER"

CO-STARRING UNINFORMED, INFLAMMATORY RHETORIC AS "THE PLATFORM"

WITH SPECIAL APPEARANCES BY LOW-BLOW INSULTS, DISABLED MOCKERY AND SEXUAL DEVIANCE

AND INTRODUCING MAKE AMERICA GREAT AGAIN AS "THE EMPTY SLOGAN"

REPULSIVE
R
TO ANYONE WHO'S NOT A DISGRUNTLED CAUCASIAN

PLANNED PROVISIONS OF TRUMPCARE

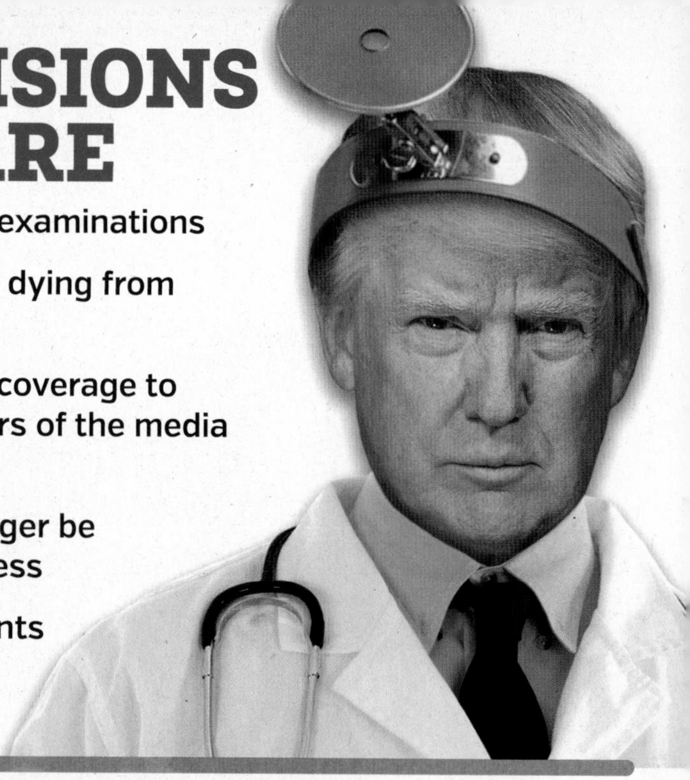

- Trump will personally administer all breast examinations
- Doctors will be required to refer to patients dying from terminal diseases as "losers"
- Health insurers will not be allowed to deny coverage to anyone, except Muslims, Mexicans, members of the media and Hillary Clinton
- Narcissistic-sociopathic disorder will no longer be recognized as an incapacitating mental illness
- There will be higher Medicare reimbursements for doctors who have Fox News on their waiting room TVs

WRITER: EVAN WAITE

MELANIA TRUMP DENIES PLAGIARIZING MICHELLE OBAMA

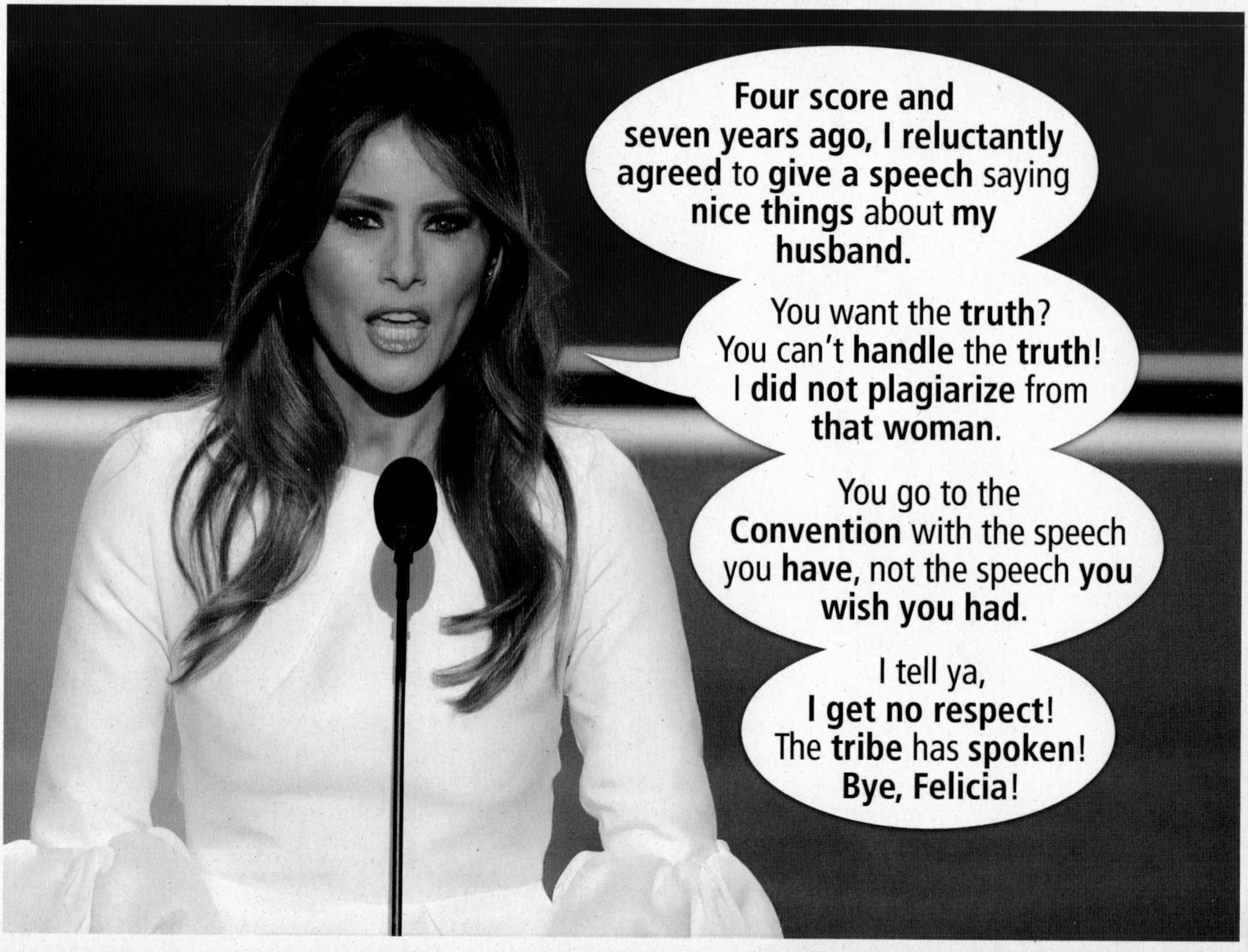
Four score and seven years ago, I reluctantly agreed to give a speech saying nice things about my husband.
You want the truth? You can't handle the truth! I did not plagiarize from that woman.
You go to the Convention with the speech you have, not the speech you wish you had.
I tell ya, I get no respect! The tribe has spoken! Bye, Felicia!

TRUMP SAYS OBAMA NOT AMERICAN THE BORN IDENTITY

Some would say that Donald Trump is a narcissistic clown, an empty suit, a shameless self-promoter, a moronic braggart, a miserable bastard with bad hair, a pompous media-whore of a man. And they'd be right! But one term no one would ever use to describe him is "credible Presidential candidate." Yet for a few fleeting weeks in 2011, The Donald talked about running for President and the gullible media played along. His campaign strategy was simple: hitch his political bandwagon onto the right-wing wacko movement that was convinced Barack Obama was born in Kenya. Trump got plenty of media coverage as he boasted it was "unbelievable" what his investigators had turned up about the President. But when the White House released President Obama's birth certificate, The Donald's run for the Presidency came to an abrupt halt. Just like this intro.

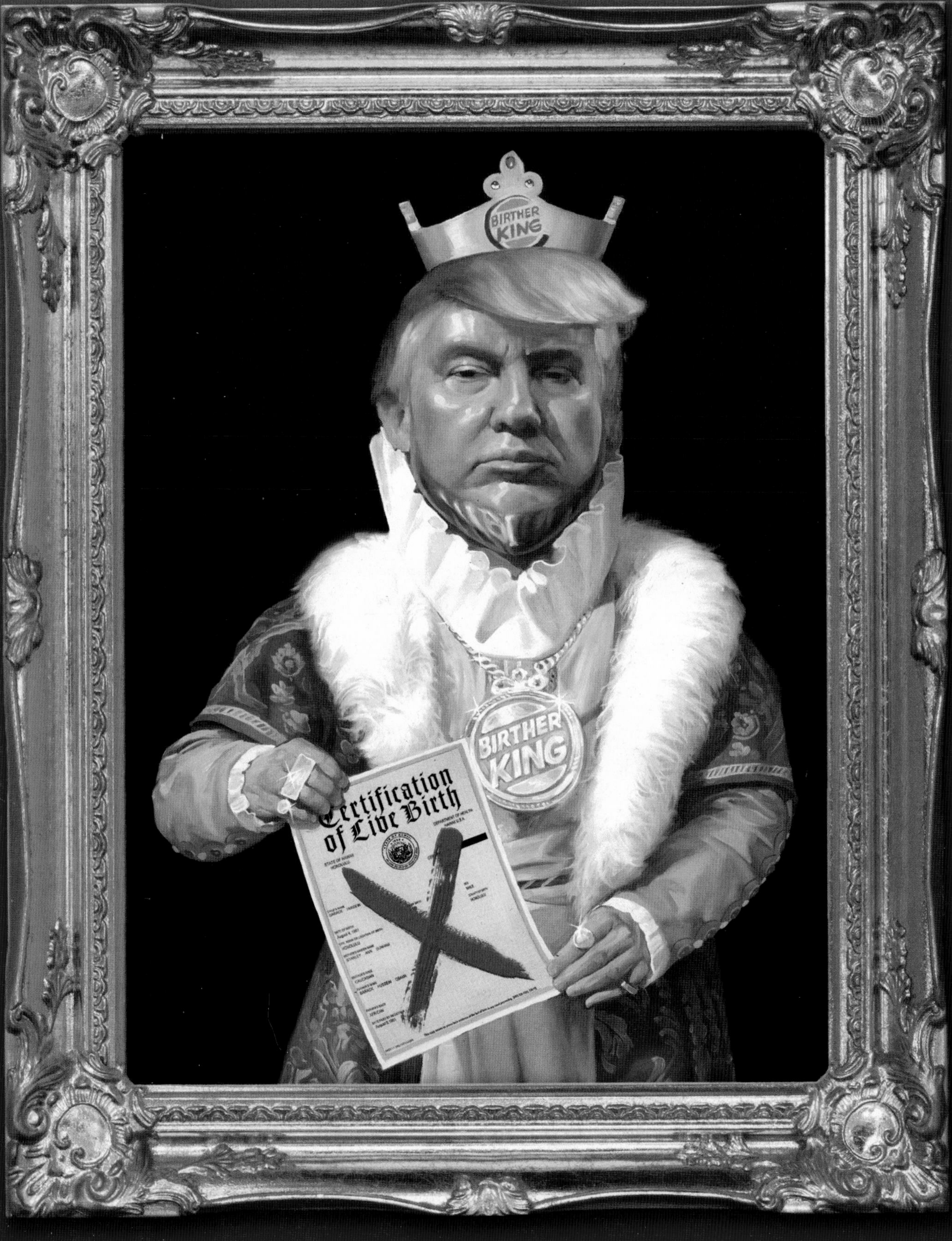
BIRTHER KING
BIRTHER KING
Certification of Live Birth

WRITER: DESMOND DEVLIN ARTIST: ROBERTO PARADA

For a while now, Donald Trump has been traveling around the country pledging to "Make America Great Again!" It's a fine campai
Latinos, Gold Star families, women and the disabled is time-consuming, so maybe he just hasn't had time to figure it all out. Well, we he

THE MAD "I WILL MAKE AMERICA

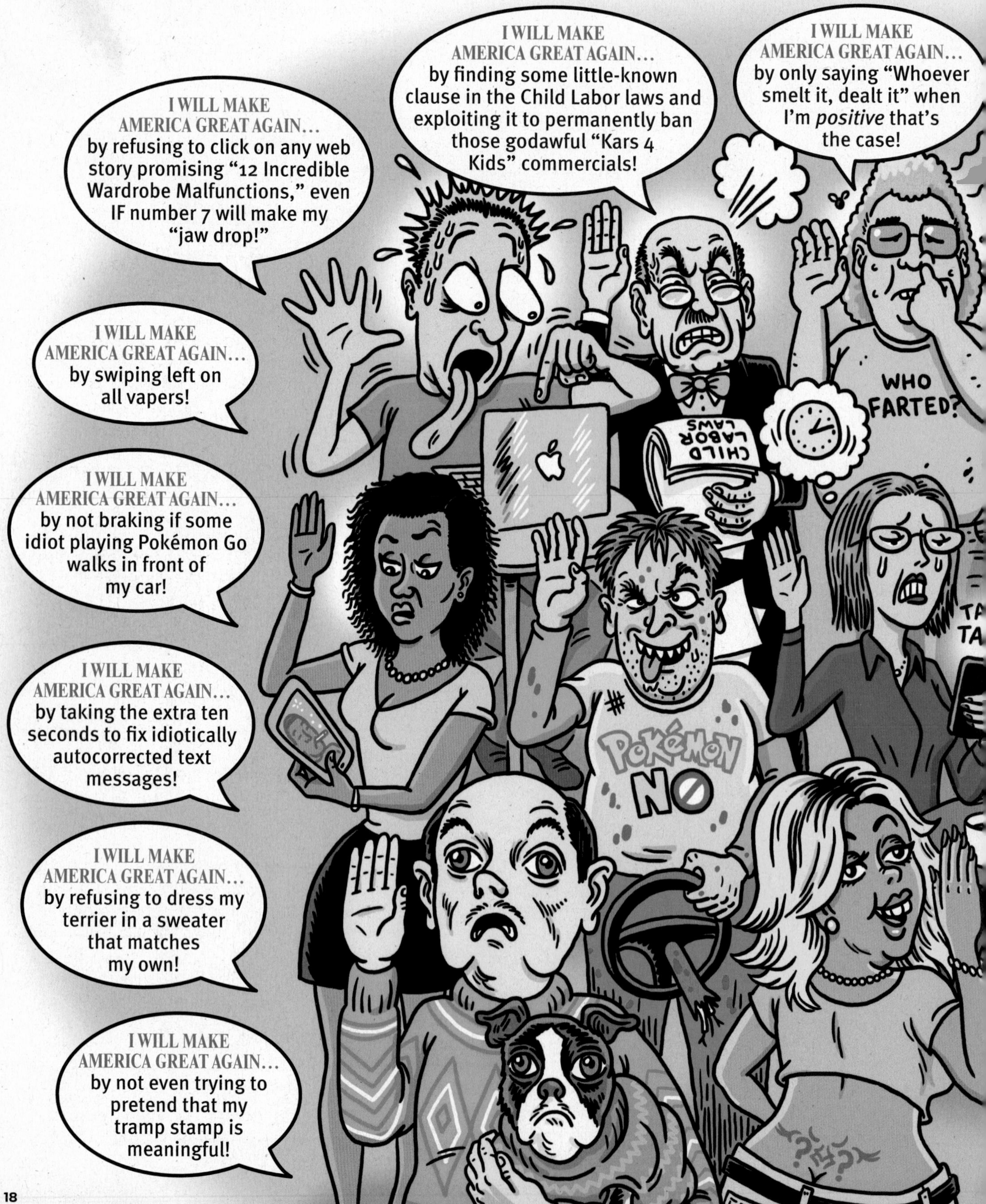
I WILL MAKE AMERICA GREAT AGAIN… by refusing to click on any web story promising "12 Incredible Wardrobe Malfunctions," even IF number 7 will make my "jaw drop!"
I WILL MAKE AMERICA GREAT AGAIN… by finding some little-known clause in the Child Labor laws and exploiting it to permanently ban those godawful "Kars 4 Kids" commercials!
I WILL MAKE AMERICA GREAT AGAIN… by only saying "Whoever smelt it, dealt it" when I'm *positive* that's the case!
WHO FARTED?
CHILD LABOR LAWS
I WILL MAKE AMERICA GREAT AGAIN… by swiping left on all vapers!
I WILL MAKE AMERICA GREAT AGAIN… by not braking if some idiot playing Pokémon Go walks in front of my car!
POKéMON NO
I WILL MAKE AMERICA GREAT AGAIN… by taking the extra ten seconds to fix idiotically autocorrected text messages!
I WILL MAKE AMERICA GREAT AGAIN… by refusing to dress my terrier in a sweater that matches my own!
I WILL MAKE AMERICA GREAT AGAIN… by not even trying to pretend that my tramp stamp is meaningful!

ogan, but Mr. Trump has been woefully short of details on how exactly he'll do this. To be fair, alienating Muslims, veterans,
t MAD know EXACTLY what's wrong with the U.S. AND how to fix it! And you will, too, once you rise, raise your right hand and recite...

GREAT AGAIN" CITIZEN'S PLEDGE

ARTIST: WARD SUTTON

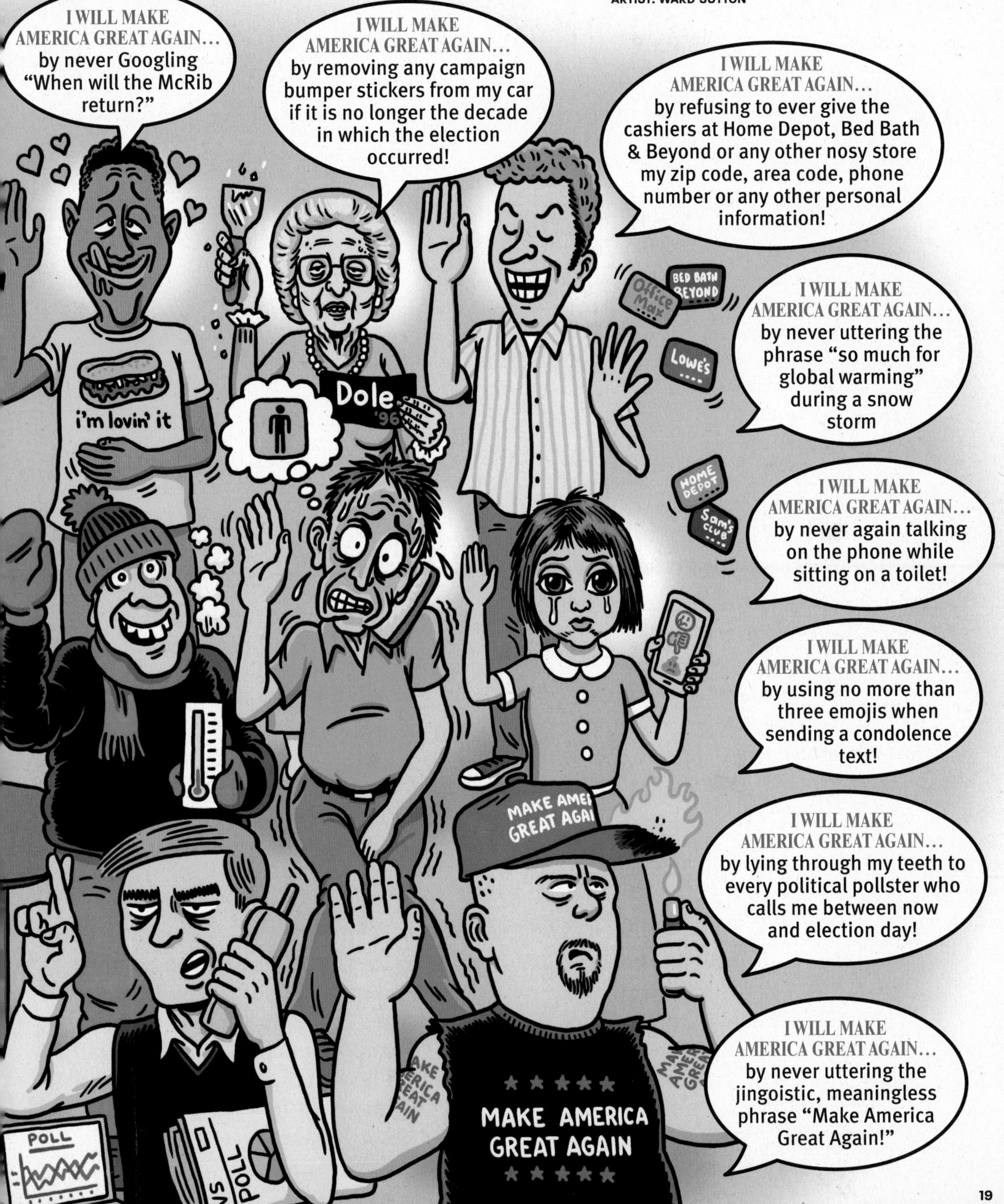
I WILL MAKE AMERICA GREAT AGAIN... by never Googling "When will the McRib return?"
i'm lovin' it
I WILL MAKE AMERICA GREAT AGAIN... by removing any campaign bumper stickers from my car if it is no longer the decade in which the election occurred!
Dole '96
I WILL MAKE AMERICA GREAT AGAIN... by refusing to ever give the cashiers at Home Depot, Bed Bath & Beyond or any other nosy store my zip code, area code, phone number or any other personal information!
BED BATH BEYOND
Office Max
Lowe's
HOME DEPOT
Sam's CLUB
I WILL MAKE AMERICA GREAT AGAIN... by never uttering the phrase "so much for global warming" during a snow storm
I WILL MAKE AMERICA GREAT AGAIN... by never again talking on the phone while sitting on a toilet!
I WILL MAKE AMERICA GREAT AGAIN... by using no more than three emojis when sending a condolence text!
I WILL MAKE AMERICA GREAT AGAIN... by lying through my teeth to every political pollster who calls me between now and election day!
POLL
I WILL MAKE AMERICA GREAT AGAIN... by never uttering the jingoistic, meaningless phrase "Make America Great Again!"
MAKE AMERICA GREAT AGAIN

O COME ALL YE HATEFUL DEPT.

TRUMP CHRISTMAS CAROLS

Oy to the World

(Sung to the tune of "Joy to the World")

Oy to the world – for Trump has won
And all – the polls – were wrong!
Let everyone
Be pissed and glum
And women and black folks shriek!
And Mormons and Muslims freak!
The en-ti-re-coun-try is up sh*t's creek!

White Country

(Sung to the tune of "White Christmas")

I'm dreaming of a white country
Just like supporters in my base
Where Latinos garden
And black folks pardon
All my insults to their race
I'm dreaming of a white country
Led by my friends on the alt-right
En-dure the riots I in-cite
And may all our citizens be white!

Build the Wall

(Sung to the tune of "Deck the Halls")

Build the wall along the border
(Trump-a-la la la, Trump la-la-la)
Wide and high and that's an order
(Trump-a-la la la, Trump la-la-la)
Immigrants will not be staying
(Trump-a-la, Trump-a-la, la-la-la)
Mexico will be stuck paying!
(Trump-a-la la la, Trump la-la-la)

They're all rapists and bad hombres
(Trump-a-la la la, Trump la-la-la)
They hate Trump just like Mitt Romney
(Trump-a-la la la, Trump la-la-la)
Don't be scared, please do not panic
(Trump-a-la, Trump-a-la, la-la-la)
'Long as you are not Hispanic!
(Trump-a-la la la, Trump la-la-la)

Rudy the Trump Supporter

(Sung to the tune of
"Rudolph the Red-Nosed Reindeer")

You know Christie and Carson
and Sessions and Mike Pence
Bannon and Priebus,
all men who make no sense…
But do you recall
The most unhinged spokesman of all?

Rudy the Trump supporter
Had a snarling ugly smirk
Invoking 9/11
You could say he was berserk

Screaming at the convention
Sounding like a man insane
Rudy was just as scary
As snakes crawling on a plane

Then Trump won election night
And soon came to say
"Rudy with your tone of hate
You might be my Sec. of State"

But Rudy was passed over
Which filled many hearts with glee
Rudy the Trump supporter
You'll go down in in-fa-my!

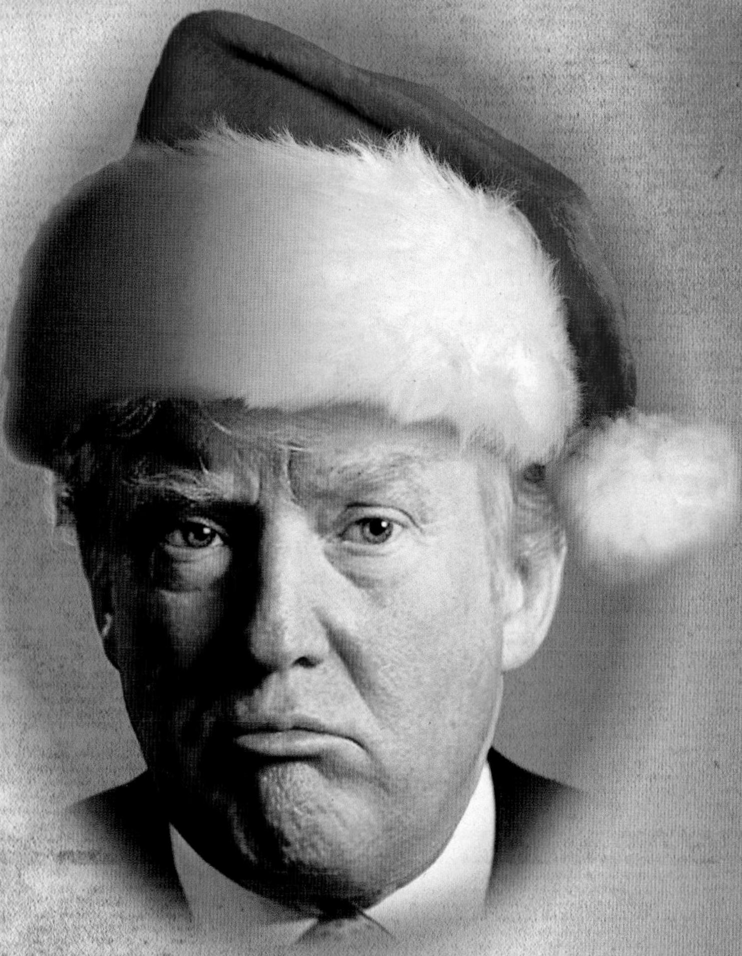

Oh Little Town of Washington

(Sung to the tune of
"Oh Little Town of Bethlehem')

Oh little town of Washington
The swamp it's time to drain
And God help us it's Reince Preibus
The guy with the weird name
And yet he rose to power
Though smart as Forrest Gump
He's such a jerk and still has work
All thanks to Donald Trump

O No Here Comes Mike Pence

(Sung to the tune of
"O Come All Ye Faithful")

Oh no, here comes Mike Pence
Scornful and self-righteous
He's gutting, he's cutting
Planned Par-ar-enthood
Mandating funerals
For aborted zygotes
Oh come let us abhor him
It's dangerous to ignore him
Just who the hell is for him?
Mike Pence, good Lord!

HOW MELANIA TRUMP PLANS TO FIGHT ONLINE BULLYING

Dressing in a bikini, pouting, begging for civility

Being a figurehead and letting Mike Pence's wife handle the whole thing

Teaming up with Amazon for a sting operation promoting "Free Shipping for Cyberbullies" — then nabbing anyone who tries to order

Asking Russian hackers to find out who the bullies are and letting Putin take it from there

Keeping her husband away from his phone as much as possible

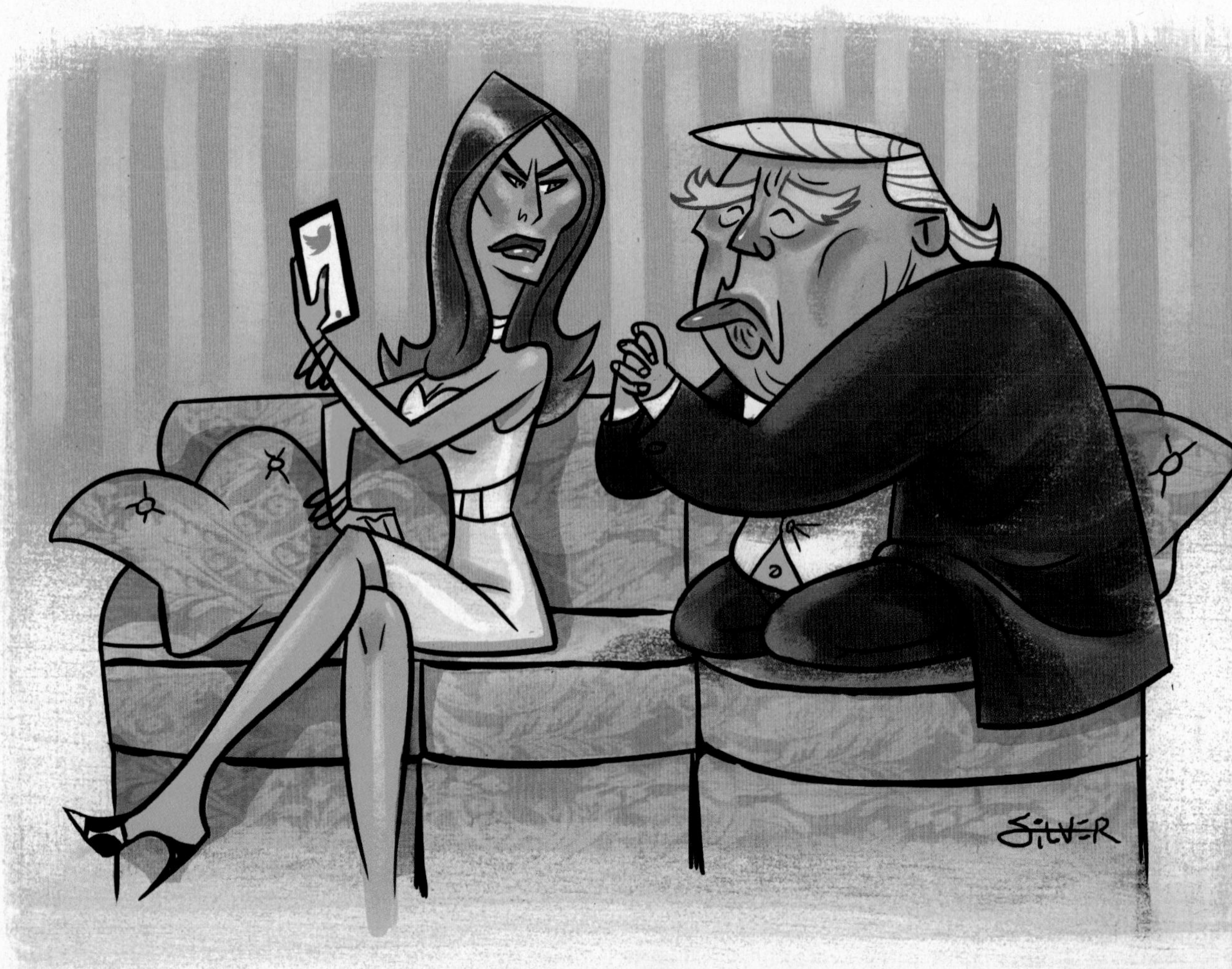
SILVER

WRITER: JEFF KRUSE ARTIST: STEPHEN SILVER

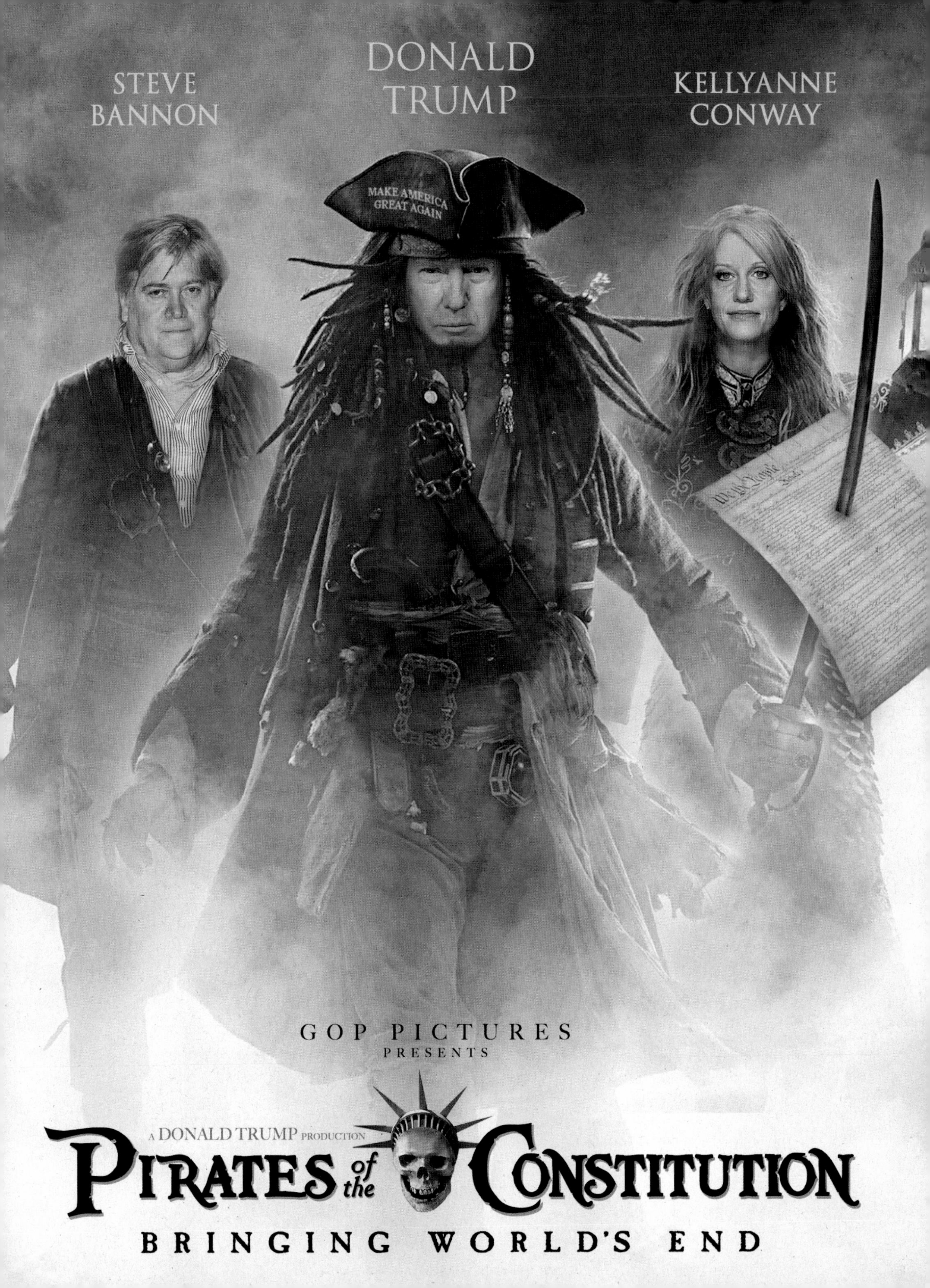
STEVE
BANNON
DONALD
TRUMP
KELLYANNE
CONWAY
MAKE AMERICA
GREAT AGAIN
GOP PICTURES
PRESENTS
A DONALD TRUMP PRODUCTION
PIRATES of the CONSTITUTION
BRINGING WORLD'S END

GETTING CANNED LAUGHTER DEPT.

...DONALD TRUMP YOU'RE

Every week ***The Apprentice*** **ends with a contestant getting pink-slipped and told why he or she doesn't measure up business-wise — but never the one person who, week after week, consistently shows bad business judgement, makes embarrassing corporate decisions and, frankly, has one of the worst résumés in corporate history! This is an easy one. We're sorry, but...**

For starting every season with 16 or 18 varied, multicultural contestants of both genders, only to pick as the winner another boring, corporate, brown-nosing white guy... **...Donald Trump, YOU'RE FIRED!**

For pretending on network TV that any real businessman in his right mind would hand over the reins of a major building project to some guy who won the job by selling four cups of lemonade in the middle of a city street... **...Donald Trump, YOU'RE FIRED!**

For being a dude with a zillion divorces, bankruptcies and/or mistresses who lectures contestants on "ethical behavior"... **...Donald Trump, YOU'RE FIRED!**

For continually claiming your show is the highest-rated show on TV, except for the seven other shows that consistently and inconveniently out-viewer you... **...Donald Trump, YOU'RE FIRED!**

For wasting sixteen weeks to impart such rare gems of Trump business wisdom as "Think big"..."Work well with others"and "Love what you do"... **...Donald Trump, YOU'RE FIRED!**

For subjecting America week after week to that moronic, gravity-defying, architecturally-unsound, can't-be-mocked-enough hairdo from no known period in coiffing history... **...Donald Trump, YOU'RE FIRED!**

SISCO

GRAND COSTUME BALL

FIRED!!!

For encouraging every other annoying, charisma-deprived *Benefactor* and *Rebel Billionaire* to clog the airways with their own lame-o business reality shows...

...Donald Trump, **YOU'RE FIRED!**

For being the only human in the history of planet Earth to own a casino that *LOST MONEY*...

...Donald Trump, **YOU'RE FIRED!**

For picking female contestants with pouty lips, do-me hair and big boobs and then chastising them for using sex to get ahead...

...Donald Trump, **YOU'RE FIRED!**

For somehow convincing the world your nickname should be "The Donald" instead of more appropriate monikers like "The Dickwad," "The Deadbeat," or "The Debt-Ridden-Diddler-of-Beauty-Pageant-Rejects..."

...Donald Trump, **YOU'RE FIRED!**

For criticizing others about "not thinking outside the box" when your sum-total marketing strategy involves pathologically slapping the word "Trump" on everything in sight...

...Donald Trump, **YOU'RE FIRED!**

For mentally ruining that hip-cool "Money, Money, Money" song by forever linking it to slow-motion images of a certain white, middle-aged, bloated, funk-free, lard-ass pucker-squinting his way out of a gold-plated helicopter...

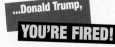
...Donald Trump, **YOU'RE FIRED!**

For somehow making *Joey* the SECOND most embarrassing show on NBC Thursday...

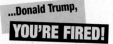
...Donald Trump,

YOU'RE FIRED!

For unironically coming to the conclusion that it's perfectly reasonable for a bankruptcy-skirting, junk-bond-peddling, deal-reneging, contract-welching business-weasel to be the spokesman for Visa credit cards...

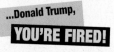
...Donald Trump, **YOU'RE FIRED!**

WRITER: RUSS COOPER
ARTIST: SAM SISCO

REVELATIONS FROM TRUMP'S VOTER FRAUD INVESTIGATION

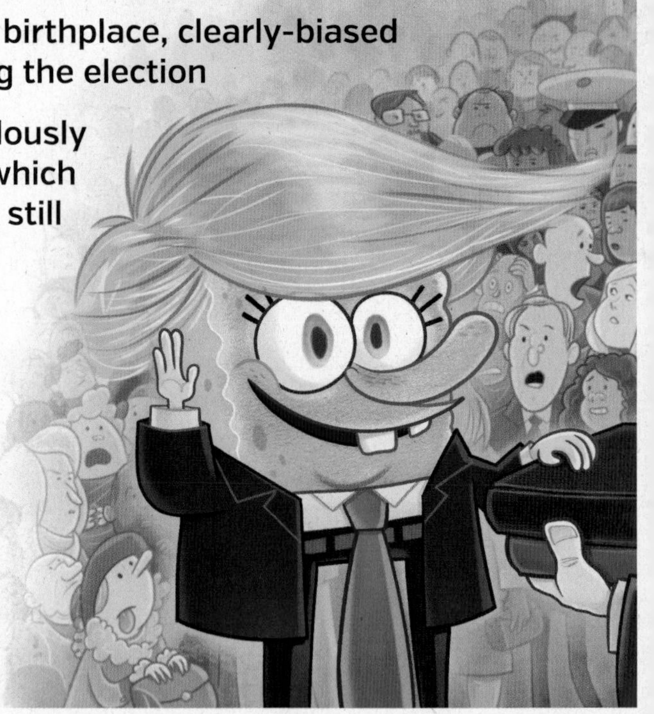

- Despite the fact that Illinois is Hillary Clinton's birthplace, clearly-biased Illinois voters did not recuse themselves during the election
- Apparently, the country is still using the ridiculously antiquated "Electoral College" system, under which a candidate who loses by millions of votes can still win the election
- There's also something really screwed up with the voting for the NBA All-Star Game when Russell Westbrook isn't even starting
- Millions of California residents cast ballots despite being born in other states
- In several Oregon precincts, gag write-in votes for Stewie Griffin were illegally changed to gag write-in votes for Spongebob

WRITER: JEFF KRUSE   ARTIST: JOSE GARIBALDI

TRUMP'S DEBATE DEMANDS

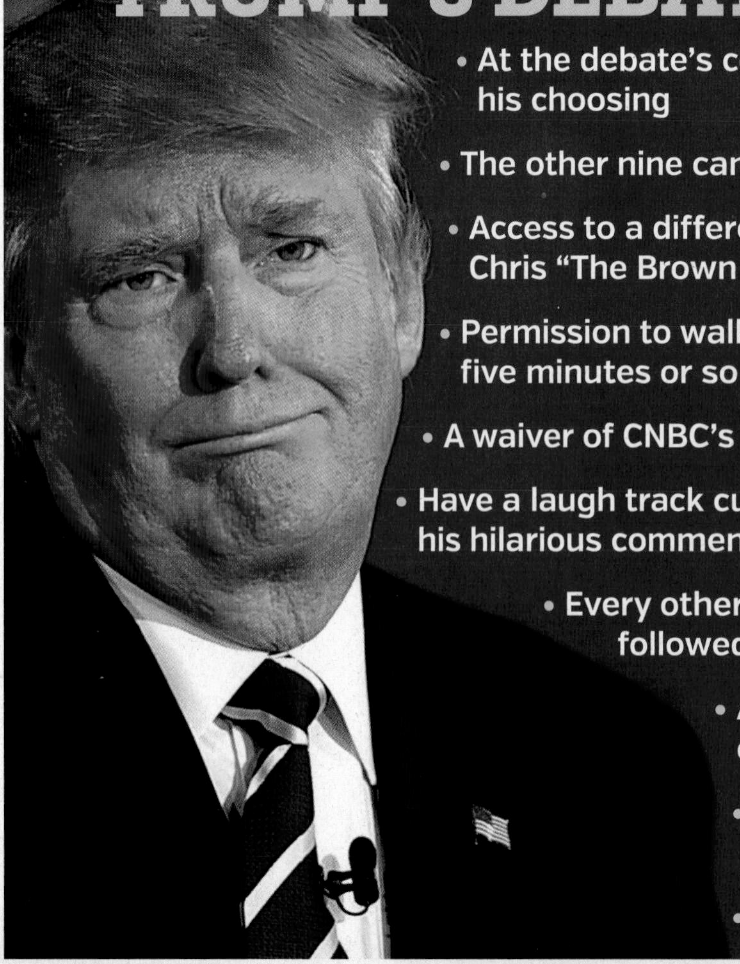

- At the debate's conclusion, he may "fire" a rival of his choosing
- The other nine candidates must share one microphone
- Access to a different bathroom than the one used by Chris "The Brown Fog" Christie
- Permission to walk over and give Jeb Bush a noogie every five minutes or so
- A waiver of CNBC's unreasonable "pants-wearing" policy
- Have a laugh track cued up for each time he makes one of his hilarious comments about Mexican rapists
- Every other candidate's responses must be followed by the "sad trombone" sound effect
- A solid-gold letter "T" must emblazon each candidate's podium
- Absolutely NO fact-checking by CNBC's moderators
- Free WiFi

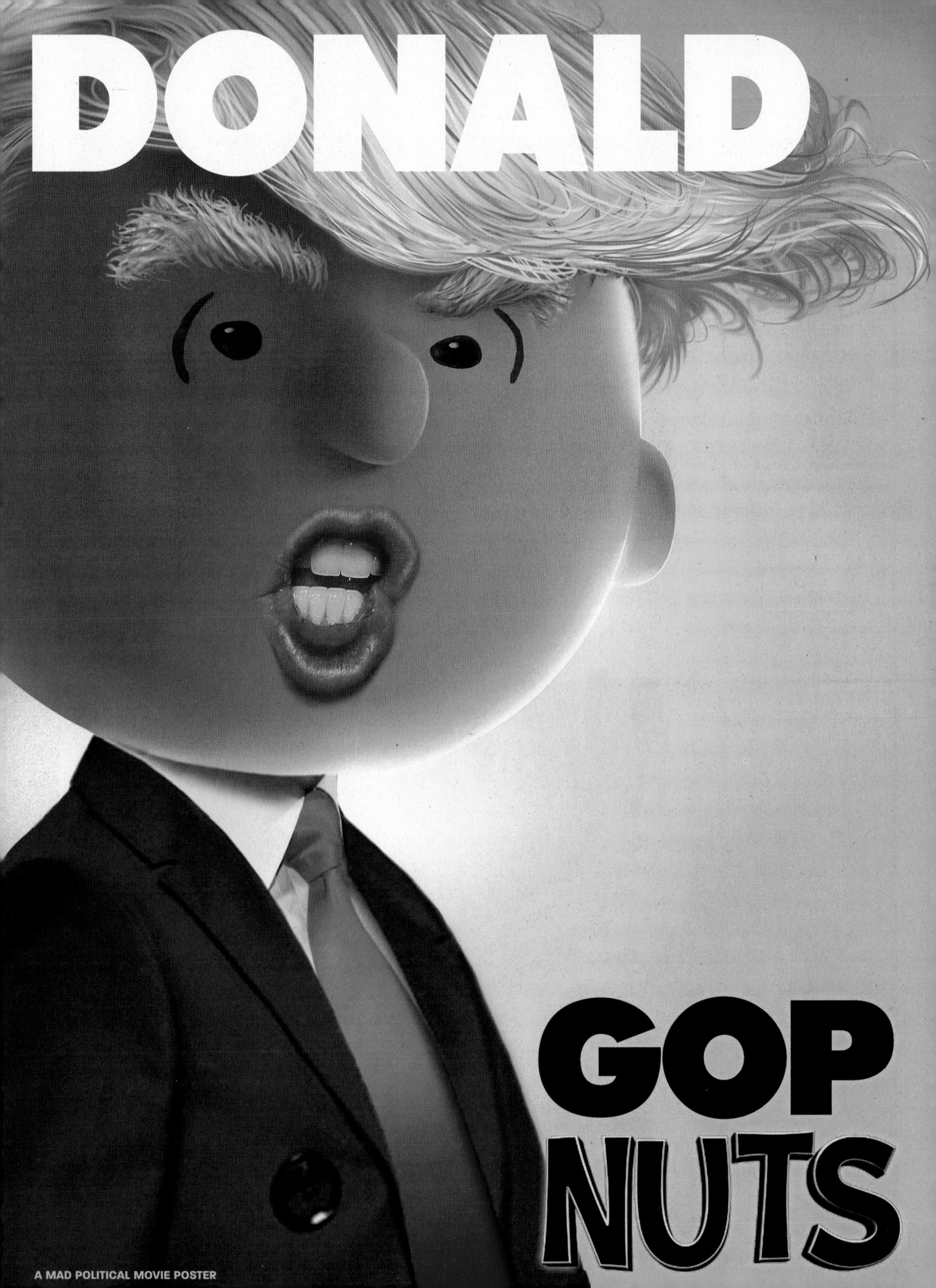
DONALD
GOP
NUTS
A MAD POLITICAL MOVIE POSTER

One Fine Morning In Florida

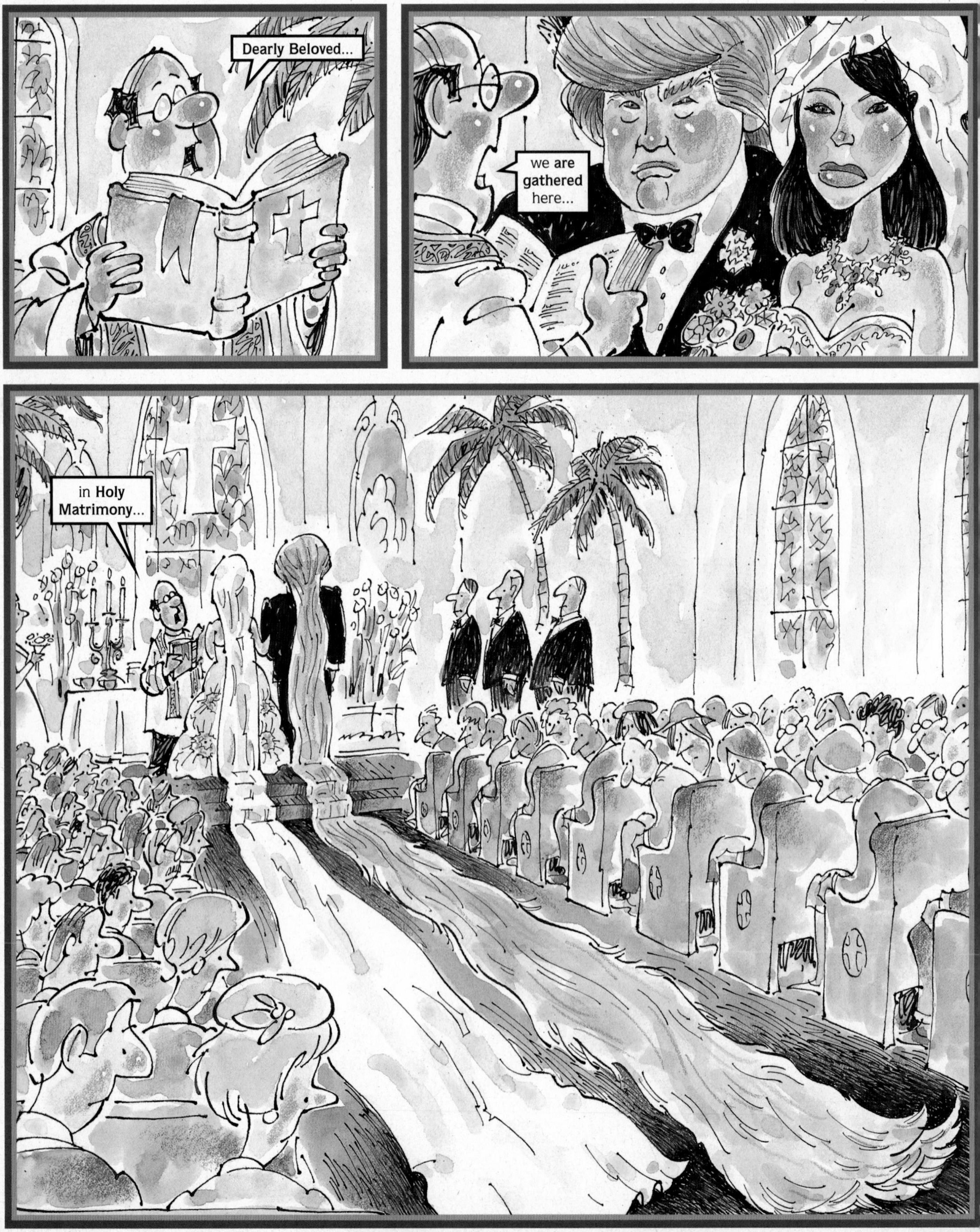
Dearly Beloved...
we are gathered here...
in Holy Matrimony...

WRITER: DUCK EDWING ARTIST: PAUL COKER

TONIGHT!

"THE PHYSICIST FISTICUFFS"

TALE OF THE TAPE

STEPHEN "ROLLING THUNDER" HAWKING VS DONALD "KID LOUDMOUTH" TRUMP

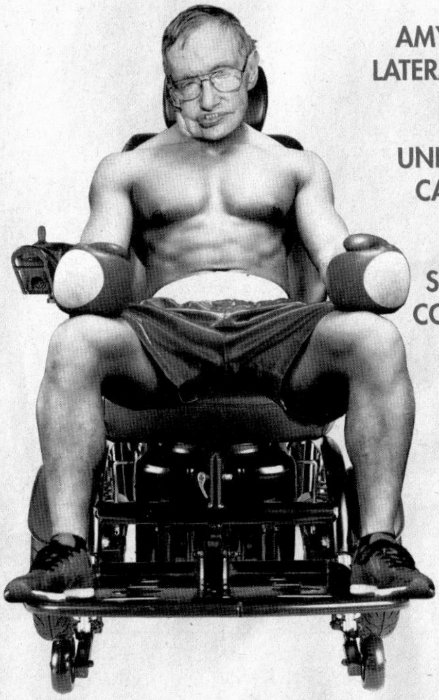

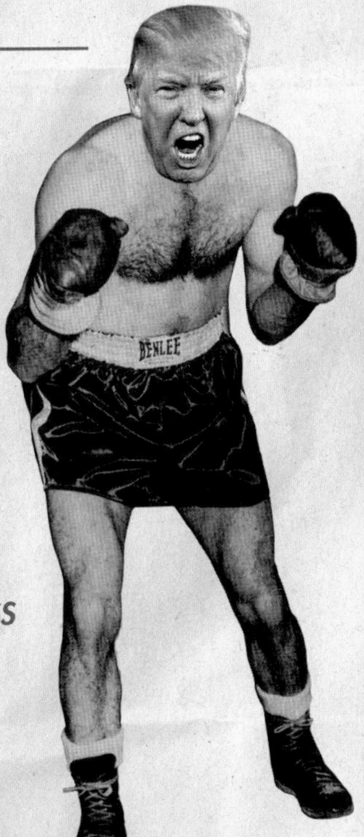
BENLEE

STEPHEN HAWKING January 8, 1942 Oxford, UK		DONALD TRUMP June 14, 1946 Queens, NY
160	**I.Q. SCORE**	16.0
AMYOTROPHIC LATERAL SCLEROSIS	**INCURABLE MALADY**	DIARRHEA MOUTH
UNIVERSITY OF CAMBRIDGE	**SCHOOL HE'S SYNONYMOUS WITH**	TRUMP UNIVERSITY
SCIENTIFIC CONSENSUS	**CONSIDERED A GENIUS BY...**	HIMSELF
A BRIEF HISTORY OF TIME	**THOUGHT-PROVOKING LITERARY WORK**	*THINK BIG AND KICK ASS*
5	**SIMPSONS APPEARANCES**	4
NO	**HAS EVER BEEN IN A FIGHT**	NO

When *The Apprentice* turned into *Celebrity Apprentice*, they only forgot one itty-bitty thing. Celebrities! Last season's washed-up wannabes and barely-weres packed all the star wattage of a sputtering bug zapper. Mr. Donald Trump is a man accustomed to the best in life. Therefore, any celebrity project bearing the Trump name should reflect the unforgettable, shared moments of human culture. The Roman Empire! The Renaissance! Shaving Vince McMahon's head on pay-per-view! So don't ask how it's happened, just root for the history-making superstars as they fight to become...

THE DEAD

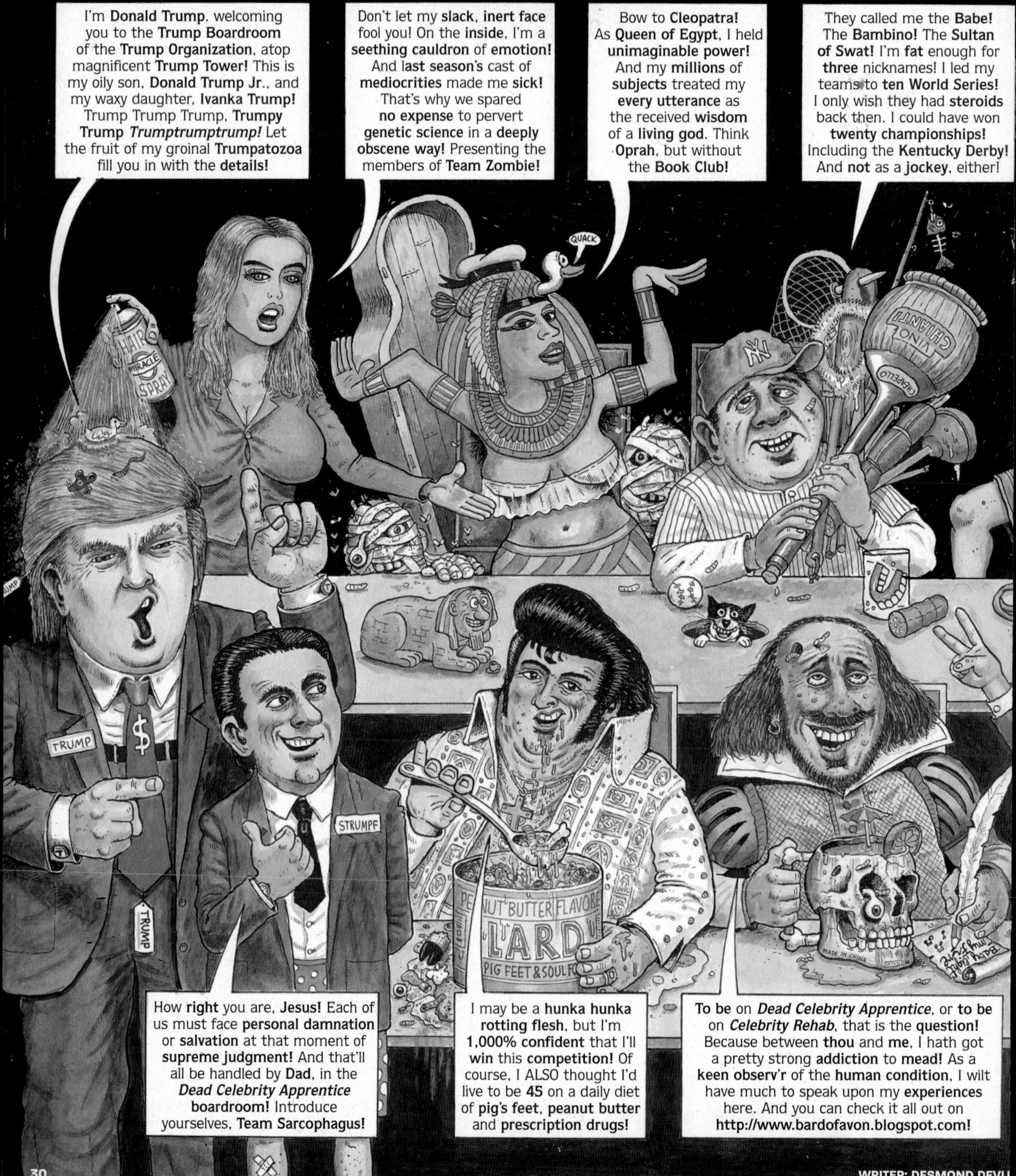
I'm Donald Trump, welcoming you to the Trump Boardroom of the Trump Organization, atop magnificent Trump Tower! This is my oily son, Donald Trump Jr., and my waxy daughter, Ivanka Trump! Trump Trump Trump, Trumpy Trump Trumptrumptrumptrump! Let the fruit of my groinal Trumpatozoa fill you in with the details!
Don't let my slack, inert face fool you! On the inside, I'm a seething cauldron of emotion! And last season's cast of mediocrities made me sick! That's why we spared no expense to pervert genetic science in a deeply obscene way! Presenting the members of Team Zombie!
Bow to Cleopatra! As Queen of Egypt, I held unimaginable power! And my millions of subjects treated my every utterance as the received wisdom of a living god. Think Oprah, but without the Book Club!
They called me the Babe! The Bambino! The Sultan of Swat! I'm fat enough for three nicknames! I led my teams to ten World Series! I only wish they had steroids back then. I could have won twenty championships! Including the Kentucky Derby! And not as a jockey, either!
QUACK
HAIR MIRACLE SPRAY
VINO CHIANTI
TRUMP
STRUMPF
TRUMP
PEANUT BUTTER FLAVORED LARD PIG FEET & SOUL F
MADE IN CHINA
How right you are, Jesus! Each of us must face personal damnation or salvation at that moment of supreme judgment! And that'll all be handled by Dad, in the Dead Celebrity Apprentice boardroom! Introduce yourselves, Team Sarcophagus!
I may be a hunka hunka rotting flesh, but I'm 1,000% confident that I'll win this competition! Of course, I ALSO thought I'd live to be 45 on a daily diet of pig's feet, peanut butter and prescription drugs!
To be on Dead Celebrity Apprentice, or to be on Celebrity Rehab, that is the question! Because between thou and me, I hath got a pretty strong addiction to mead! As a keen observ'r of the human condition, I wilt have much to speak upon my experiences here. And you can check it all out on http://www.bardofavon.blogspot.com!

WRITER: DESMOND DEVLI

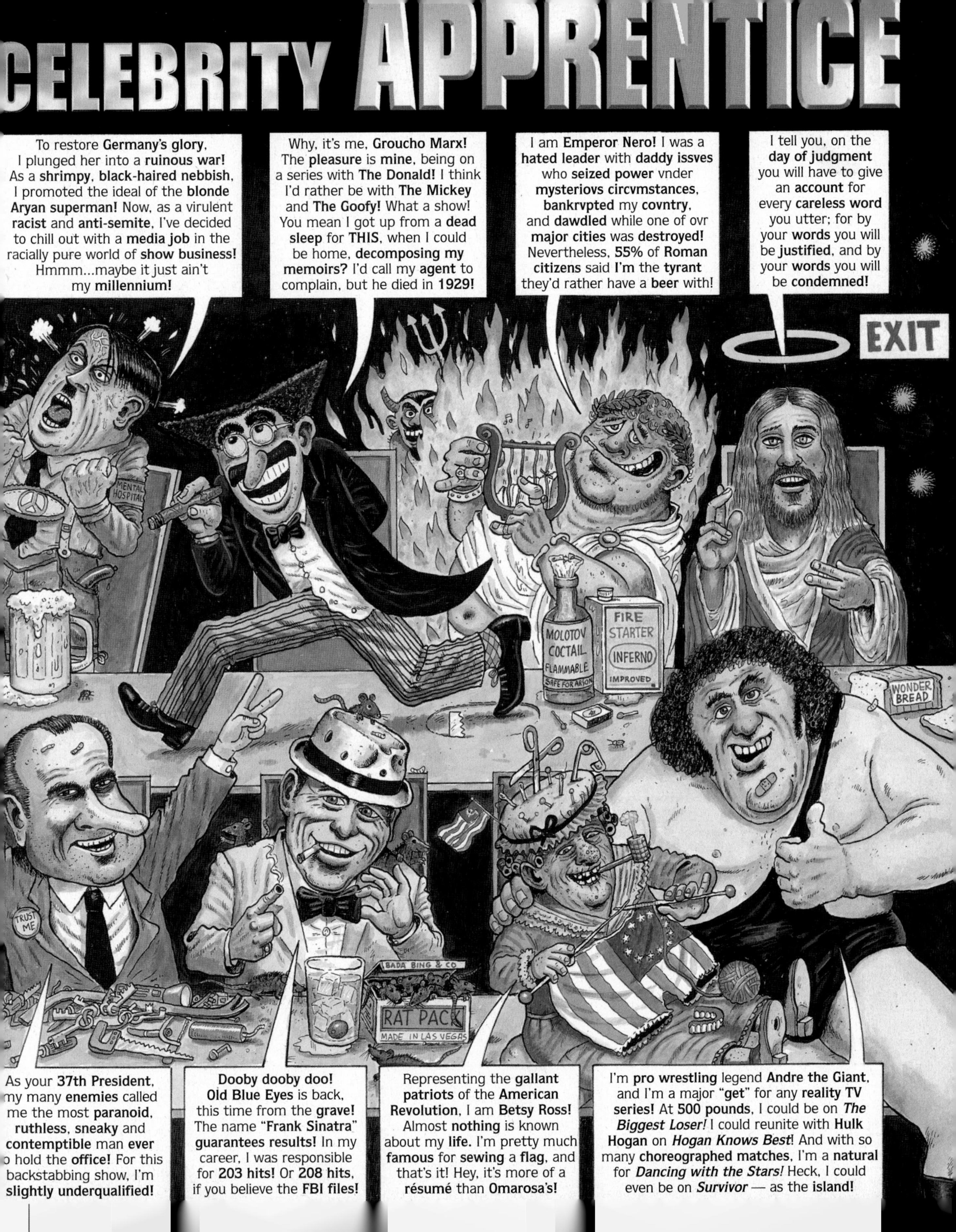

CELEBRITY APPRENTICE
To restore **Germany's glory**, I plunged her into a **ruinous war!** As a **shrimpy, black-haired nebbish**, I promoted the ideal of the **blonde Aryan superman!** Now, as a virulent **racist** and **anti-semite**, I've decided to chill out with a **media job** in the racially pure world of **show business!** Hmmm...maybe it just ain't my **millennium!**
Why, it's me, **Groucho Marx!** The **pleasure** is **mine**, being on a series with **The Donald!** I think I'd rather be with **The Mickey** and **The Goofy!** What a show! You mean I got up from a **dead sleep** for **THIS**, when I could be home, **decomposing my memoirs?** I'd call my **agent** to complain, but he died in **1929!**
I am **Emperor Nero!** I was a **hated leader** with **daddy issves** who **seized power** vnder **mysteriovs circvmstances**, **bankrvpted** my **covntry**, and **dawdled** while one of ovr **major cities** was **destroyed!** Nevertheless, **55%** of **Roman citizens** said **I'm** the **tyrant** they'd rather have a **beer** with!
I tell you, on the **day of judgment** you will have to give an **account** for every **careless word** you utter; for by your **words** you will be **justified**, and by your **words** you will be **condemned!**
EXIT
MENTAL HOSPITAL
MOLOTOV COCTAIL FLAMMABLE SAFE FOR ARSON
FIRE STARTER INFERNO IMPROVED
WONDER BREAD
TRUST ME
BADA BING & CO
RAT PACK MADE IN LAS VEGAS
As your **37th President**, my many **enemies** called me the most **paranoid**, **ruthless**, **sneaky** and **contemptible** man **ever** to hold the **office!** For this backstabbing show, I'm **slightly underqualified!**
Dooby dooby doo! Old Blue Eyes is back, this time from the **grave!** The name **"Frank Sinatra" guarantees results!** In my career, I was responsible for **203 hits!** Or **208 hits**, if you believe the **FBI files!**
Representing the **gallant patriots** of the **American Revolution**, I am **Betsy Ross!** Almost **nothing** is known about my **life**. I'm pretty much **famous** for **sewing** a **flag**, and that's it! Hey, it's more of a **résumé** than **Omarosa's!**
I'm **pro wrestling** legend **Andre the Giant**, and I'm a major **"get"** for any **reality TV series!** At **500 pounds**, I could be on ***The Biggest Loser!*** I could reunite with **Hulk Hogan** on *Hogan Knows Best*! And with so many **choreographed matches**, I'm a **natural** for *Dancing with the Stars!* Heck, I could even be on *Survivor* — as the **island!**

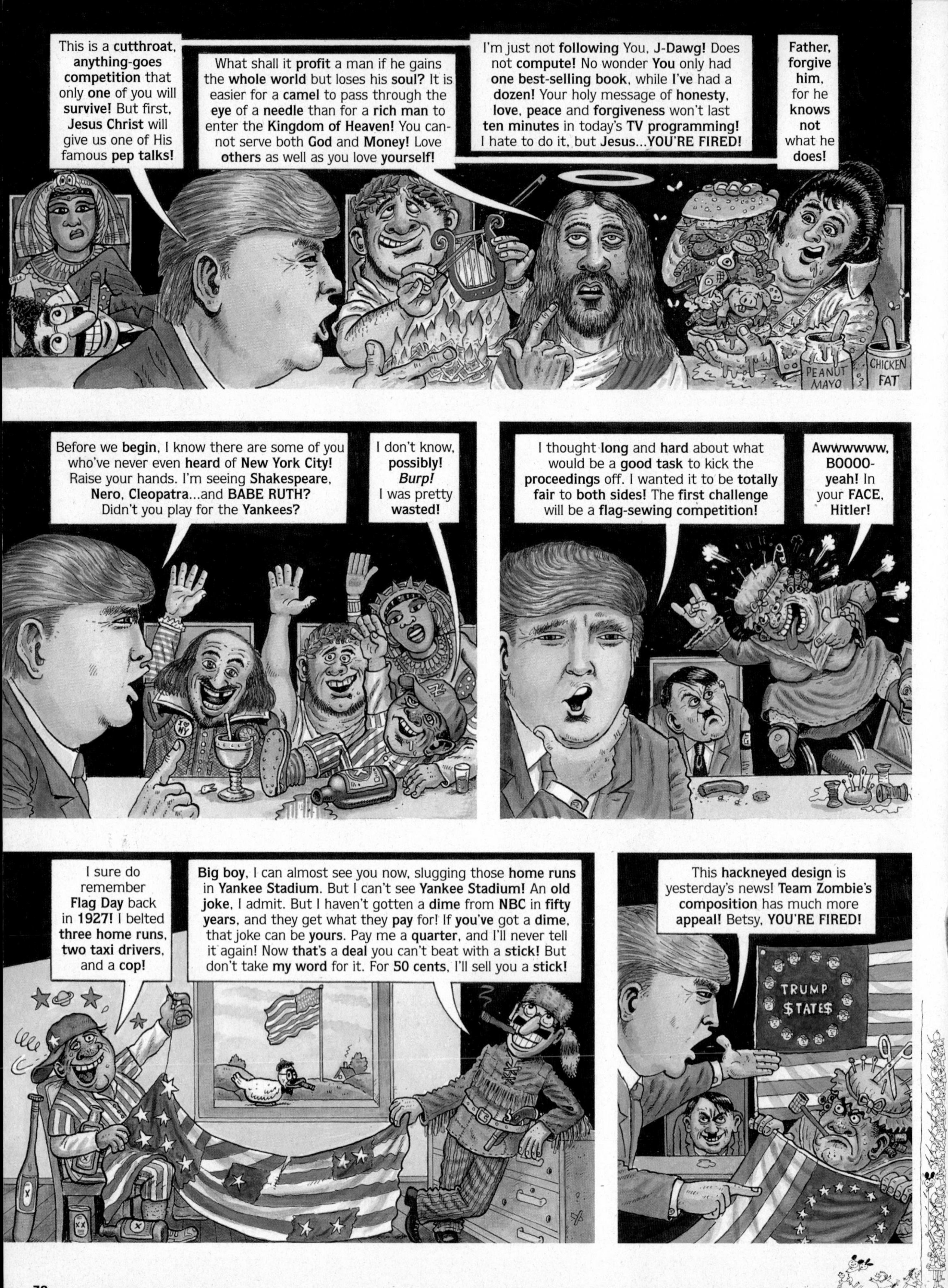
This is a cutthroat, anything-goes competition that only one of you will survive! But first, Jesus Christ will give us one of His famous pep talks!
What shall it profit a man if he gains the whole world but loses his soul? It is easier for a camel to pass through the eye of a needle than for a rich man to enter the Kingdom of Heaven! You cannot serve both God and Money! Love others as well as you love yourself!
I'm just not following You, J-Dawg! Does not compute! No wonder You only had one best-selling book, while I've had a dozen! Your holy message of honesty, love, peace and forgiveness won't last ten minutes in today's TV programming! I hate to do it, but Jesus...YOU'RE FIRED!
Father, forgive him, for he knows not what he does!
PEANUT MAYO
CHICKEN FAT
Before we begin, I know there are some of you who've never even heard of New York City! Raise your hands. I'm seeing Shakespeare, Nero, Cleopatra...and BABE RUTH? Didn't you play for the Yankees?
I don't know, possibly! Burp! I was pretty wasted!
I thought long and hard about what would be a good task to kick the proceedings off. I wanted it to be totally fair to both sides! The first challenge will be a flag-sewing competition!
Awwwwww, BOOOO-yeah! In your FACE, Hitler!
I sure do remember Flag Day back in 1927! I belted three home runs, two taxi drivers, and a cop!
Big boy, I can almost see you now, slugging those home runs in Yankee Stadium. But I can't see Yankee Stadium! An old joke, I admit. But I haven't gotten a dime from NBC in fifty years, and they get what they pay for! If you've got a dime, that joke can be yours. Pay me a quarter, and I'll never tell it again! Now that's a deal you can't beat with a stick! But don't take my word for it. For 50 cents, I'll sell you a stick!
This hackneyed design is yesterday's news! Team Zombie's composition has much more appeal! Betsy, YOU'RE FIRED!
TRUMP $TATE$

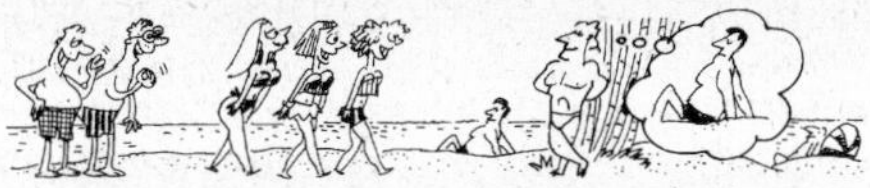

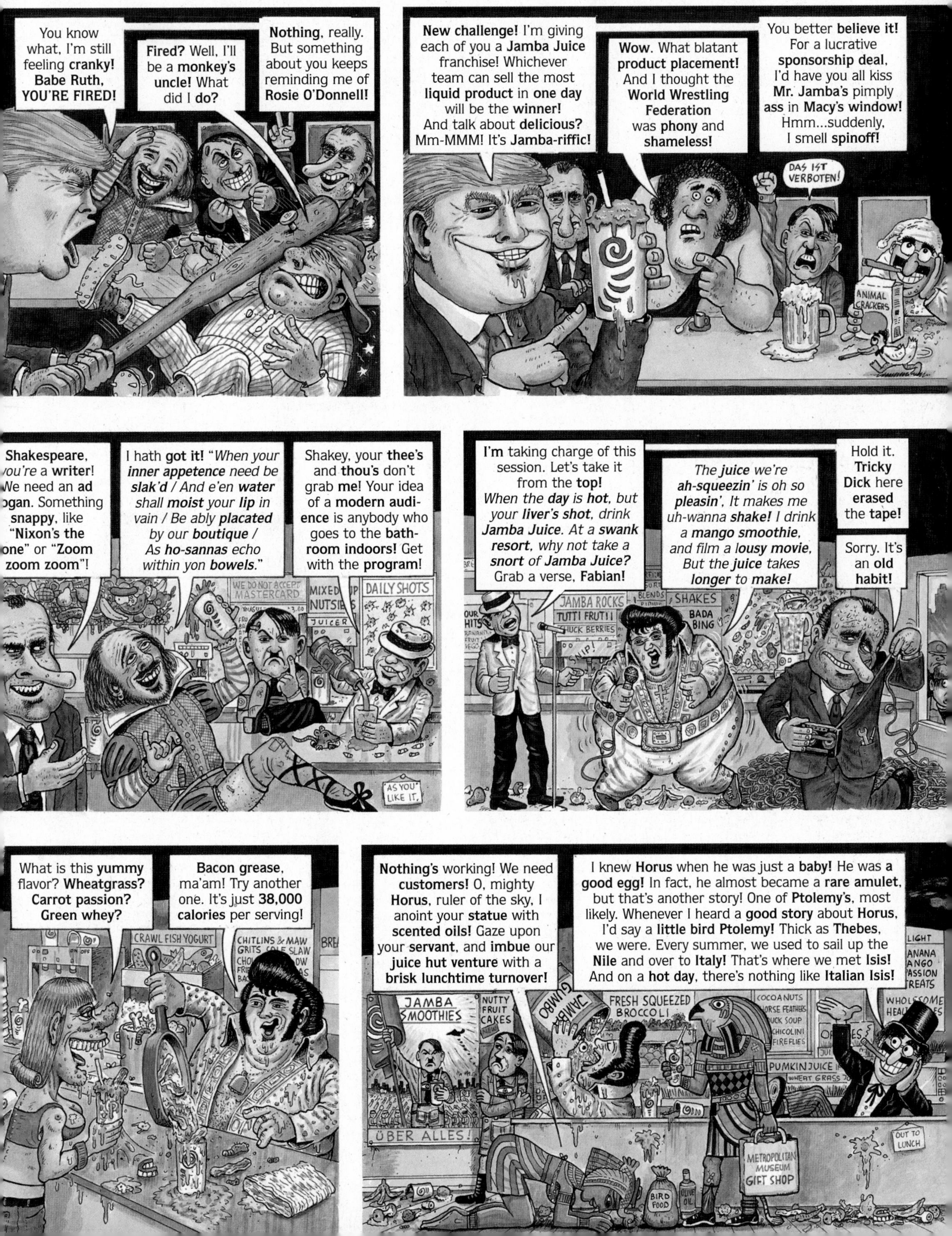
You know what, I'm still feeling **cranky! Babe Ruth, YOU'RE FIRED!**
Fired? Well, I'll be a **monkey's uncle!** What did I **do?**
Nothing, really. But something about you keeps reminding me of **Rosie O'Donnell!**
New challenge! I'm giving each of you a **Jamba Juice** franchise! Whichever team can sell the most **liquid product** in **one day** will be the **winner!** And talk about **delicious?** Mm-MMM! It's **Jamba-riffic!**
Wow. What blatant **product placement!** And I thought the **World Wrestling Federation** was **phony** and **shameless!**
You better **believe it!** For a lucrative **sponsorship deal**, I'd have you all kiss **Mr. Jamba's** pimply **ass** in **Macy's window!** Hmm...suddenly, I smell **spinoff!**
DAS IST VERBOTEN!
ANIMAL CRACKERS
Shakespeare, ou're a **writer!** e need an **ad** ogan. Something **snappy**, like **"Nixon's the** one" or **"Zoom zoom zoom"**!
I hath **got it!** "*When your* ***inner appetence*** *need be* ***slak'd*** */ And e'en* ***water*** *shall* ***moist*** *your* ***lip*** *in vain / Be ably* ***placated*** *by our* ***boutique*** */ As* ***ho-sannas*** *echo within yon* ***bowels***."
Shakey, your **thee's** and **thou's** don't grab **me!** Your idea of a **modern audience** is anybody who goes to the **bathroom indoors!** Get with the **program!**
WE DO NOT ACCEPT MASTERCARD
MIXED UP NUTSIES
DAILY SHOTS
JUICER
AS YOU LIKE IT
I'm taking charge of this session. Let's take it from the **top!** *When the* ***day*** *is* ***hot***, *but your* ***liver's shot***, *drink* ***Jamba Juice***. *At a* ***swank resort***, *why not take a* ***snort*** *of* ***Jamba Juice?*** Grab a verse, **Fabian!**
The ***juice*** *we're* ***ah-squeezin'*** *is oh so* ***pleasin'***, *It makes me uh-wanna* ***shake!*** *I drink a* ***mango smoothie***, *and film a* ***lousy movie***, *But the* ***juice*** *takes* ***longer*** *to* ***make!***
Hold it. **Tricky Dick** here **erased** the **tape!**
Sorry. It's an **old habit!**
JAMBA ROCKS
TUTTI FRUTTI
SHAKES
BADA BING
SNIP!
What is this **yummy** flavor? **Wheatgrass? Carrot passion? Green whey?**
Bacon grease, ma'am! Try another one. It's just **38,000 calories** per serving!
CRAWL FISH YOGURT
CHITLINS & MAW GRITS COLE SLAW
Nothing's working! We need **customers!** O, mighty **Horus**, ruler of the sky, I anoint your **statue** with **scented oils!** Gaze upon your **servant**, and **imbue** our **juice hut venture** with a **brisk lunchtime turnover!**
I knew **Horus** when he was just a **baby!** He was **a good egg!** In fact, he almost became a **rare amulet**, but that's another story! One of **Ptolemy's**, most likely. Whenever I heard a **good story** about **Horus**, I'd say a **little bird Ptolemy!** Thick as **Thebes**, we were. Every summer, we used to sail up the **Nile** and over to **Italy!** That's where we met **Isis!** And on a **hot day**, there's nothing like **Italian Isis!**
JAMBA SMOOTHIES
NUTTY FRUIT CAKES
FRESH SQUEEZED BROCCOLI
COCOANUTS
CHICOLINI FIREFLIES
PUMKIN JUICE
ÜBER ALLES!
OUT TO LUNCH
METROPOLITAN MUSEUM GIFT SHOP
BIRD FOOD
OLIVE OIL

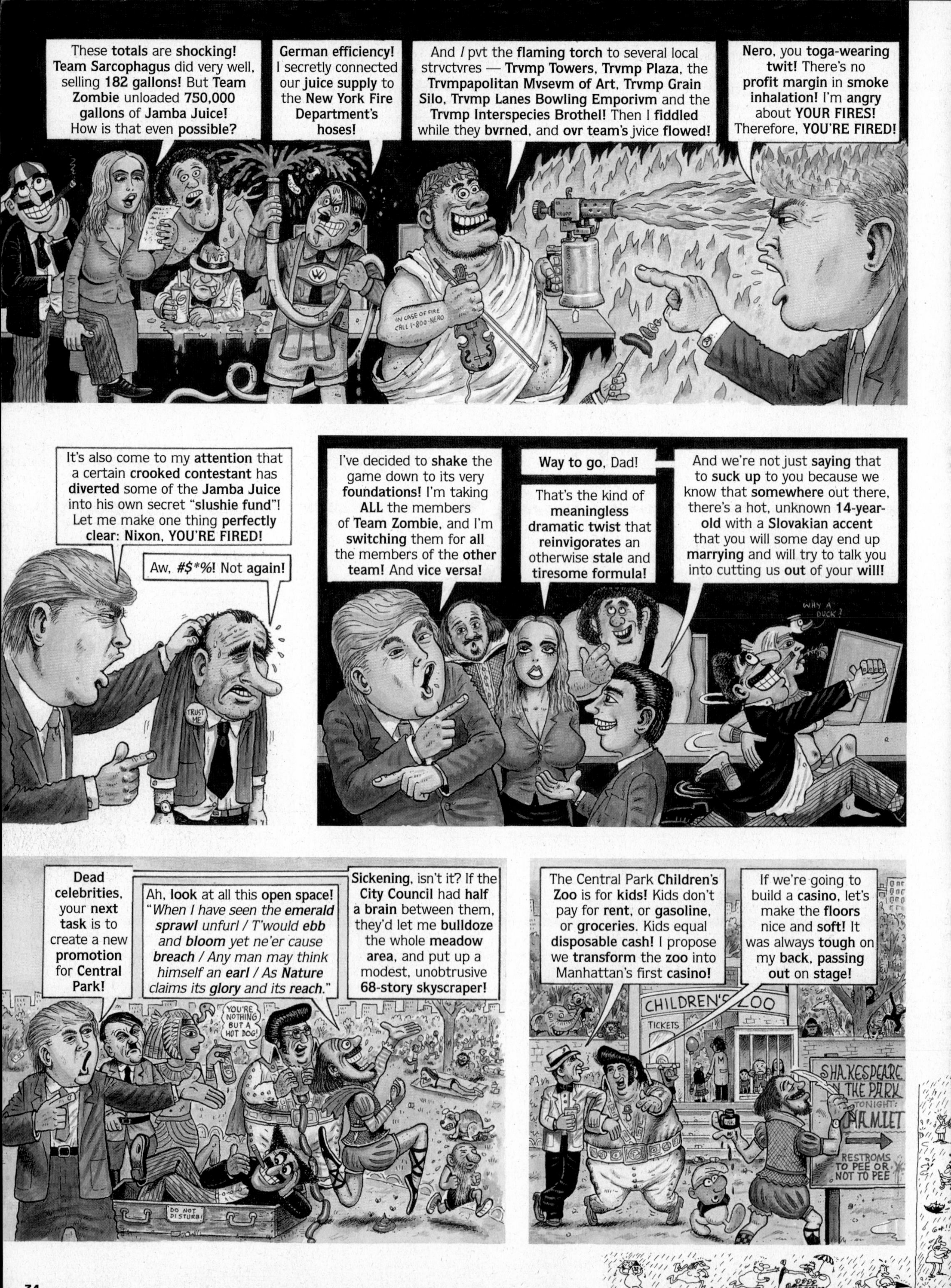
These **totals** are **shocking! Team Sarcophagus** did very well, selling **182 gallons!** But **Team Zombie** unloaded **750,000 gallons** of **Jamba Juice!** How is that even **possible?**
German efficiency! I secretly connected our **juice supply** to the **New York Fire Department's hoses!**
KRUPP
IN CASE OF FIRE CALL 1-800-NERO
And *I* pvt the **flaming torch** to several local strvctvres — **Trvmp Towers**, **Trvmp Plaza**, the **Trvmpapolitan Mvsevm of Art**, **Trvmp Grain Silo**, **Trvmp Lanes Bowling Emporivm** and the **Trvmp Interspecies Brothel!** Then I **fiddled** while they **bvrned**, and **ovr team's** jvice **flowed!**
Nero, you **toga-wearing twit!** There's no **profit margin** in **smoke inhalation!** I'm **angry** about **YOUR FIRES!** Therefore, **YOU'RE FIRED!**
It's also come to my **attention** that a certain **crooked contestant** has **diverted** some of the **Jamba Juice** into his own secret "**slushie fund**"! Let me make one thing **perfectly clear: Nixon, YOU'RE FIRED!**
Aw, ***#$*%!*** Not **again!**
TRUST ME
I've decided to **shake** the game down to its very **foundations!** I'm taking **ALL** the members of **Team Zombie**, and I'm **switching** them for **all** the members of the **other team!** And **vice versa!**
Way to go, Dad!
That's the kind of **meaningless dramatic twist** that **reinvigorates** an otherwise **stale** and **tiresome formula!**
And we're not just **saying** that to **suck up** to you because we know that **somewhere** out there, there's a hot, unknown **14-year-old** with a **Slovakian accent** that you will some day end up **marrying** and will try to talk you into cutting us **out** of your **will!**
WHY A DUCK?
Dead celebrities, your **next task** is to create a new **promotion** for **Central Park!**
Ah, **look** at all this **open space!** "*When I have seen the **emerald sprawl** unfurl / T'would **ebb** and **bloom** yet ne'er cause **breach** / Any man may think himself an **earl** / As **Nature** claims its **glory** and its **reach**.*"
Sickening, isn't it? If the **City Council** had **half a brain** between them, they'd let me **bulldoze** the whole **meadow area**, and put up a modest, unobtrusive **68-story skyscraper!**
YOU'RE NOTHING BUT A HOT DOG!
DO NOT DISTURB!
The Central Park **Children's Zoo** is for **kids!** Kids don't pay for **rent**, or **gasoline**, or **groceries**. Kids equal **disposable cash!** I propose we **transform** the **zoo** into Manhattan's first **casino!**
If we're going to build a **casino**, let's make the **floors** nice and **soft!** It was always **tough** on my **back**, **passing out** on stage!
CHILDREN'S ZOO
TICKETS
SHAKESPEARE IN THE PARK
TONIGHT: HAMLET
RESTROOMS TO PEE OR NOT TO PEE

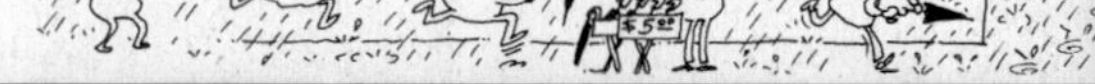

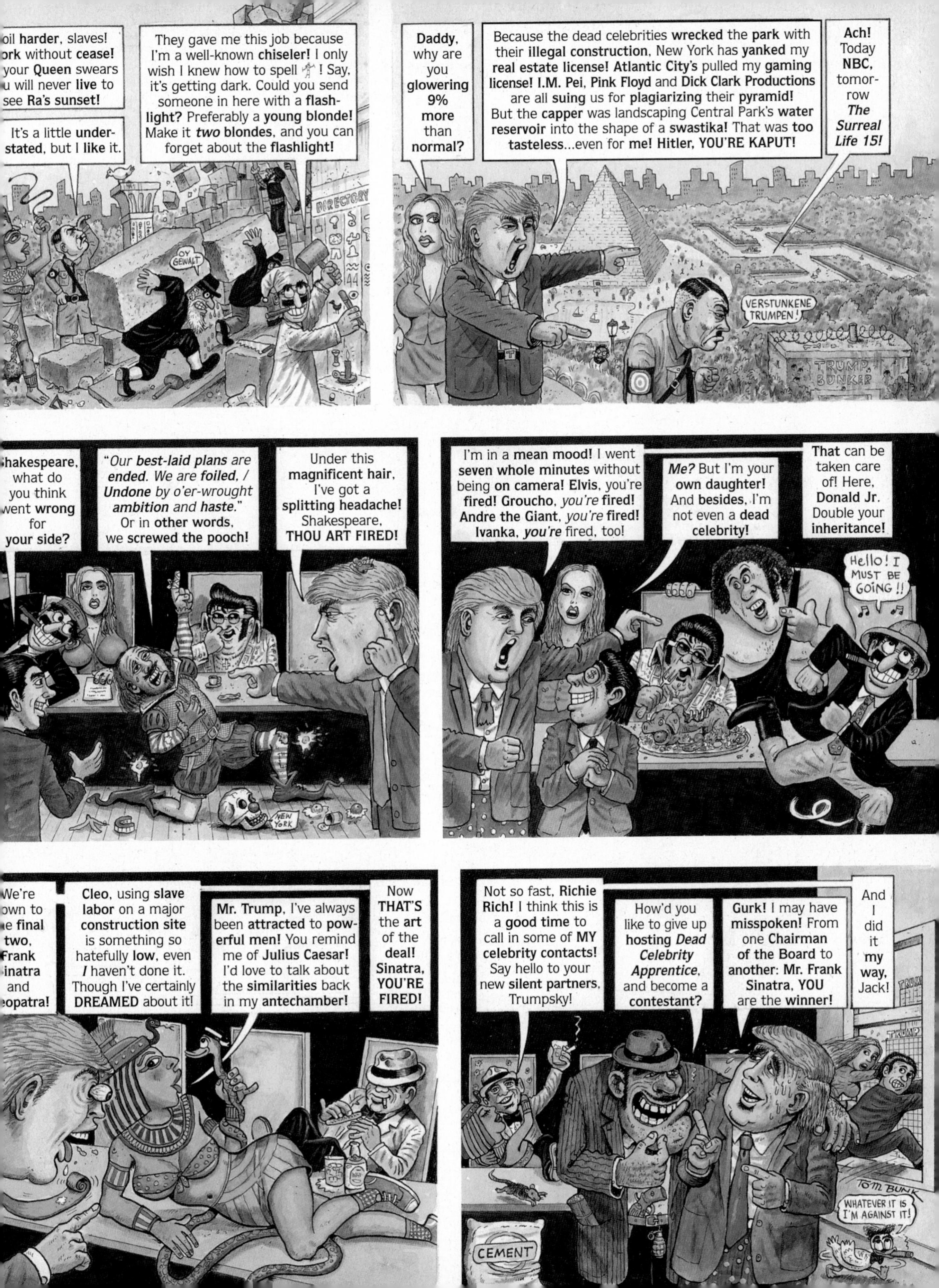

oil harder, slaves! ork without cease! your Queen swears u will never live to see Ra's sunset!
They gave me this job because I'm a well-known chiseler! I only wish I knew how to spell ! Say, it's getting dark. Could you send someone in here with a flash-light? Preferably a young blonde! Make it two blondes, and you can forget about the flashlight!
It's a little under-stated, but I like it.
DIRECTORY
OY GEWALT
Daddy, why are you glowering 9% more than normal?
Because the dead celebrities wrecked the park with their illegal construction, New York has yanked my real estate license! Atlantic City's pulled my gaming license! I.M. Pei, Pink Floyd and Dick Clark Productions are all suing us for plagiarizing their pyramid! But the capper was landscaping Central Park's water reservoir into the shape of a swastika! That was too tasteless...even for me! Hitler, YOU'RE KAPUT!
Ach! Today NBC, tomorrow The Surreal Life 15!
VERSTUNKENE TRUMPEN!
TRUMP BUNKER
hakespeare, what do you think went wrong for your side?
"Our best-laid plans are ended. We are foiled, / Undone by o'er-wrought ambition and haste." Or in other words, we screwed the pooch!
Under this magnificent hair, I've got a splitting headache! Shakespeare, THOU ART FIRED!
NEW YORK
I'm in a mean mood! I went seven whole minutes without being on camera! Elvis, you're fired! Groucho, you're fired! Andre the Giant, you're fired! Ivanka, you're fired, too!
Me? But I'm your own daughter! And besides, I'm not even a dead celebrity!
That can be taken care of! Here, Donald Jr. Double your inheritance!
Hello! I MUST BE GOING!!
We're own to e final two, Frank inatra and eopatra!
Cleo, using slave labor on a major construction site is something so hatefully low, even I haven't done it. Though I've certainly DREAMED about it!
Mr. Trump, I've always been attracted to pow-erful men! You remind me of Julius Caesar! I'd love to talk about the similarities back in my antechamber!
Now THAT'S the art of the deal! Sinatra, YOU'RE FIRED!
Not so fast, Richie Rich! I think this is a good time to call in some of MY celebrity contacts! Say hello to your new silent partners, Trumpsky!
How'd you like to give up hosting Dead Celebrity Apprentice, and become a contestant?
Gurk! I may have misspoken! From one Chairman of the Board to another: Mr. Frank Sinatra, YOU are the winner!
And I did it my way, Jack!
TRUMP
CEMENT
TOM BUNK
WHATEVER IT IS I'M AGAINST IT!

CLASH DISMISSED DEPT.

They were locked in a bitter war of words for months. It was hurtful, it was ugly. But why? That is the question we keep coming back to. Why can't two of America's most "beloved" celebrities just get along? Are they that diametrically opposite that they can't help but despise the other? Or is it their similarity that fuels their hatred? We report, you decide with this invaluable reference chart...

THE STARTLING SIMILARITIES (AND DIFFERENCES) BETWEEN DONALD TRUMP AND ROSIE O'DONNELL

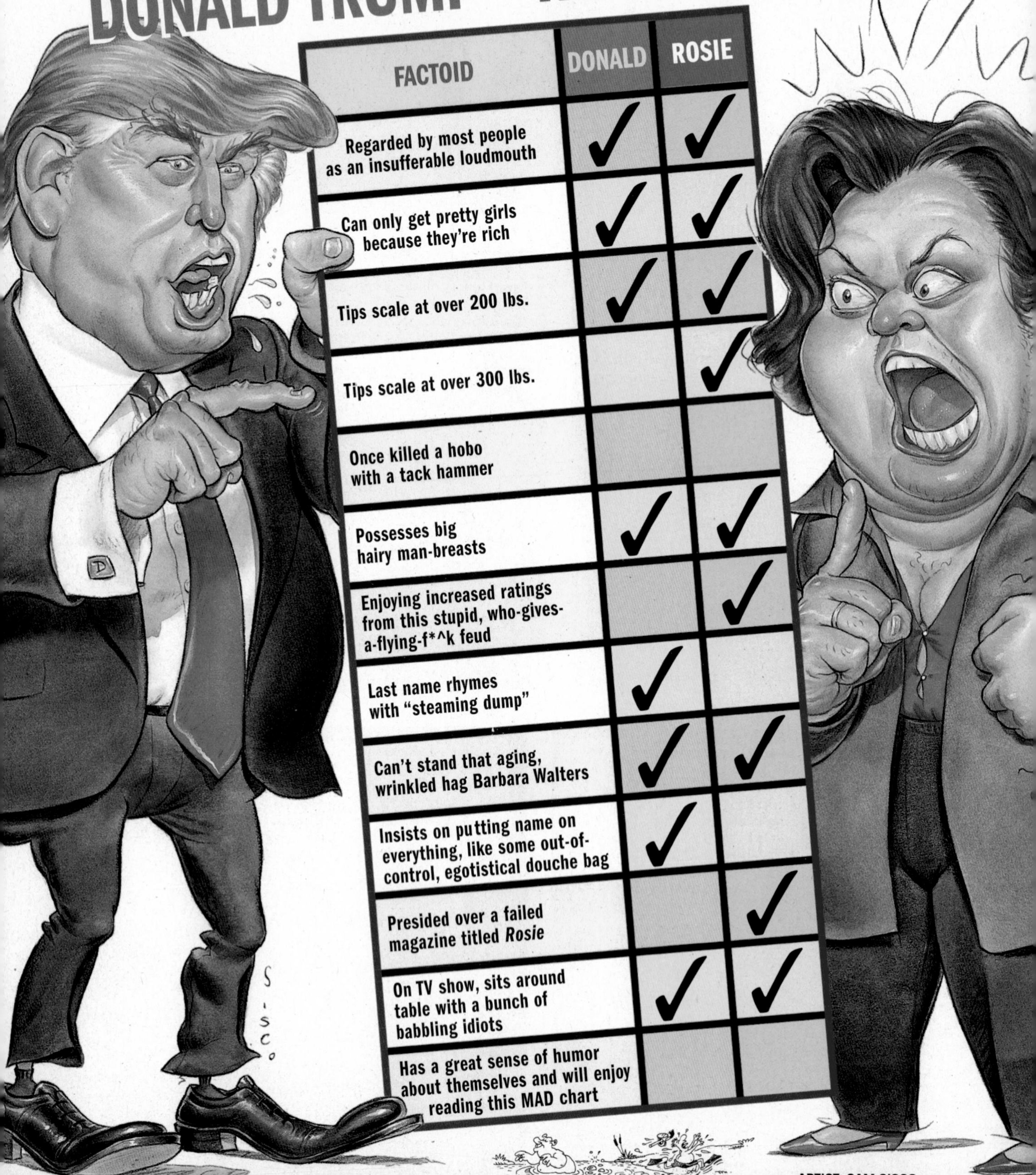

FACTOID	DONALD	ROSIE
Regarded by most people as an insufferable loudmouth	✓	✓
Can only get pretty girls because they're rich	✓	✓
Tips scale at over 200 lbs.	✓	✓
Tips scale at over 300 lbs.		✓
Once killed a hobo with a tack hammer		
Possesses big hairy man-breasts	✓	✓
Enjoying increased ratings from this stupid, who-gives-a-flying-f*^k feud		✓
Last name rhymes with "steaming dump"	✓	
Can't stand that aging, wrinkled hag Barbara Walters	✓	✓
Insists on putting name on everything, like some out-of-control, egotistical douche bag	✓	
Presided over a failed magazine titled *Rosie*		✓
On TV show, sits around table with a bunch of babbling idiots	✓	✓
Has a great sense of humor about themselves and will enjoy reading this MAD chart		

ARTIST: SAM SISCO

Donald Trump's New Presidential Seal

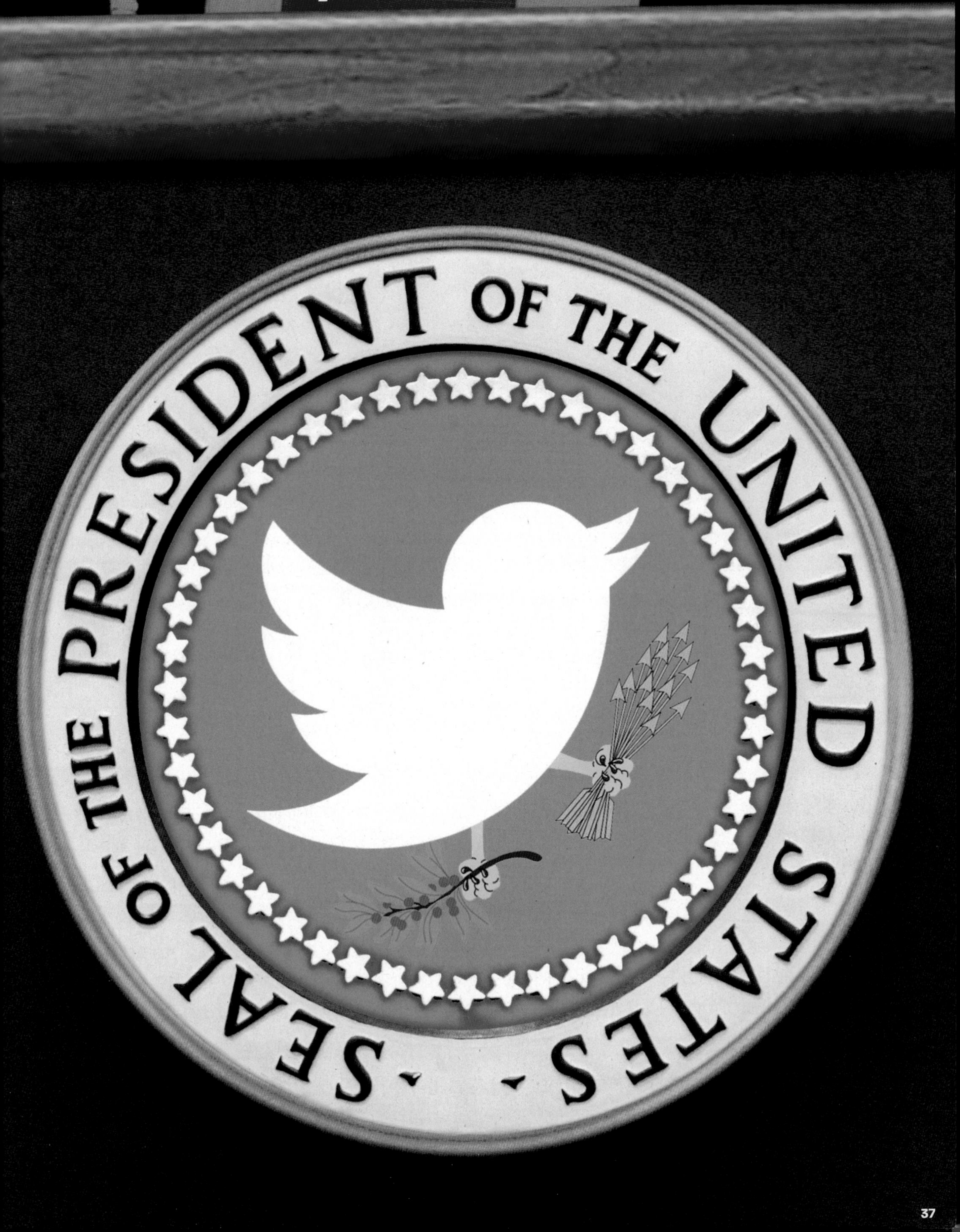
SEAL OF THE PRESIDENT OF THE UNITED STATES

THE DEVOLUTION OF TRUMP

WRITER AND ARTIST: J.C. DUFFY

TRUMP TWEETS
THANKSGIVING

Saw @PresidentObama pardon the turkey. Unimpressed. I like turkeys that DON'T get captured!

Love the kids' table — it's the perfect place to scout out my fourth wife!

So excited for @MelaniaTrump's Thanksgiving specialty: frozen corn & Crispix with ketchup. Now that's eating!

Not going to @DonaldJTrumpJr's for Thanksgiving. Last year he served the endangered elephant he shot. Gamey!

A great day to remember how the Indians welcomed the Pilgrims to America, but NOT Muslims or Syrian refugees. Smart!

If you're committing hate crimes in my name, please stop. It's Thanksgiving, for God's sake! You can always pick it back up tomorrow!

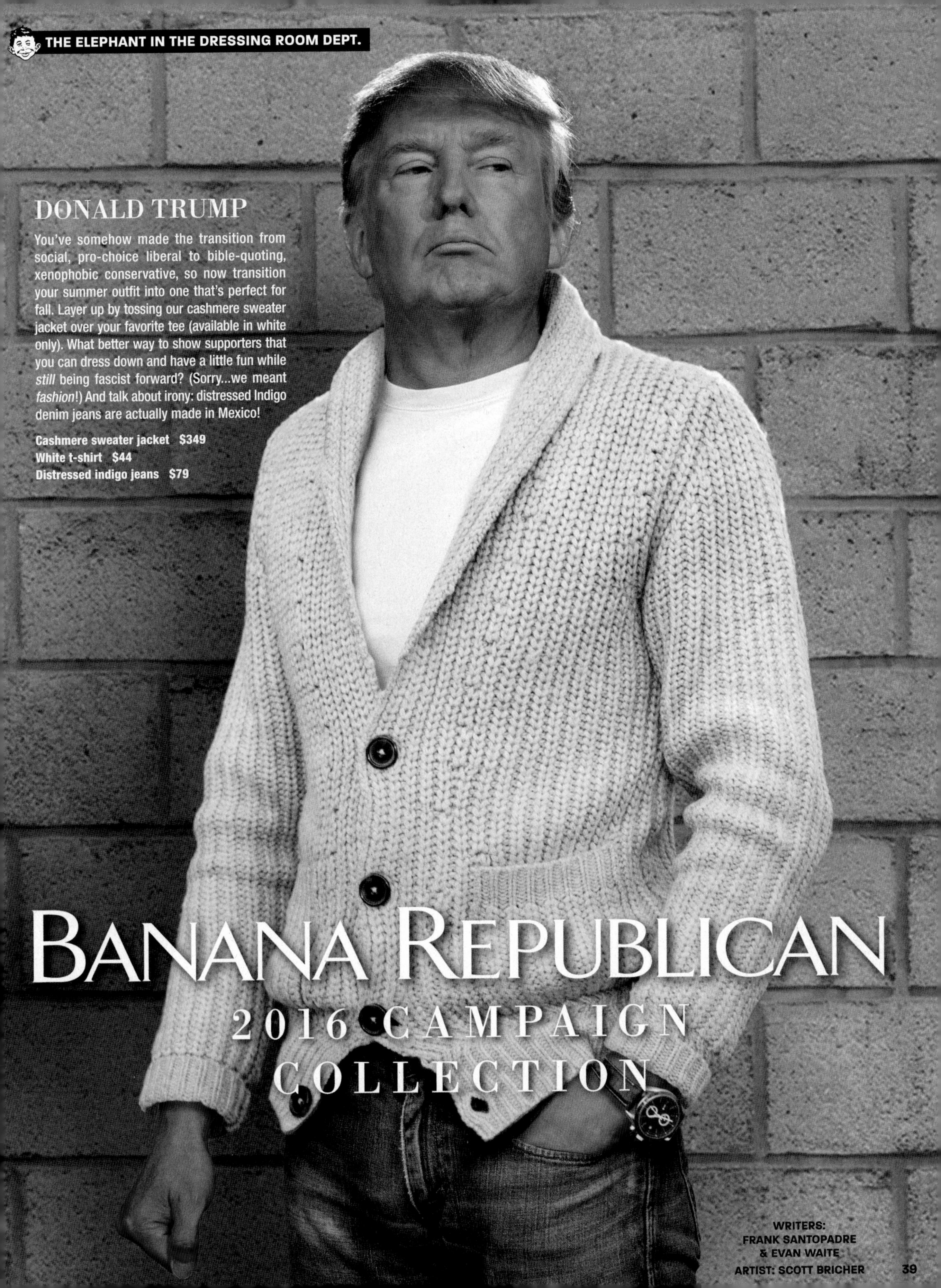

BANANA REPUBLICAN

2016 CAMPAIGN COLLECTION

DONALD TRUMP

You've somehow made the transition from social, pro-choice liberal to bible-quoting, xenophobic conservative, so now transition your summer outfit into one that's perfect for fall. Layer up by tossing our cashmere sweater jacket over your favorite tee (available in white only). What better way to show supporters that you can dress down and have a little fun while *still* being fascist forward? (Sorry...we meant *fashion*!) And talk about irony: distressed Indigo denim jeans are actually made in Mexico!

Cashmere sweater jacket $349
White t-shirt $44
Distressed indigo jeans $79

WRITERS:
FRANK SANTOPADRE
& EVAN WAITE
ARTIST: SCOTT BRICHER

MARCO RUBIO

You're not especially bright, charismatic or experienced, yet your party's puppet masters have anointed you as the "establishment candidate," so you don't want to let them down. No worries! In our hand-stitched jacket and colorful gingham shirt, you'll stand out like a black dude at a Tea Party rally, while tailored trousers offer pockets deep enough to hold wads of Koch Brothers cash! Finally, our classic cowboy boots with Cuban heels not only make you look taller in the saddle, but are great for kicking your fellow Latinos out of the country you're so fortunate to call home.

Hand-stitched jacket $209
Gingham shirt $57
Boots $179

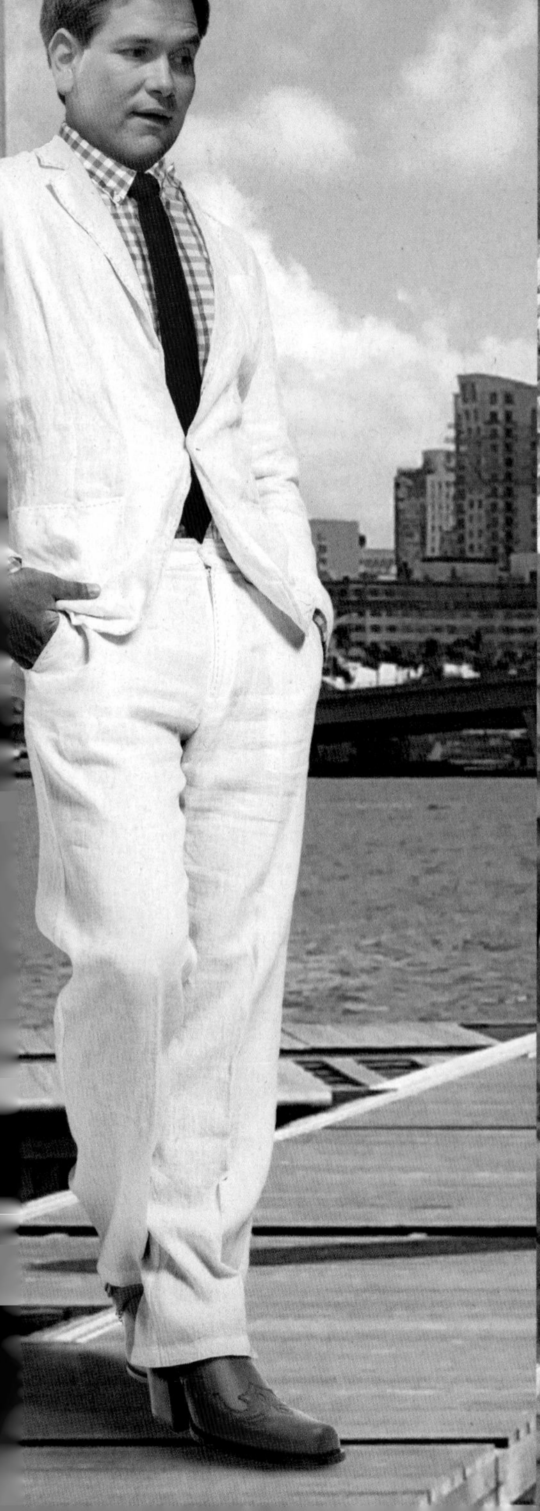

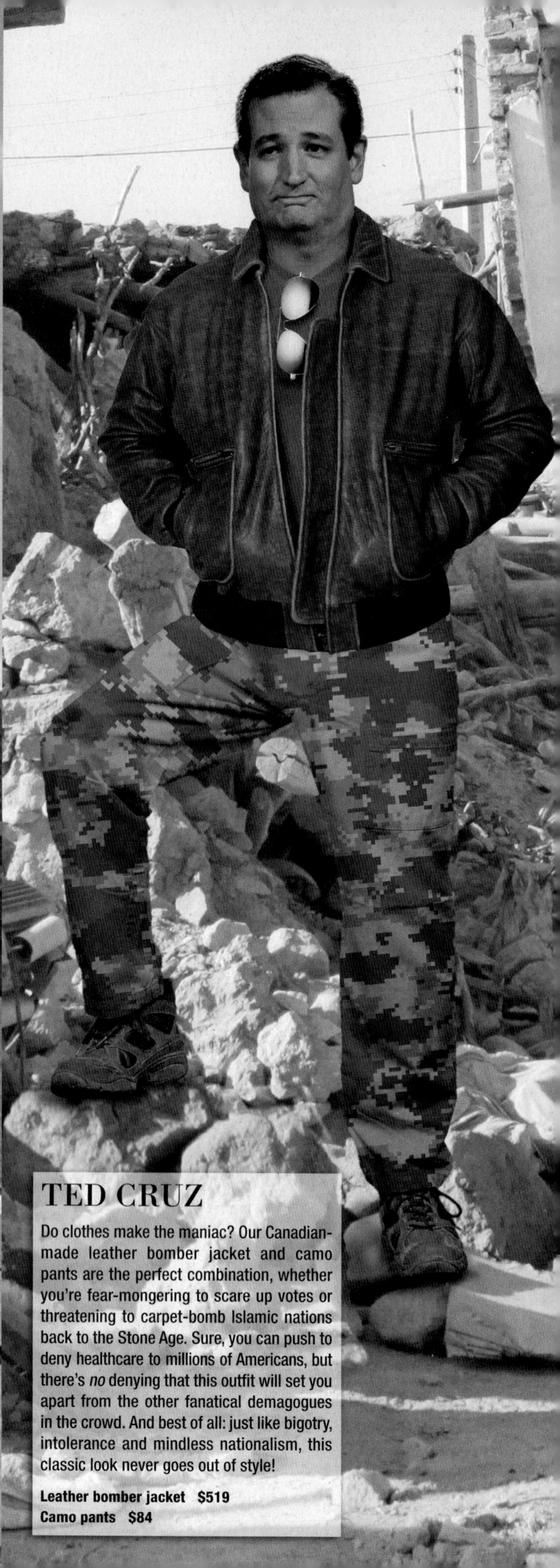

TED CRUZ

Do clothes make the maniac? Our Canadian-made leather bomber jacket and camo pants are the perfect combination, whether you're fear-mongering to scare up votes or threatening to carpet-bomb Islamic nations back to the Stone Age. Sure, you can push to deny healthcare to millions of Americans, but there's *no* denying that this outfit will set you apart from the other fanatical demagogues in the crowd. And best of all: just like bigotry, intolerance and mindless nationalism, this classic look never goes out of style!

Leather bomber jacket $519
Camo pants $84

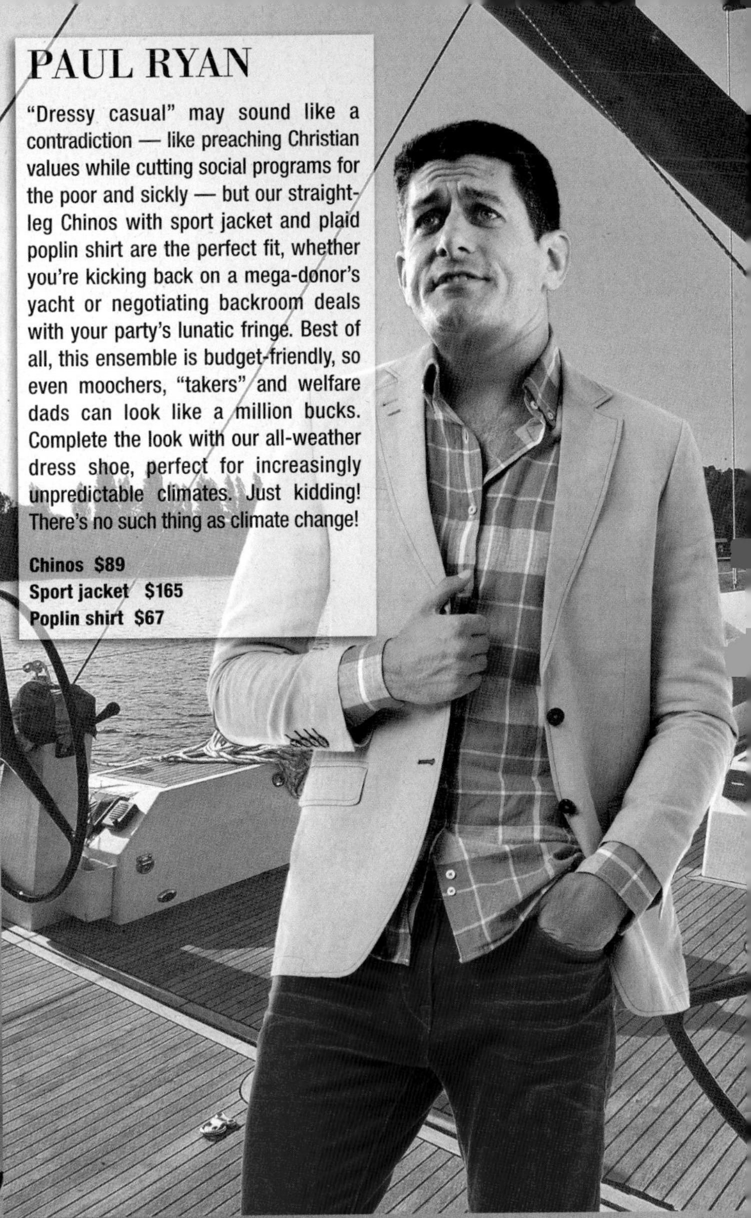

PAUL RYAN

"Dressy casual" may sound like a contradiction — like preaching Christian values while cutting social programs for the poor and sickly — but our straight-leg Chinos with sport jacket and plaid poplin shirt are the perfect fit, whether you're kicking back on a mega-donor's yacht or negotiating backroom deals with your party's lunatic fringe. Best of all, this ensemble is budget-friendly, so even moochers, "takers" and welfare dads can look like a million bucks. Complete the look with our all-weather dress shoe, perfect for increasingly unpredictable climates. Just kidding! There's no such thing as climate change!

Chinos $89
Sport jacket $165
Poplin shirt $67

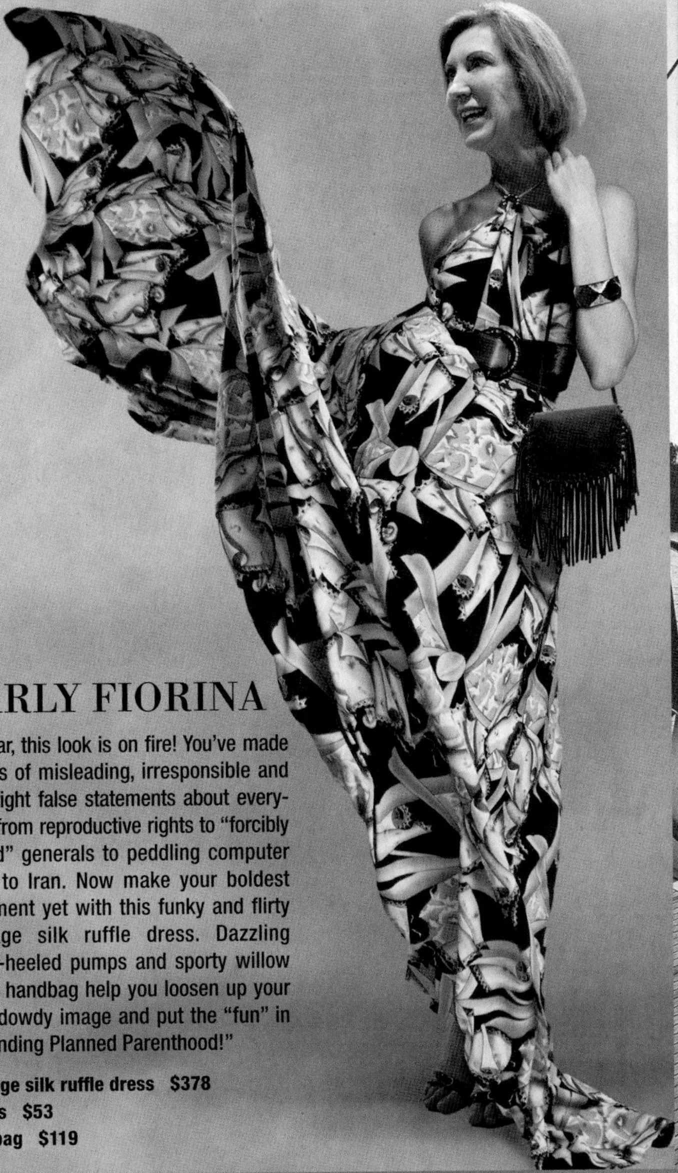

:ARLY FIORINA

ar, liar, this look is on fire! You've made ızens of misleading, irresponsible and ɔwnright false statements about every-ing from reproductive rights to "forcibly ·tired" generals to peddling computer ırts to Iran. Now make your boldest atement yet with this funky and flirty eritage silk ruffle dress. Dazzling tten-heeled pumps and sporty willow inge handbag help you loosen up your our, dowdy image and put the "fun" in lefunding Planned Parenthood!"

eritage silk ruffle dress $378
umps $53
andbag $119

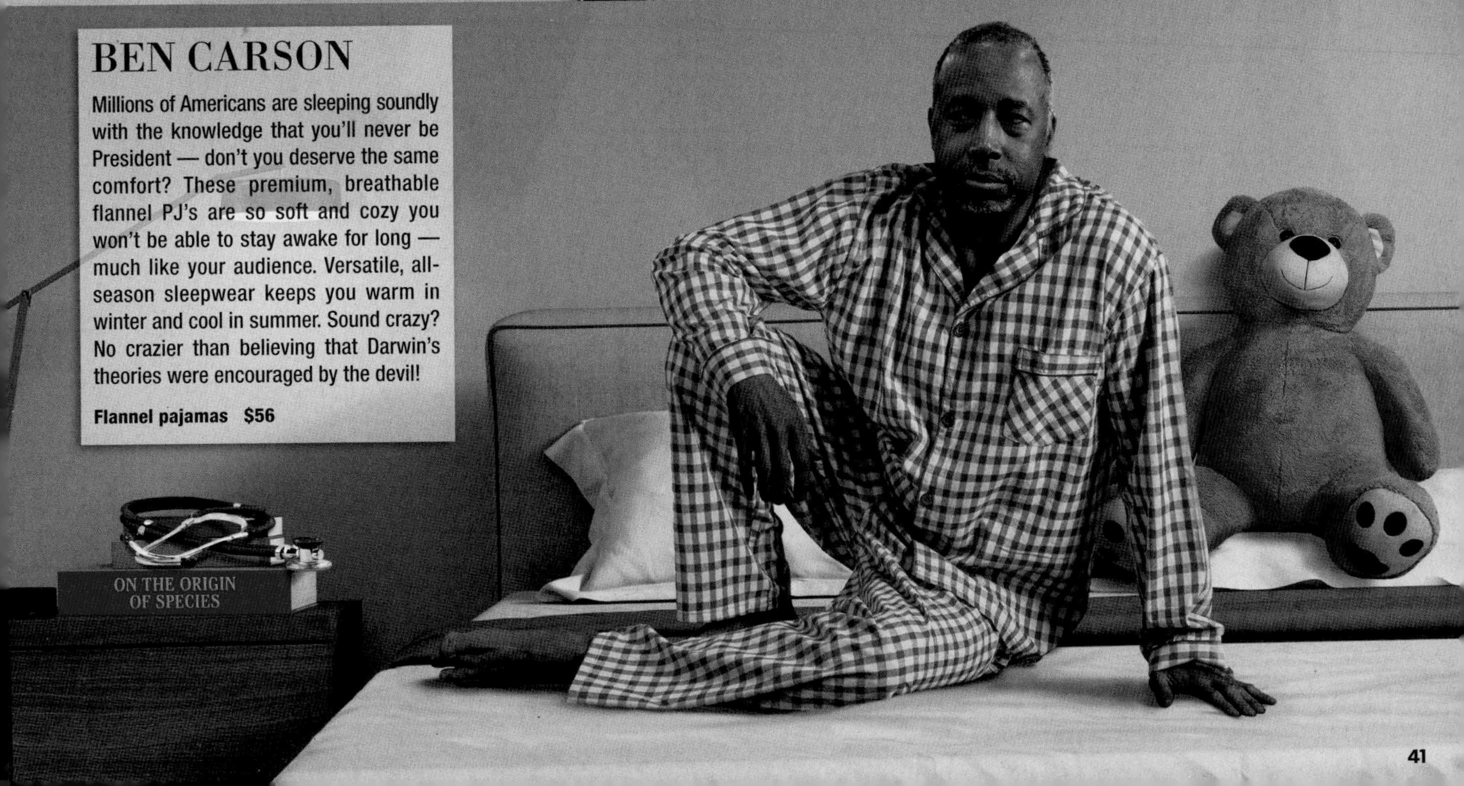
ON THE ORIGIN
OF SPECIES

BEN CARSON

Millions of Americans are sleeping soundly with the knowledge that you'll never be President — don't you deserve the same comfort? These premium, breathable flannel PJ's are so soft and cozy you won't be able to stay awake for long — much like your audience. Versatile, all-season sleepwear keeps you warm in winter and cool in summer. Sound crazy? No crazier than believing that Darwin's theories were encouraged by the devil!

Flannel pajamas $56

CHRIS CHRISTIE

Dodging investigations, insulting reporters, bullying teachers...your busy lifestyle demands an active wardrobe made of light, breathable fabric — especially when breathing *itself* is such a challenge. Our taut patterned shorts and retro *On the Waterfront* cropped tanktop allow you to wave your veto pen at sensible gun legislation without hardly breaking a sweat. Finish it off with our sporty suede slip-ons. You may not be able to see your feet, but take our word for it — you're stylin'!

Rayon patterned shorts $56
Retro fitted tanktop $39
Suede slip-ons $97

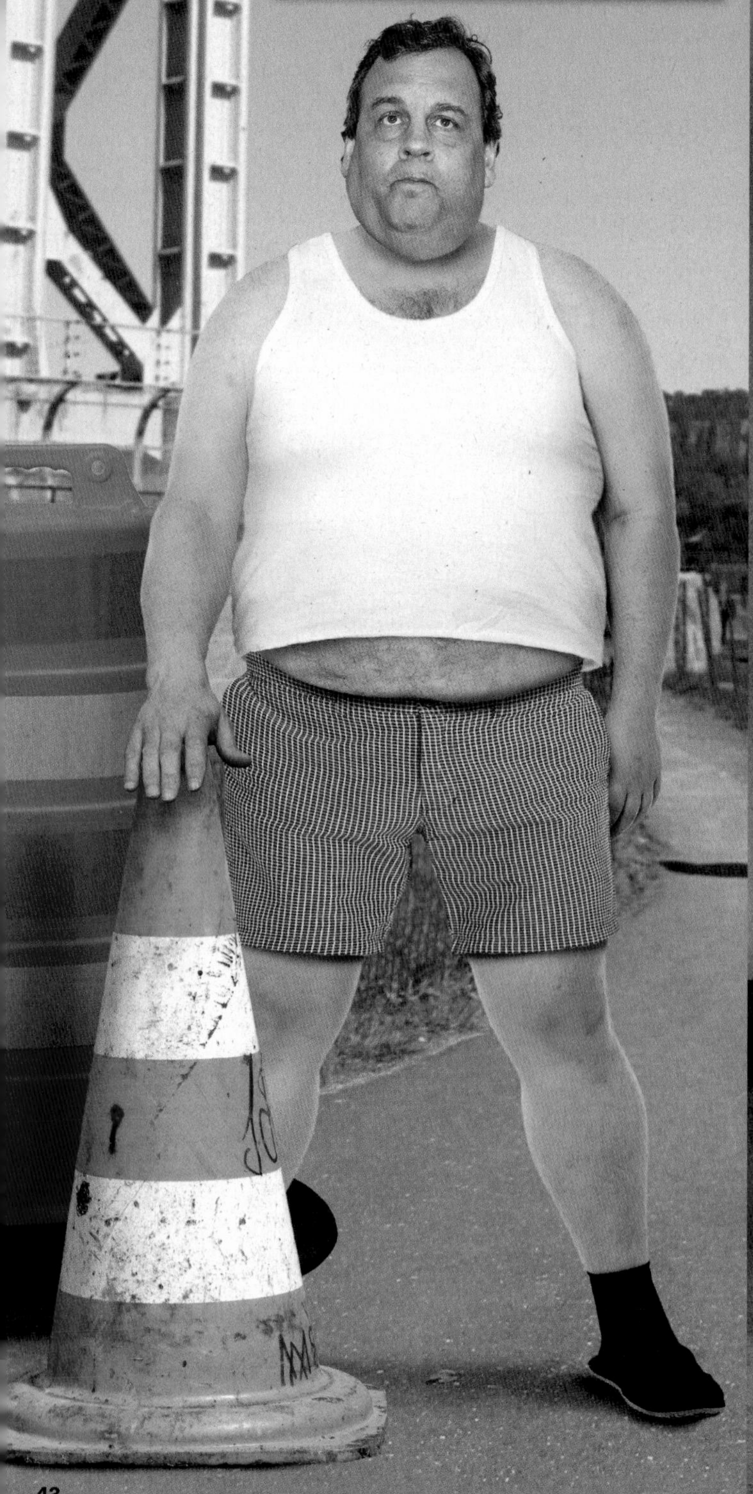

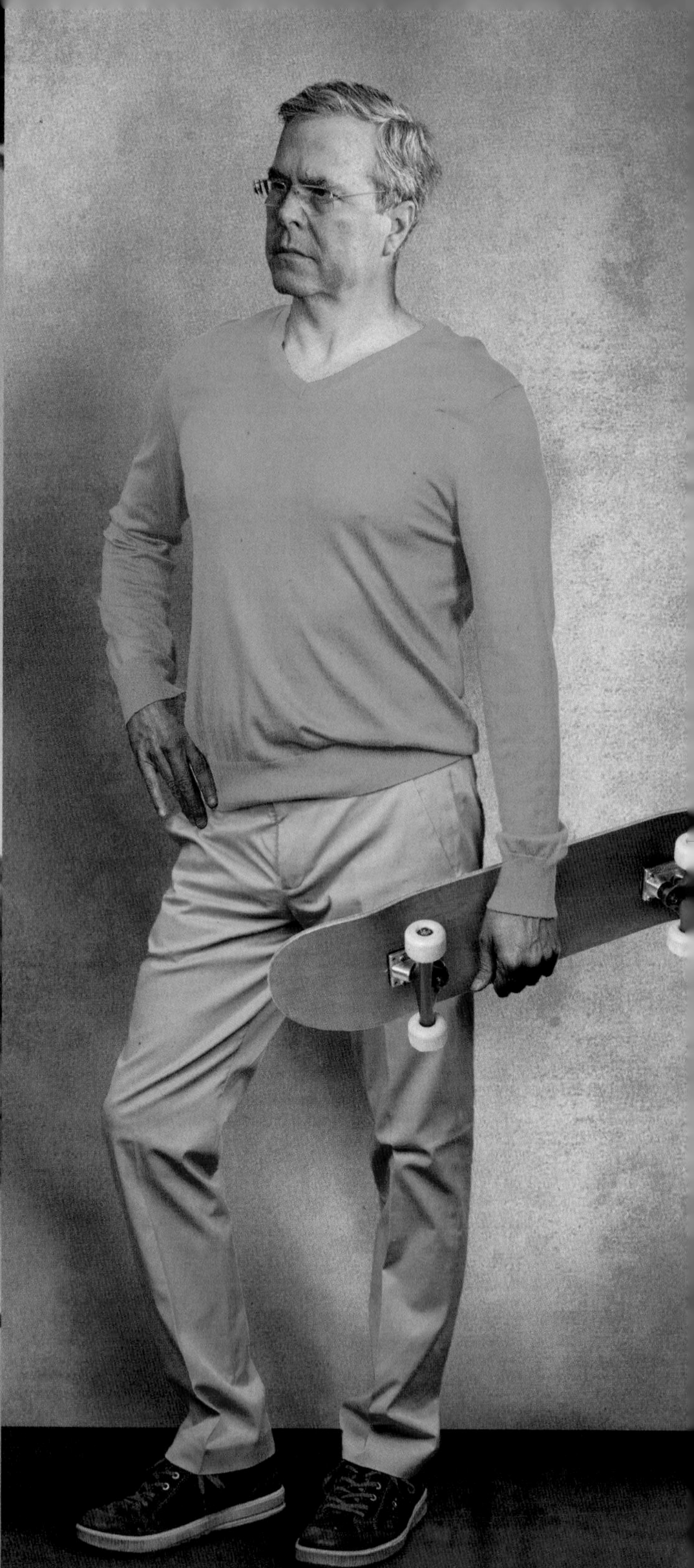

JEB BUSH

Just because you've blown through millions of dollars in a disastrous election bid doesn't mean you have to spend a fortune on clothing. With our affordable cashmere vee pullover and vintage straight chinos, you can at least dress the part, just like the "smarter" Bush brother! Even better, the sweater is reversible, just like your stance on immigration reform. Finally, our low-cut nubuck sneaker offers cushioned arch support, whether you're running from your brother's war record or simply running your own campaign into the ground.

Cashmere vee pullover $49
Vintage straight chinos $77
Low-cut nubuck sneakers $109

One Fine Morning In the Windy City

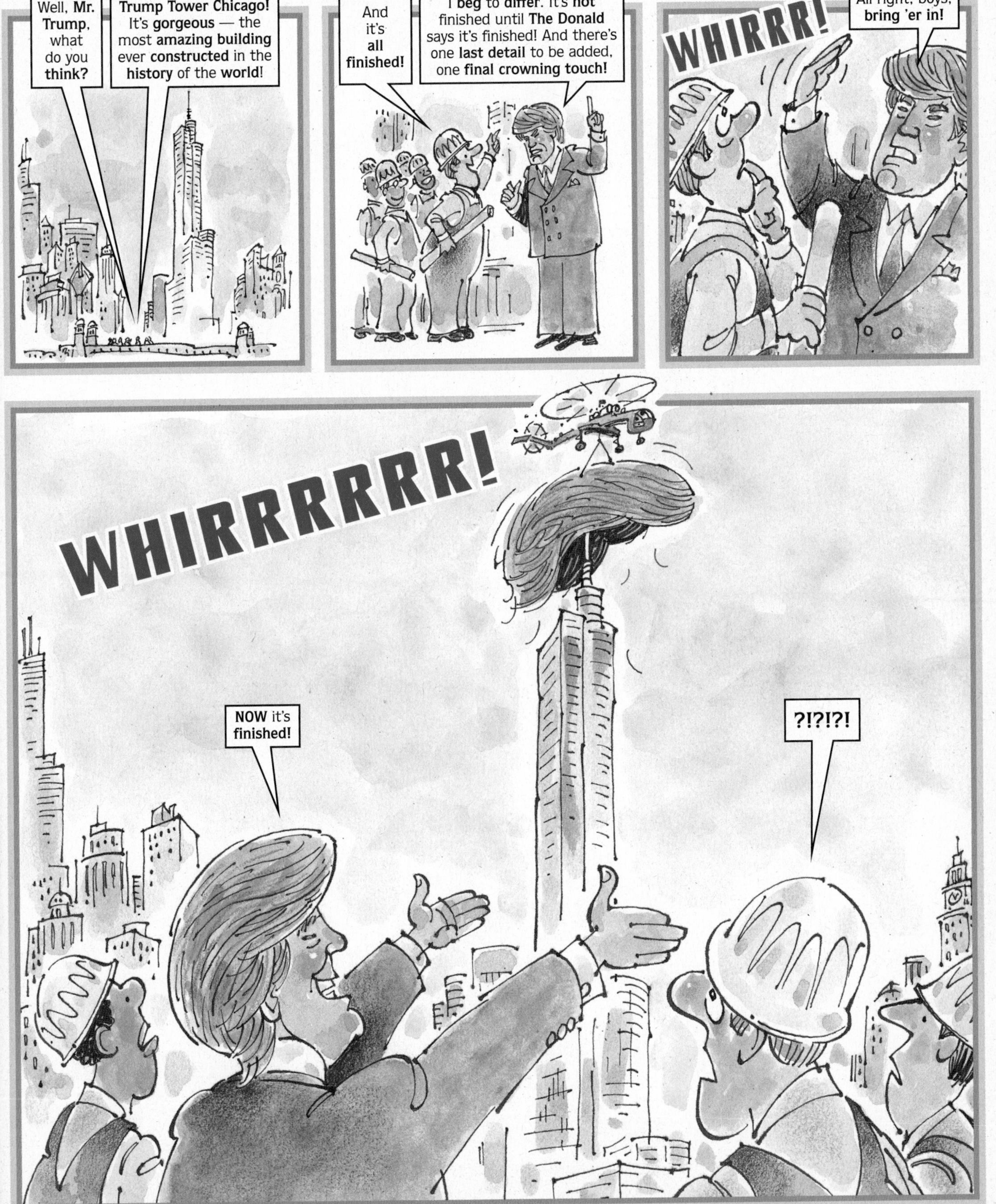
Well, Mr. Trump, what do you think?
Trump Tower Chicago! It's gorgeous — the most amazing building ever constructed in the history of the world!
And it's all finished!
I beg to differ. It's not finished until The Donald says it's finished! And there's one last detail to be added, one final crowning touch!
WHIRRR!
All right, boys, bring 'er in!
WHIRRRRRRR!
NOW it's finished!
?!?!?!

WRITER: SCOTT MENDENHALL ARTIST: PAUL COKER

TONIGHT!
"THE BORDER WAR"
TALE OF THE TAPE

DONALD "EL CRAPPO" TRUMP VS JOAQUIN "EL CHAPO" GUZMAN

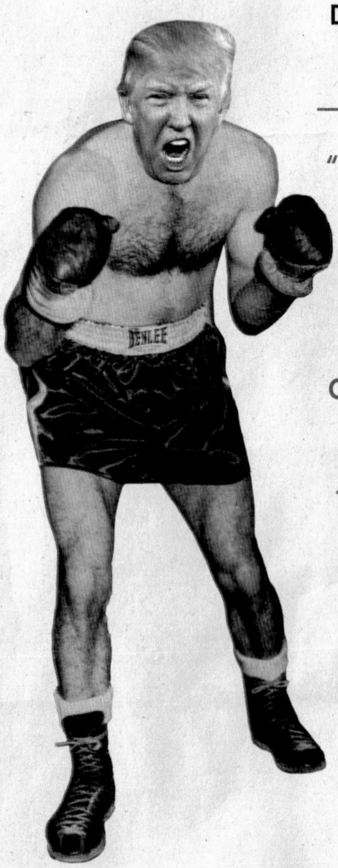

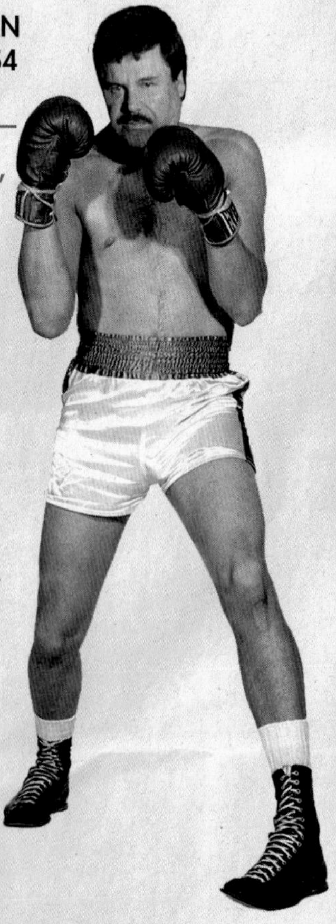

DONALD TRUMP June 14, 1946 Queens, NY		JOAQUIN GUZMAN December 25, 1954 La Tuna, MX
"YOU'RE FIRED!"	CATCHPHRASE	"DIG MY TUNNEL, POR FAVOR!"
$9 BILLION (UNVERIFIED)	NET WORTH	$1 BILLION (UNVERIFIED)
THE TRUMP ORGANIZATION	NOTORIOUS GROUP HE LEADS	THE SINALOA CARTEL
TRUMP TOWER	INFAMOUS CONSTRUCTION	ESCAPE TUNNEL
THE CELEBRITY APPRENTICE	MIND-KILLING PRODUCT	COCAINE
NO	BELOVED BY MEXICANS, DESPITE BEING VILE	YES
0	NUMBER OF LEGITIMATE PRESIDENTIAL RUNS	0

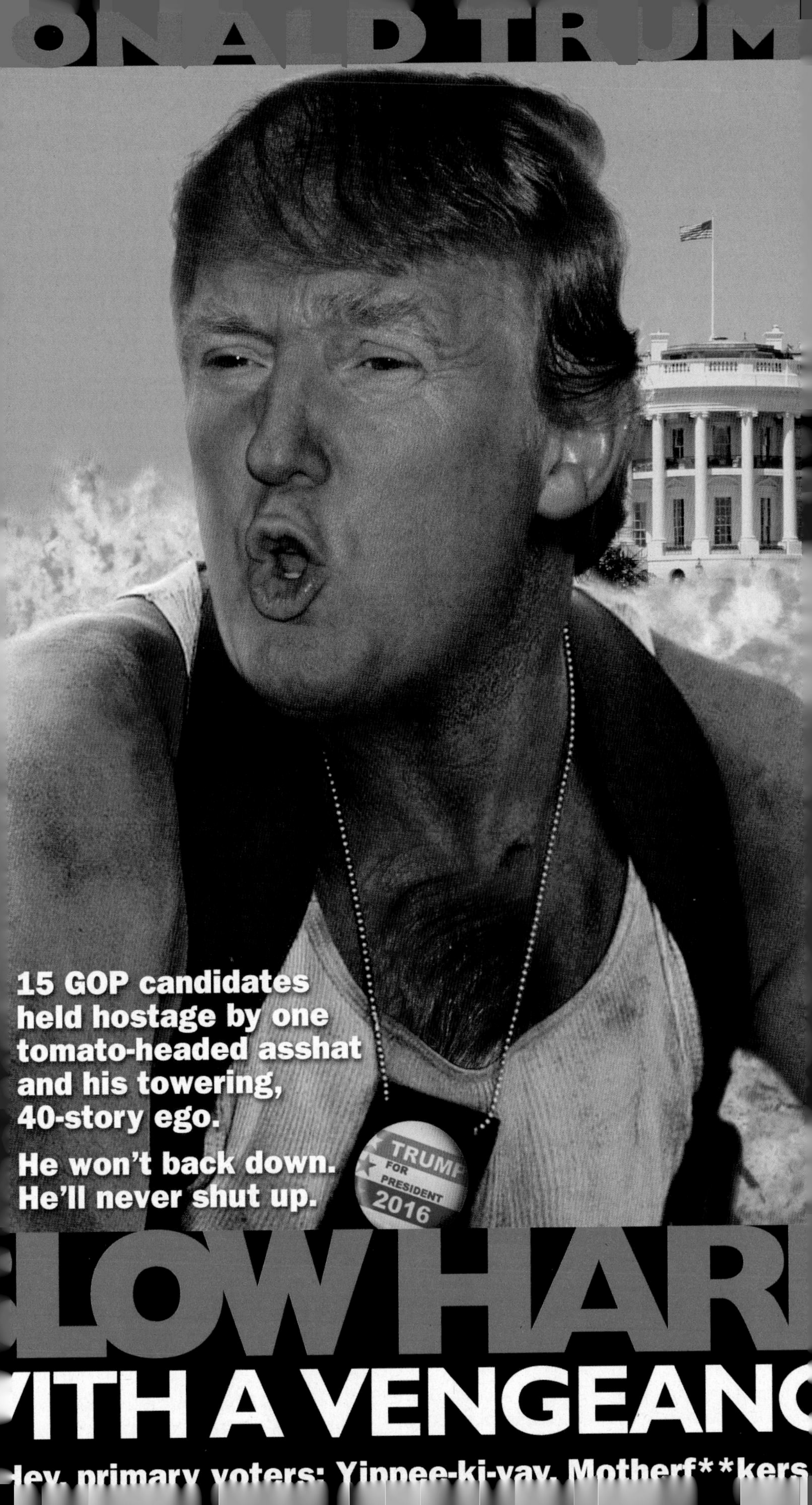
ONALD TRUM
15 GOP candidates held hostage by one tomato-headed asshat and his towering, 40-story ego.
He won't back down. He'll never shut up.
TRUMP FOR PRESIDENT 2016
LOW HAR
ITH A VENGEANC
ey, primary voters: Yippee-ki-yay, Motherf**kers

THE INGRATE WHITE WAY DEPT.

Trump Criticizes Other Broadway Shows Besides HAMILTON

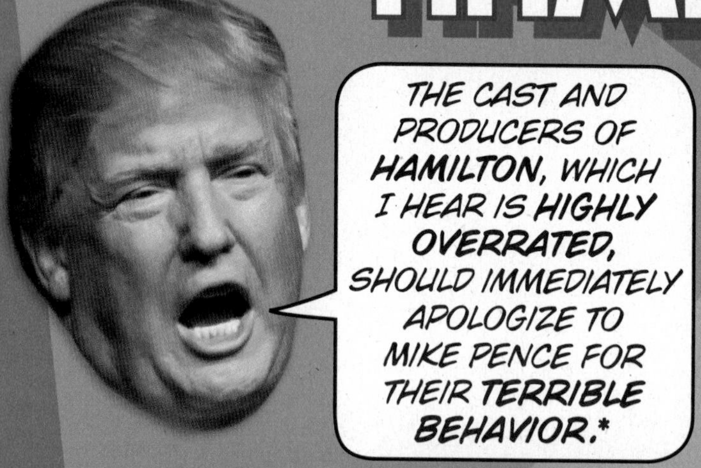
THE CAST AND PRODUCERS OF HAMILTON, WHICH I HEAR IS HIGHLY OVERRATED, SHOULD IMMEDIATELY APOLOGIZE TO MIKE PENCE FOR THEIR TERRIBLE BEHAVIOR.*

*actual tweet from November 20, 2016

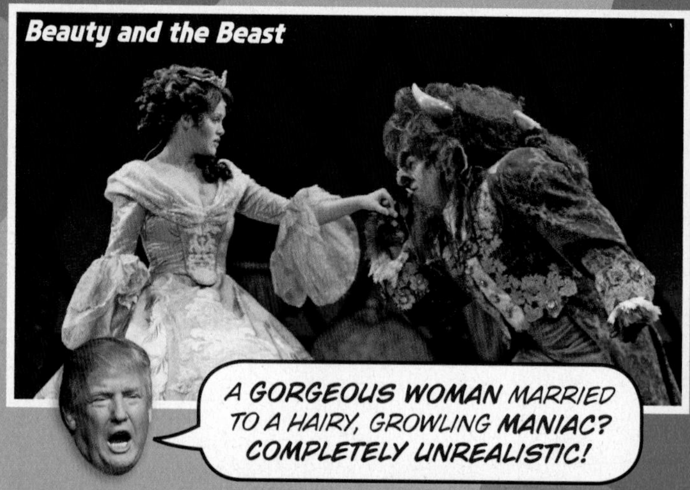
Beauty and the Beast
A GORGEOUS WOMAN MARRIED TO A HAIRY, GROWLING MANIAC? COMPLETELY UNREALISTIC!

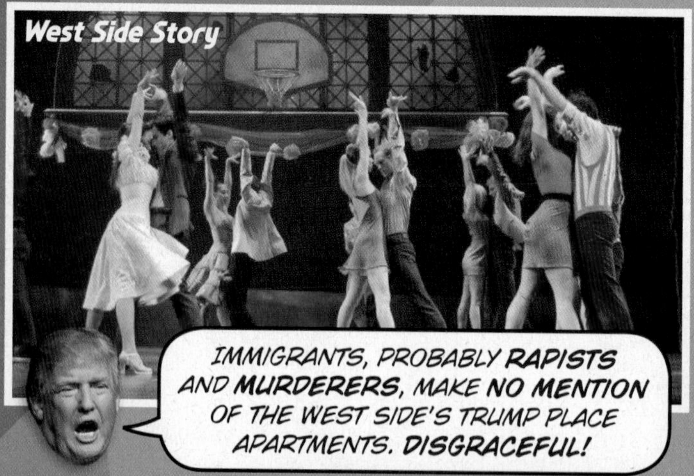
West Side Story
IMMIGRANTS, PROBABLY RAPISTS AND MURDERERS, MAKE NO MENTION OF THE WEST SIDE'S TRUMP PLACE APARTMENTS. DISGRACEFUL!

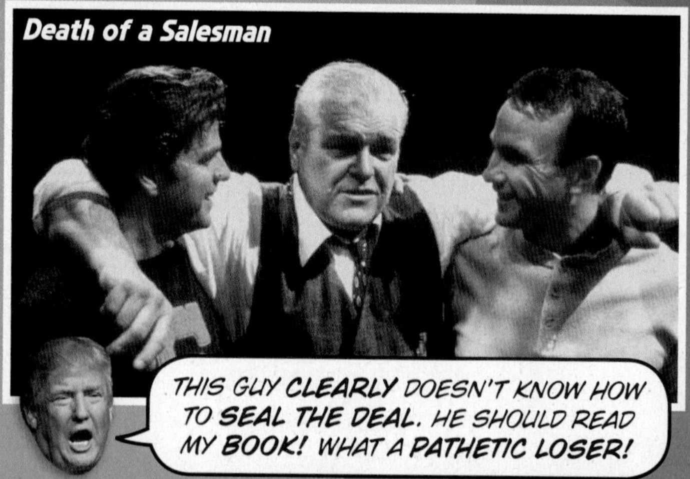
Death of a Salesman
THIS GUY CLEARLY DOESN'T KNOW HOW TO SEAL THE DEAL. HE SHOULD READ MY BOOK! WHAT A PATHETIC LOSER!

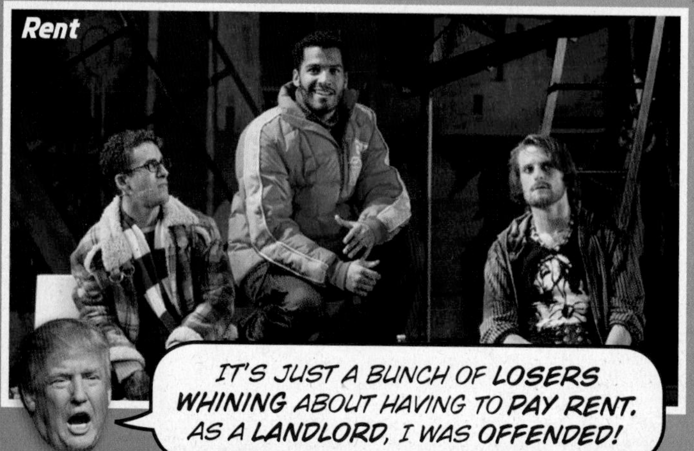
Rent
IT'S JUST A BUNCH OF LOSERS WHINING ABOUT HAVING TO PAY RENT. AS A LANDLORD, I WAS OFFENDED!

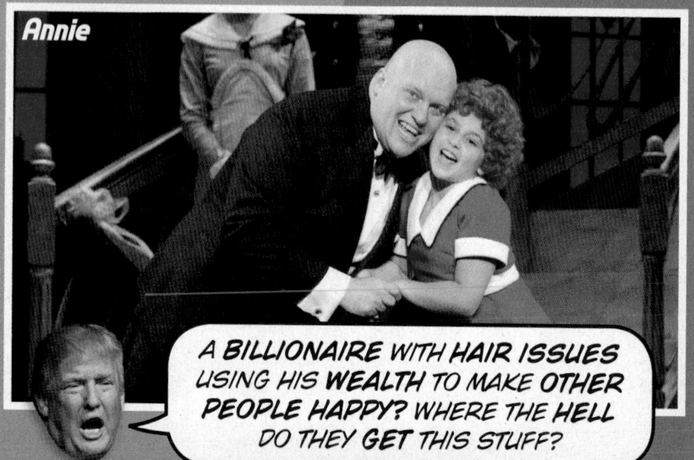
Annie
A BILLIONAIRE WITH HAIR ISSUES USING HIS WEALTH TO MAKE OTHER PEOPLE HAPPY? WHERE THE HELL DO THEY GET THIS STUFF?

7 WAYS THAT DONALD TRUMP CELEBRATED HIS 70TH BIRTHDAY

MAKE
AMERICA
GREAT AGAIN

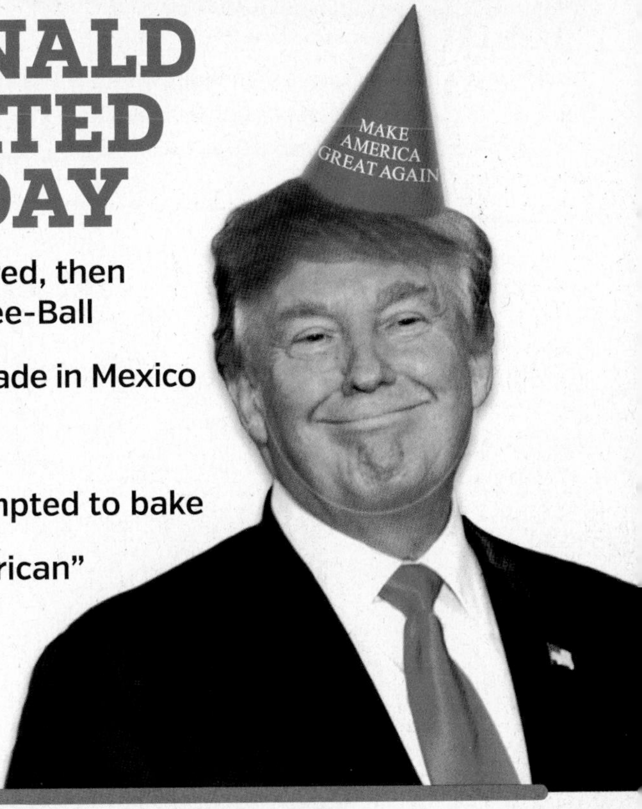

- Spending the day recklessly fomenting racial hatred, then hitting up Dave & Buster's for a few rounds of Skee-Ball
- Angrily beating on a piñata because, well, it was made in Mexico
- Tweeting out 70 new bulls#!t lies about Obama
- Trying to choke down the cake that Melania attempted to bake
- Opening the birthday card from his "African-American"
- Having his pal, Dr.Ben Carson, check his prostate
- Honestly, we have no idea, but there is "something going on"

TRUMP UNVEILS HIS NEW CAMPAIGN TEAM

SARAH PALIN
Implosion Coordinator

LANCE ARMSTRONG
Mendacity Supervisor

VLADIMIR PUTIN
Foreign Policy Advisor

CURT SCHILLING
Social Media Strategist

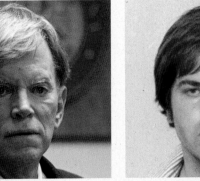

DAVID DUKE
African-American Outreach Liaison

JOHN HINCKLEY JR.
"Second Amendement People" Aide

It's time to make the funny pages great again! So let's turn back the clock (and social progress) as we grimly smile at the antics of America's First Dad and Mom, and their adorable scamps...

THE TRUM

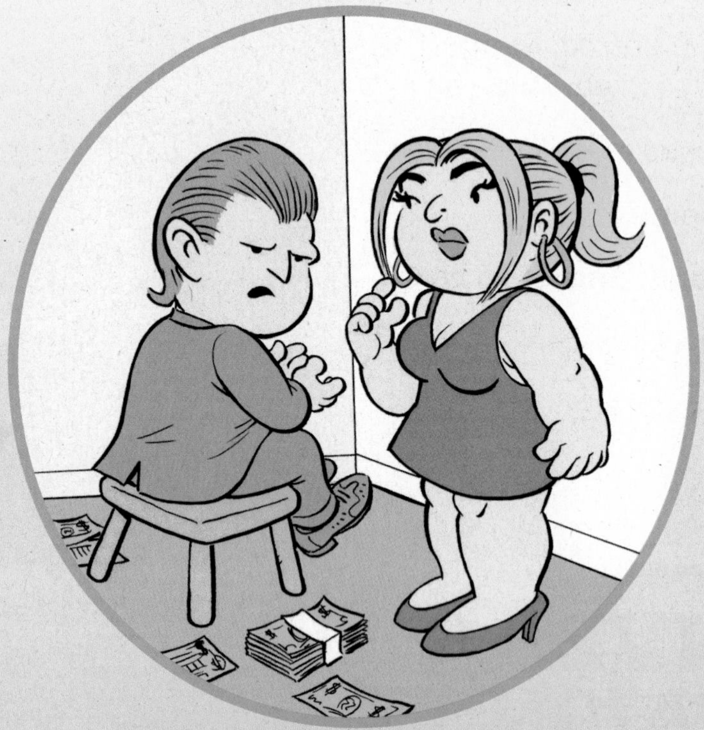

"Dad's punishing me for sayin' the seven dirty words. 'Live, from New York, it's Saturday Night!'"

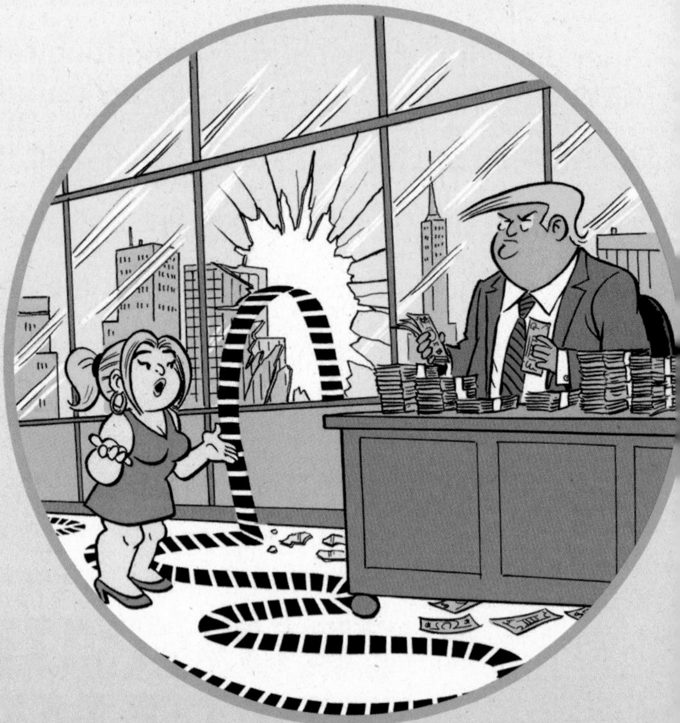

"Daddy, where'd Chris Christie go?"

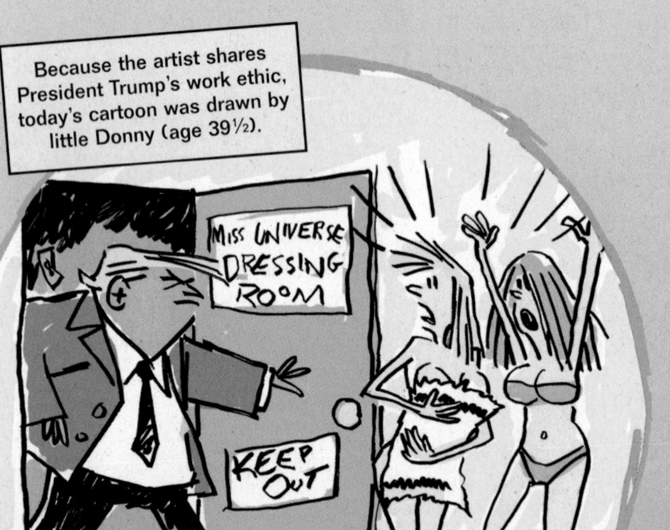
Because the artist shares President Trump's work ethic, today's cartoon was drawn by little Donny (age 39½).
MISS UNIVERSE DRESSING ROOM
KEEP OUT

My Father is the #1 best at international relations!

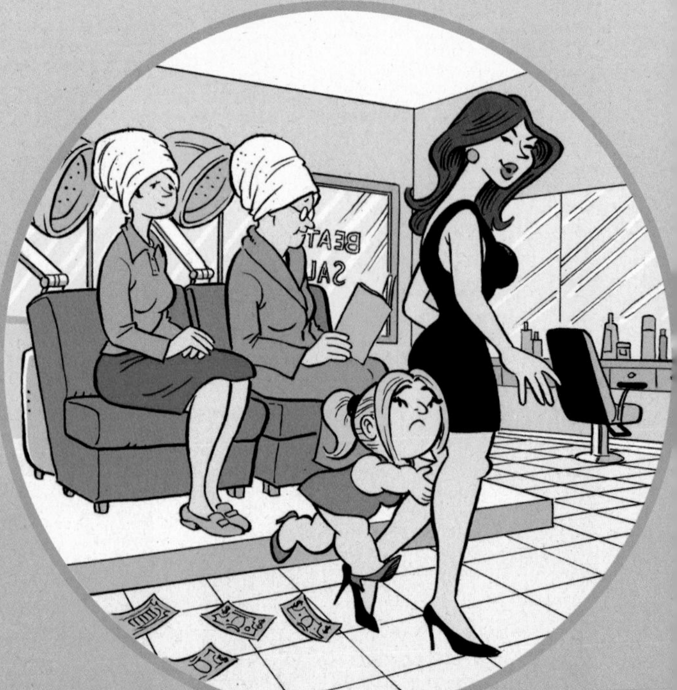

"No, sweetie, not EVERYTHING is radical Islamic terrorism."

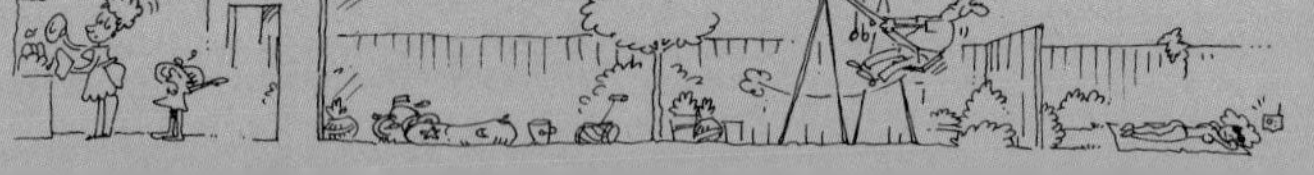

IP FAMILY CIRCUS

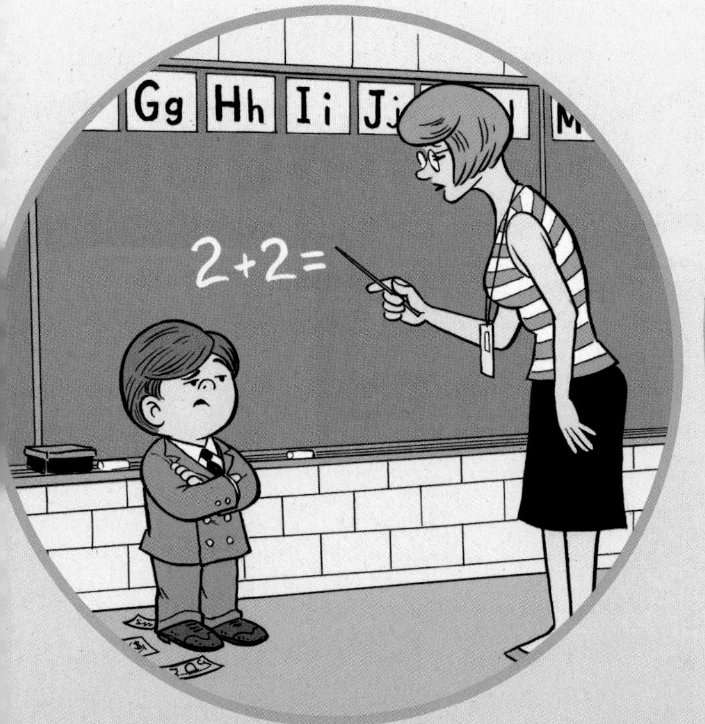
Gg Hh Ii
2+2=

"2+2 is 4, which is what my daddy said you are after he saw you at the last parent-teacher conference."

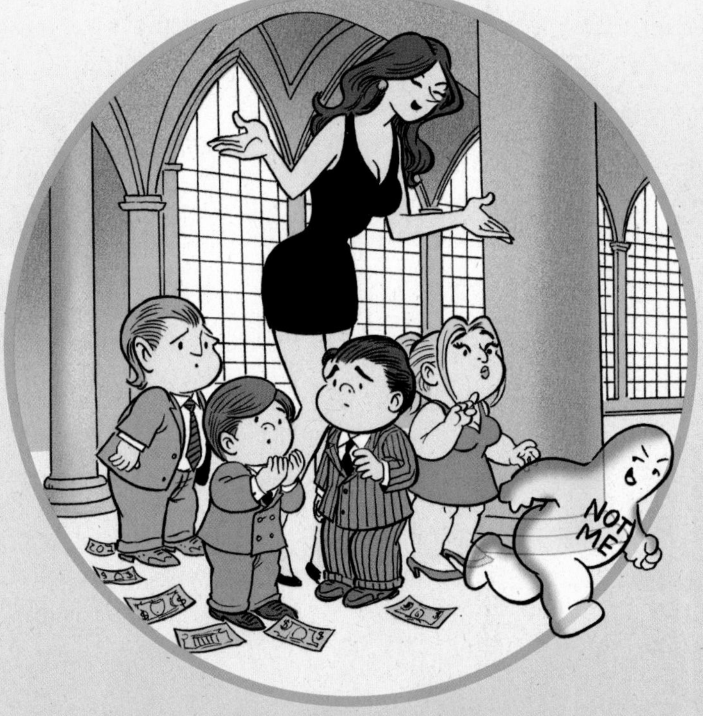
NOT ME

"Who thinks your father can bring this divided nation together?"

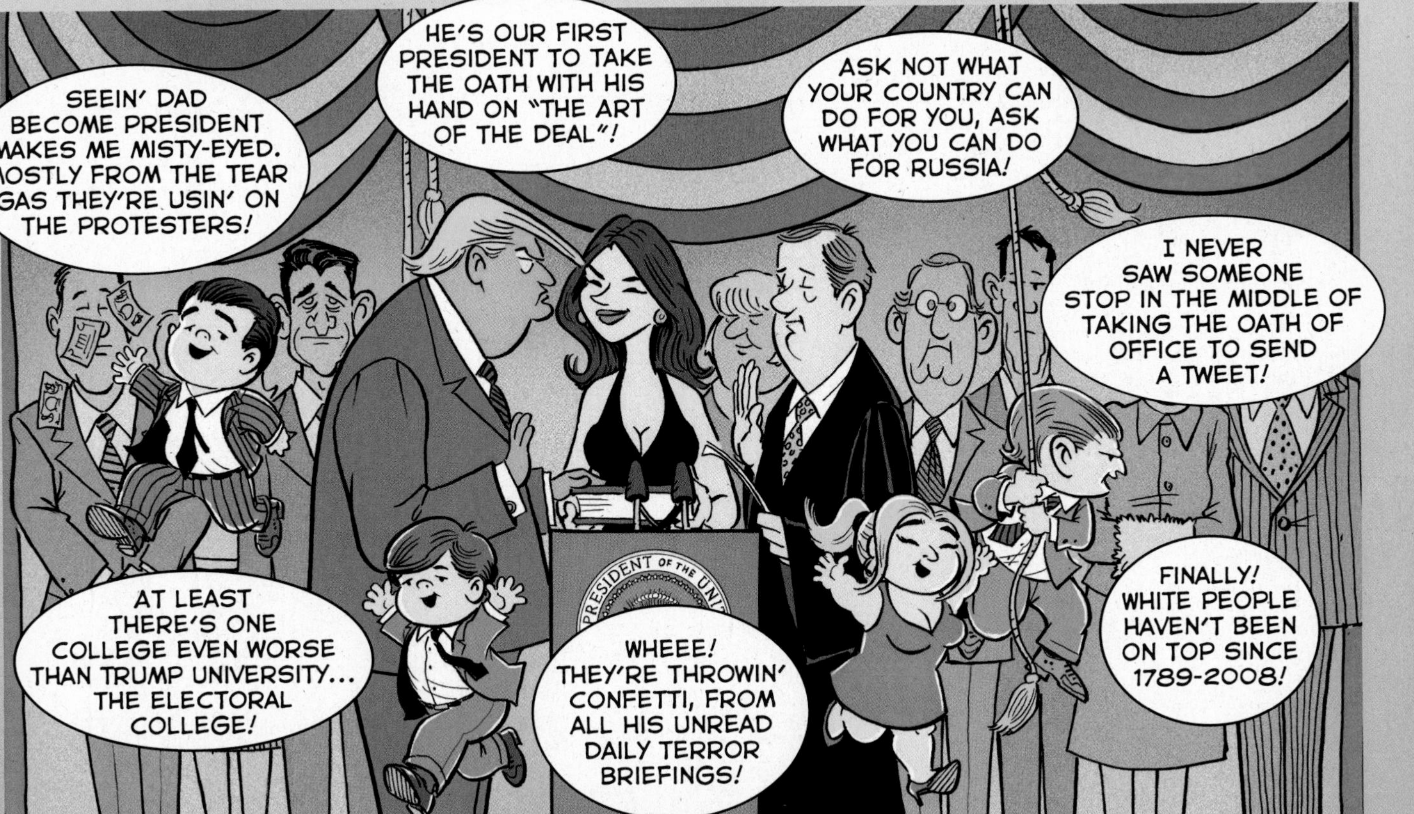
SEEIN' DAD BECOME PRESIDENT MAKES ME MISTY-EYED. MOSTLY FROM THE TEAR GAS THEY'RE USIN' ON THE PROTESTERS!
HE'S OUR FIRST PRESIDENT TO TAKE THE OATH WITH HIS HAND ON "THE ART OF THE DEAL"!
ASK NOT WHAT YOUR COUNTRY CAN DO FOR YOU, ASK WHAT YOU CAN DO FOR RUSSIA!
I NEVER SAW SOMEONE STOP IN THE MIDDLE OF TAKING THE OATH OF OFFICE TO SEND A TWEET!
AT LEAST THERE'S ONE COLLEGE EVEN WORSE THAN TRUMP UNIVERSITY... THE ELECTORAL COLLEGE!
WHEEE! THEY'RE THROWIN' CONFETTI, FROM ALL HIS UNREAD DAILY TERROR BRIEFINGS!
FINALLY! WHITE PEOPLE HAVEN'T BEEN ON TOP SINCE 1789-2008!

WRITER: DESMOND DEVLIN ARTIST: TOM RICHMOND

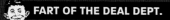
The Startling Similarities and Differences Between
TRUMP'S PRESS CONFERENCE
and
A BUS STATION BATHROOM

	Trump's Press Conference	Bus Station Bathroom
Is full of ugly sounds that you'll never be able to unhear	✓	✓
Makes you question the existence of a just and loving God	✓	✓
Features a high degree of decorum and respect for those who have gone before	—	—
There's someone on staff capable of cleaning up the resulting messes	—	✓
Is a good setting for learning facts about geopolitical complexities	—	—
S#!t, s#!t and more s#!t!	✓	✓

HATS OFF TO TRUMP FOR DENOUNCING THE KKK

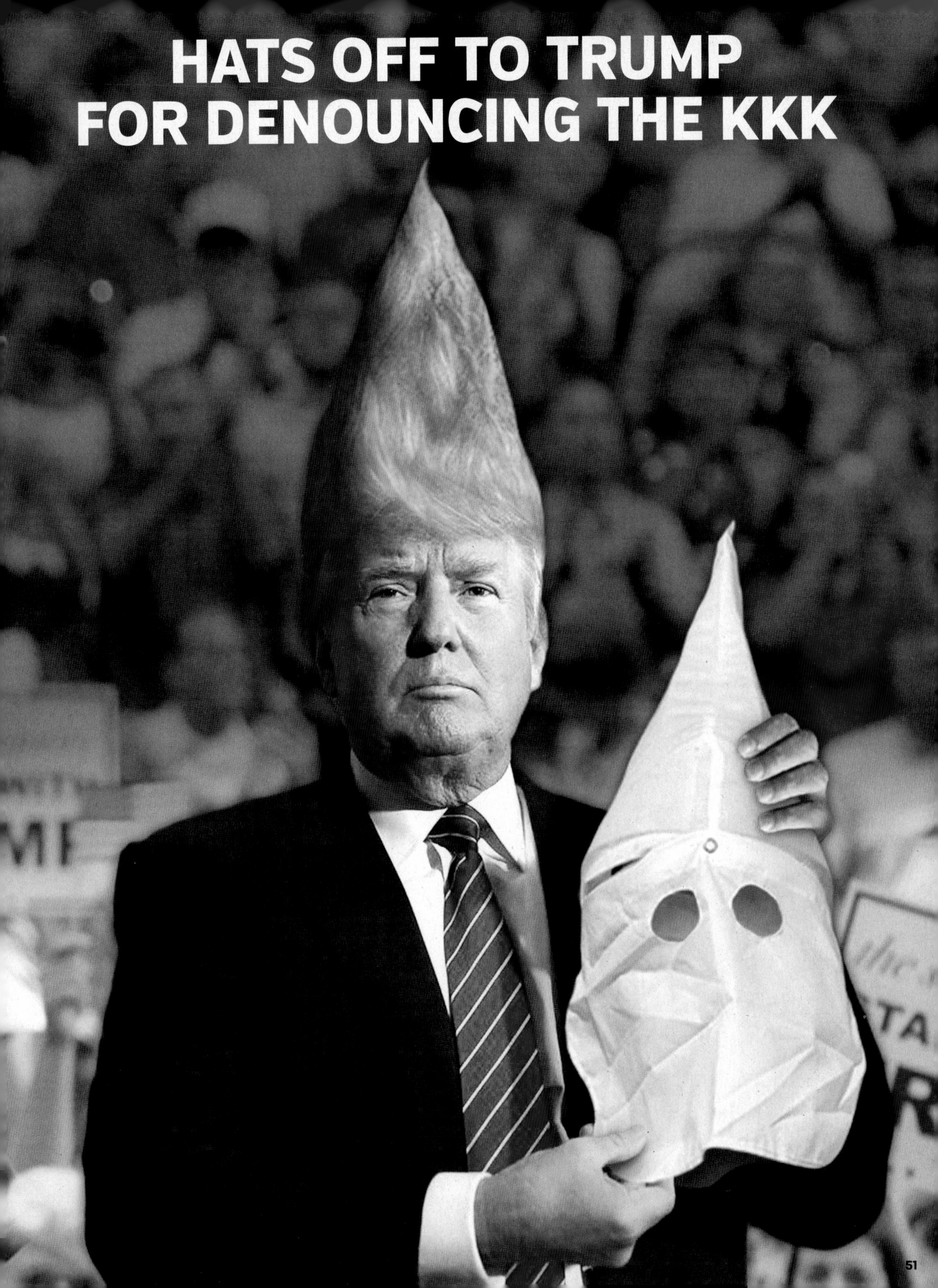

DONALD TRUMP'S ADVISORS INNER CIRCLE JERKS

Some people say "winning is everything." Those people are dumb. But when you get in league with an unqualified, borderline-psychotic political candidate just so you can win, when you sell out your core principles and use all your political skills to help that candidate capture the Presidency of the United States, you're not just dumb, you're immoral. And so it is with the men and women who chose to overlook Donald Trump's racist, misogynistic, xenophobic words and deeds and set about electing him President. "Born-again Christian" Mike Pence had no problem ignoring Trump's vulgarity and mockery of the handicapped. Kellyanne Conway gave him a pass when he said he likes to grab women's pu**ies, and Senator Ted Cruz evidently had no trouble with Trump bizarrely implicating his father in killing JFK. There were others, and they all checked their values at the door.

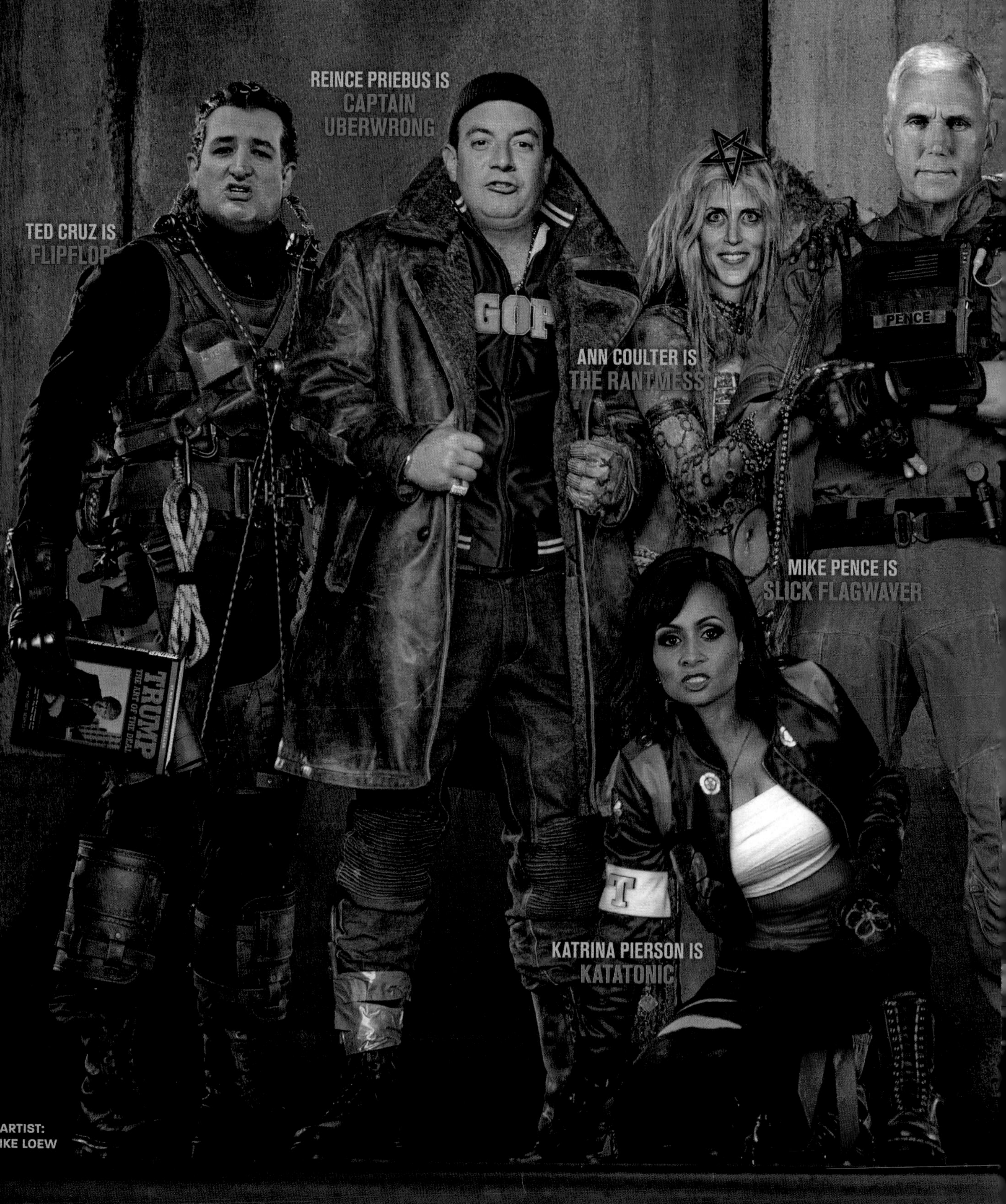
REINCE PRIEBUS IS CAPTAIN UBERWRONG
TED CRUZ IS FLIPFLOP
GOP
ANN COULTER IS THE RANT MESS
PENCE
MIKE PENCE IS SLICK FLAGWAVER
TRUMP THE ART OF THE DEAL
T
KATRINA PIERSON IS KATATONIC

ARTIST:
MIKE LOEW

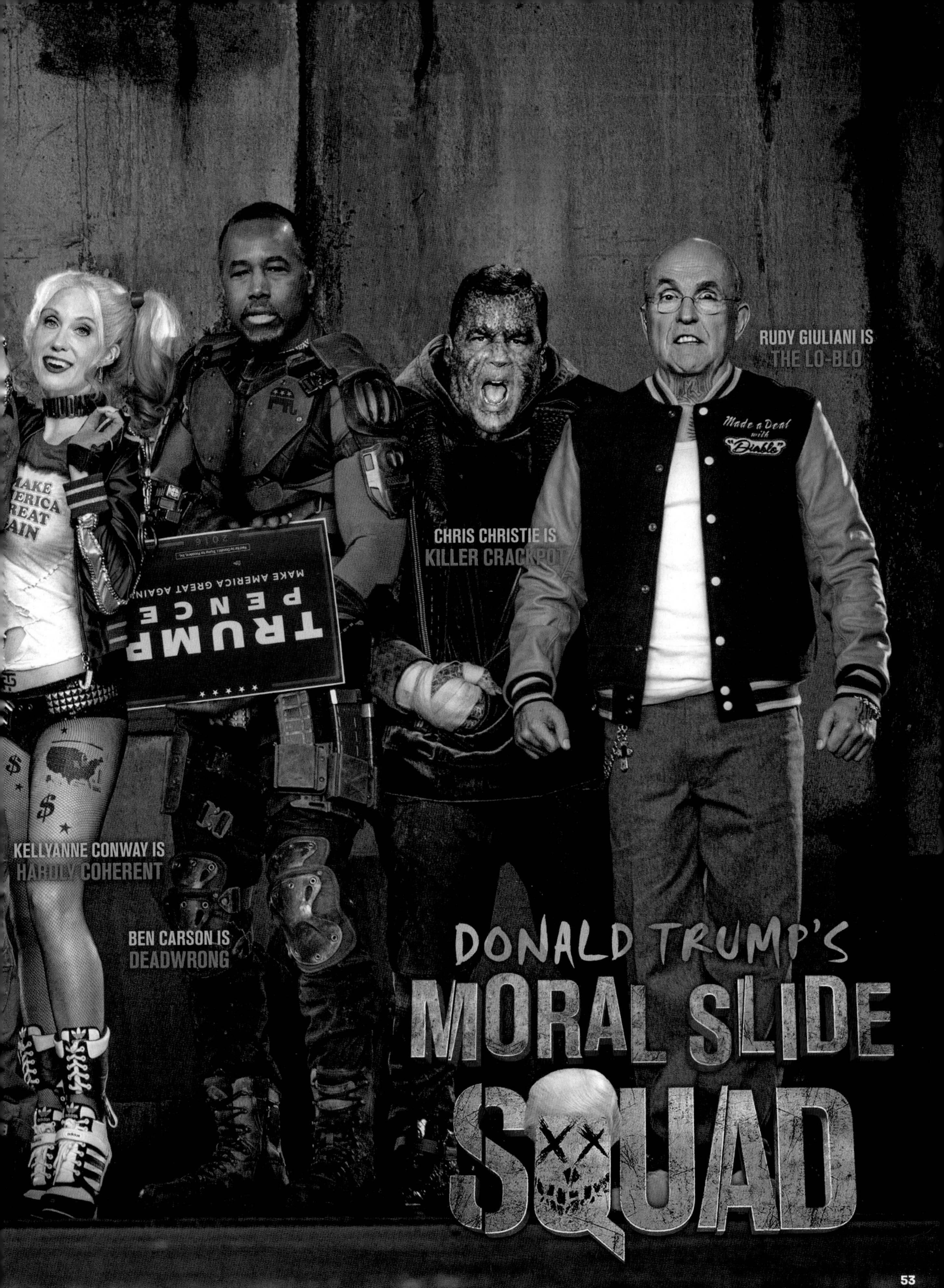
RUDY GIULIANI IS
THE LO-BLO
Made a Deal with "Diablo"
CHRIS CHRISTIE IS
KILLER CRACKPOT
TRUMP
PENCE
MAKE AMERICA GREAT AGAIN
2016
KELLYANNE CONWAY IS
HARDLY COHERENT
BEN CARSON IS
DEADWRONG
DONALD TRUMP'S
MORAL SLIDE
SQUAD

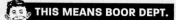
Deplorable People

Donald
"Grab 'em by the p*ssy" **Trump**

THE MOST SEXIST MAN ALIVE!

"Nobody respects women more than me!"

ON HILLARY CLINTON
"Such a nasty woman."

ON FORMER MISS UNIVERSE ALICIA MACHADO
"She was like an eating machine."

ON CARLY FIORINA
"Look at that face! Would anyone vote for that?"

WHY WON'T TRUMP RELEASE HIS TAXES?

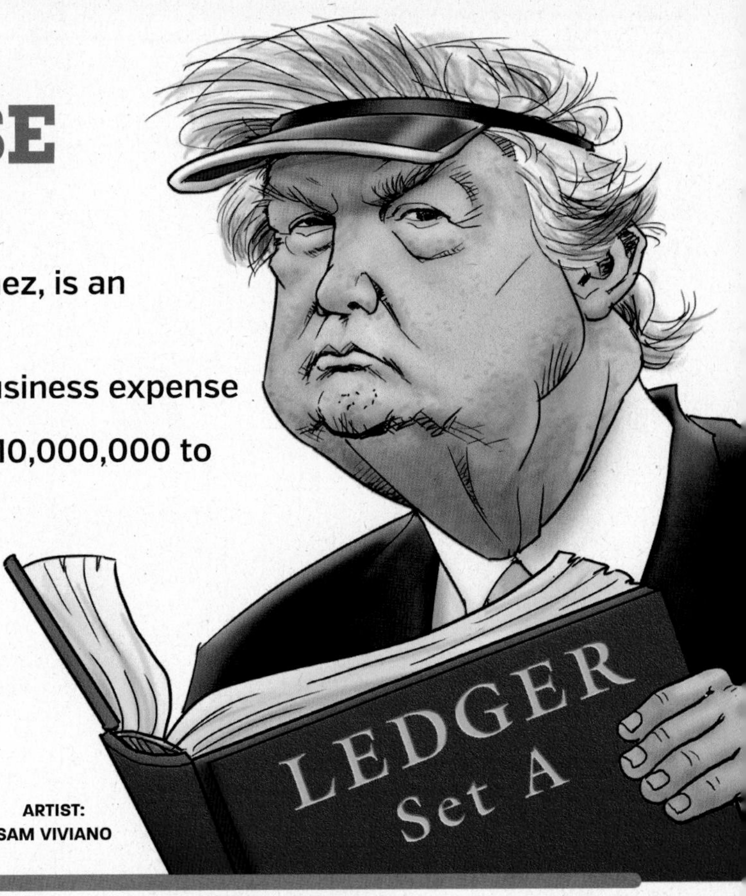
LEDGER
Set A

- His longtime accountant, Muhammad Sanchez, is an illegal Mexican-Muslim
- In 2005, he tried to write Melania off as a business expense
- There's the matter of his 2013 payment of $10,000,000 to a "Pladimir Vutin"
- Since 1976, he's listed his occupation as "Money-Grubbing Con Man"
- Hillary Clinton released hers — proving that only crooked losers release their taxes
- If he does, he'll be exposed as a devious, hypocritical, tax-dodging scumsack

ARTIST:
SAM VIVIANO

SILVER LININGS OF TRUMP'S PRESIDENCY

- Anyone who's tired of our national anthem will enjoy the new one, "Государственный гимн Российской Федерации"
- America will never have another election that's so divisive and vitriolic, because America will never have another election
- History won't repeat itself, because the second host of *The Celebrity Apprentice* can't become President
- You'll soon breeze through customs lines when returning to the U.S. — because foreigners will have stopped coming here altogether
- America will be great again — duh!

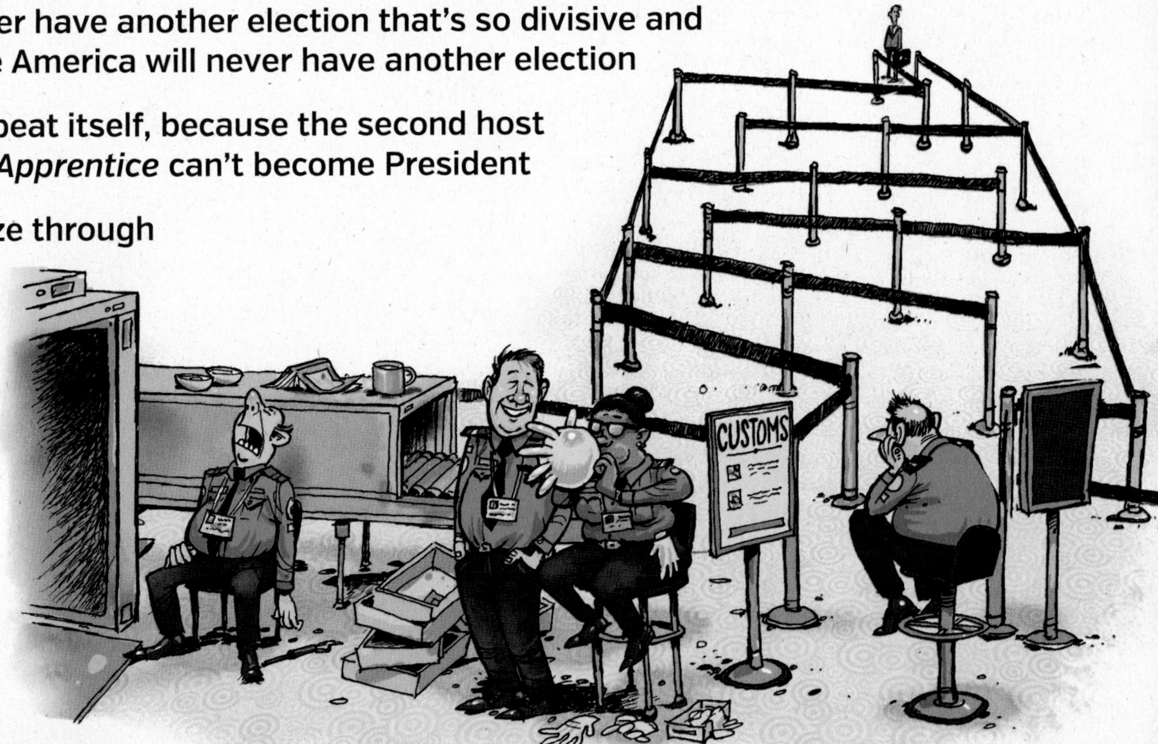
CUSTOMS

WRITER: AABYE-GAYLE D. FRANCIS-FAVILLA
ARTIST: RICH POWELL

THE REPUBLICAN PRESIDENTIAL CANDIDATES

GOP'S A CROWD

Jesus only needed 12 apostles, yet in 2016 the Republicans needed at least 16 candidates for President. We're not sure what our point is, but we thought it interesting to note. Indeed, there were so many crackpots, losers and hacks in the race, we couldn't even fit them all in this painting! One more point: the selection of Mr. Trump to be at the center of this painting was not accidental. Every time he opened his mouth, at least one person in America exclaimed, "That guy's running for President!?! Jesus Christ!"

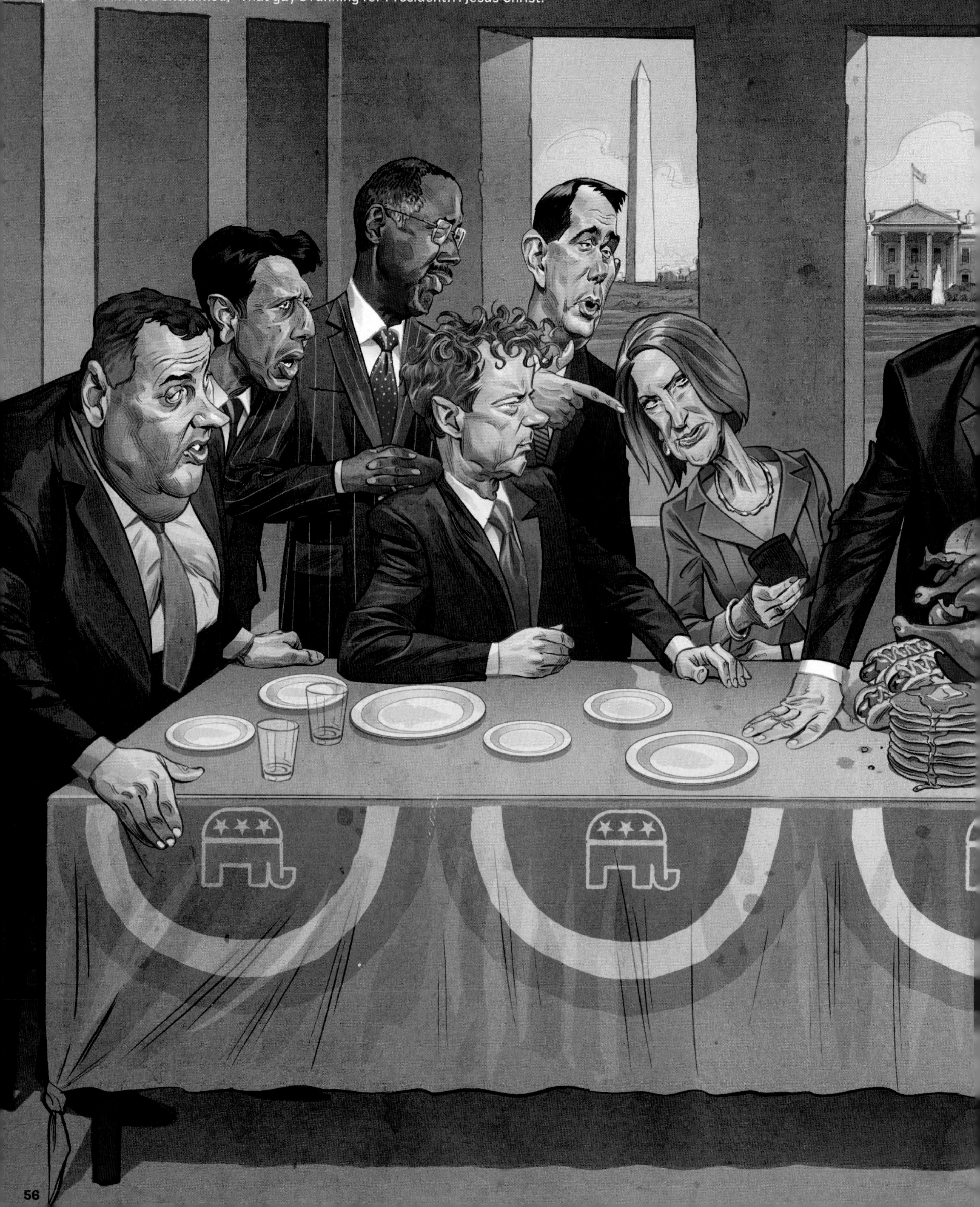

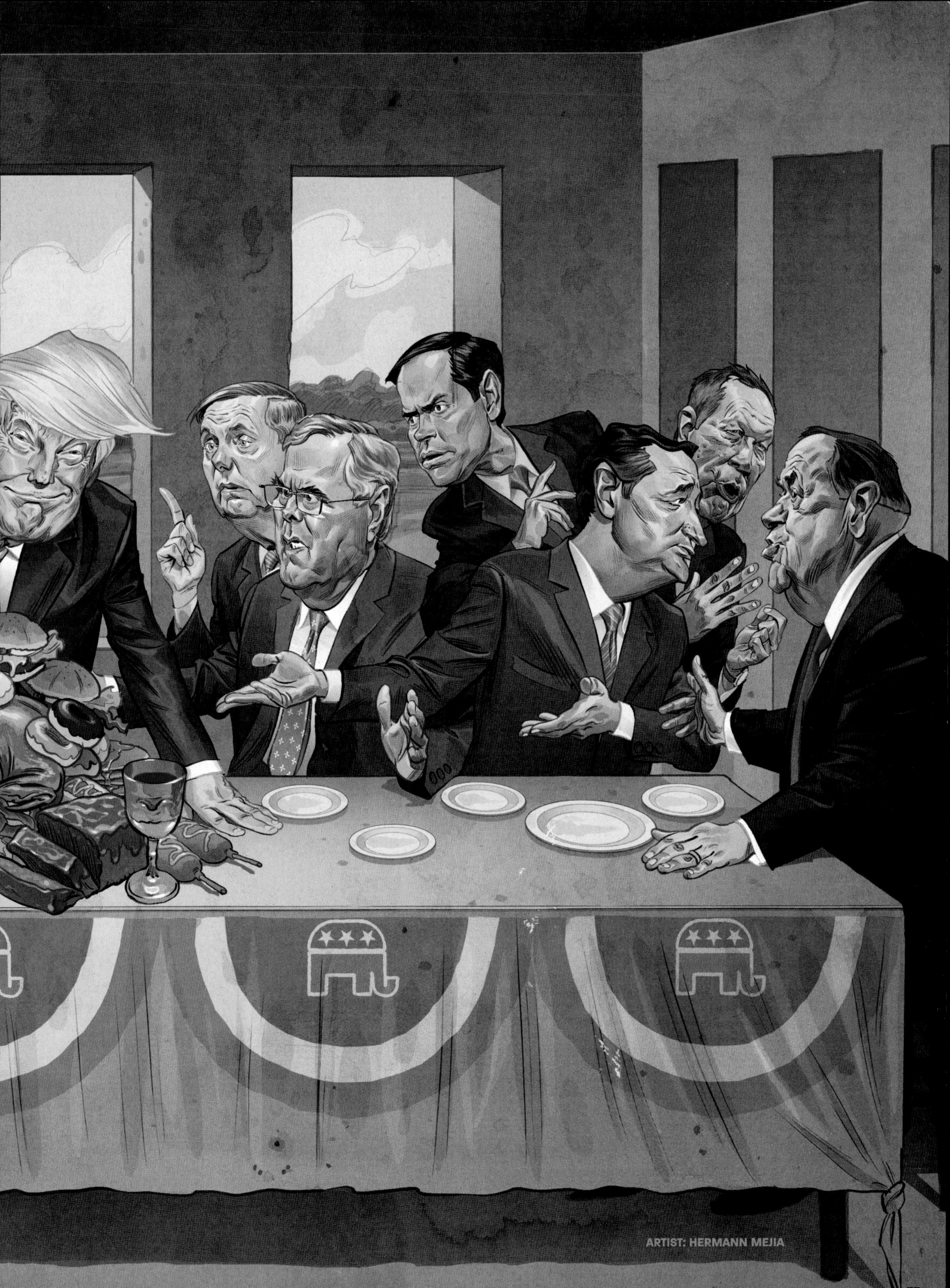

ARTIST: HERMANN MEJIA

HILLARY AND DONALD SAY "POSITIVE THINGS" ABOUT EACH OTHER

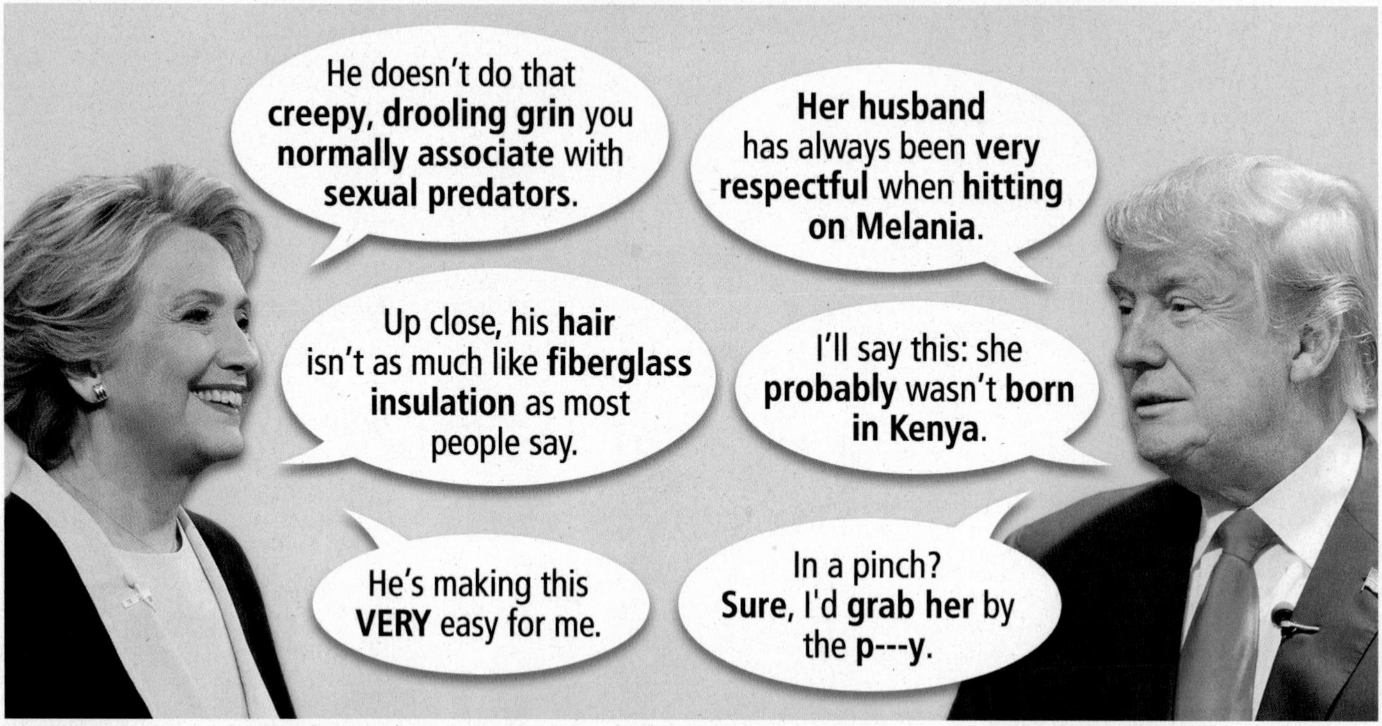
He doesn't do that creepy, drooling grin you normally associate with sexual predators.
Her husband has always been very respectful when hitting on Melania.
Up close, his hair isn't as much like fiberglass insulation as most people say.
I'll say this: she probably wasn't born in Kenya.
He's making this VERY easy for me.
In a pinch? Sure, I'd grab her by the p---y.

CELEBRITIES WITHOUT THEIR MAKEUP: TRUMP EDITION

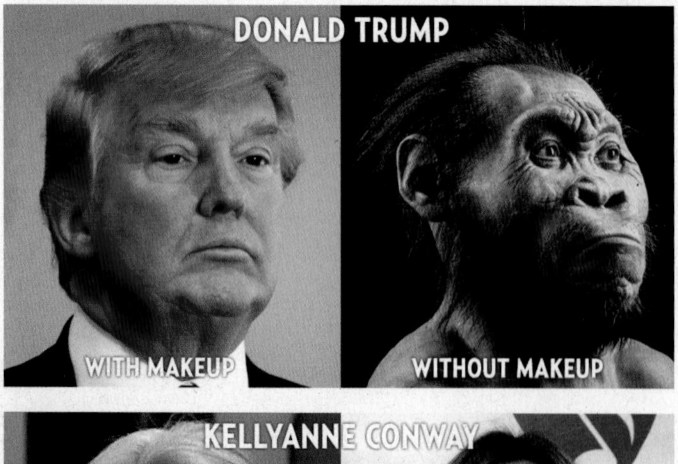
DONALD TRUMP
WITH MAKEUP
WITHOUT MAKEUP

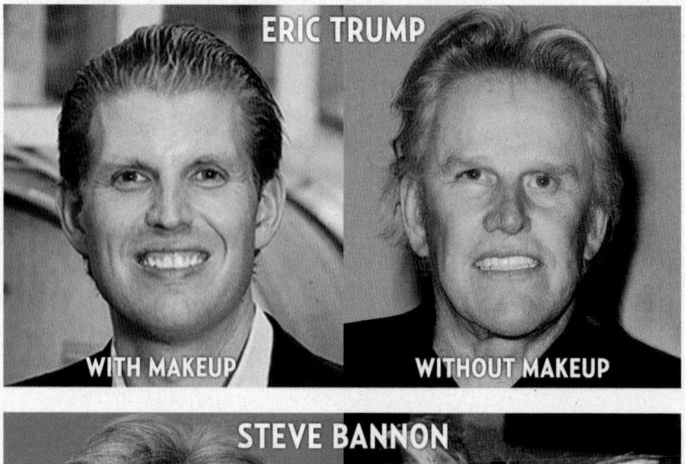
ERIC TRUMP
WITH MAKEUP
WITHOUT MAKEUP

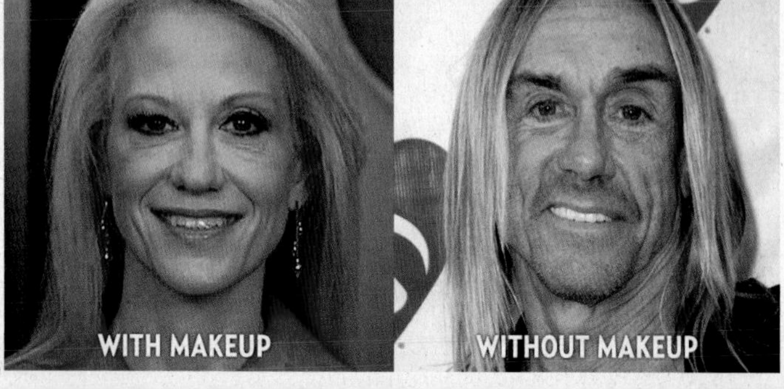
KELLYANNE CONWAY
WITH MAKEUP
WITHOUT MAKEUP

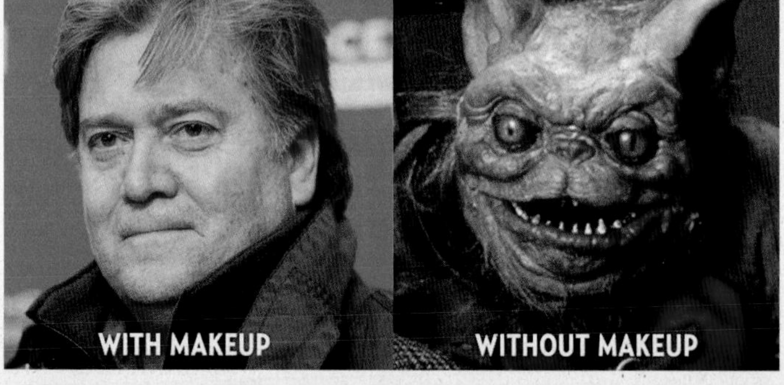
STEVE BANNON
WITH MAKEUP
WITHOUT MAKEUP

TRUMP ROAST DEPT.

ANOTHER MORNING ON FIFTH AVENUE

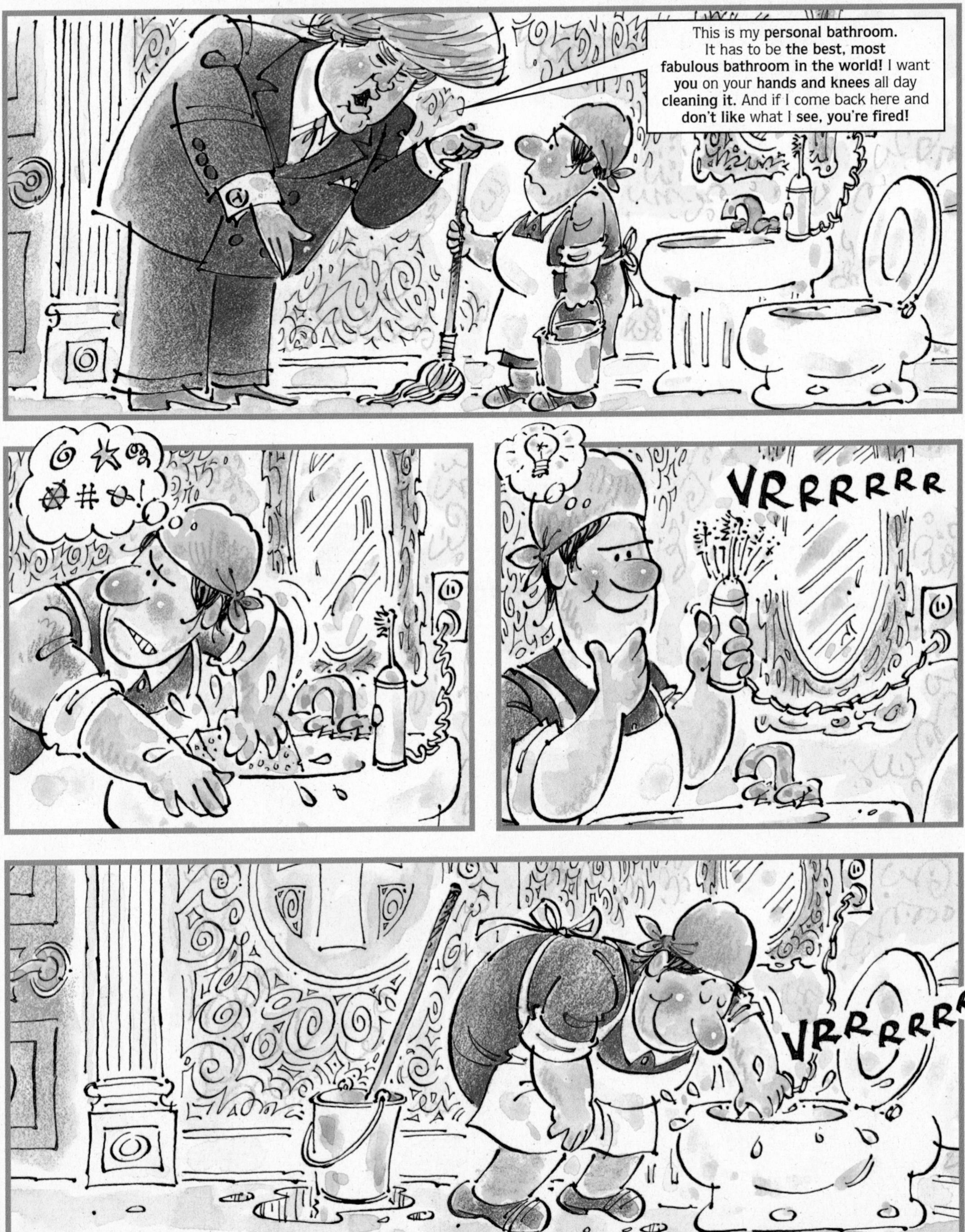
This is my personal bathroom. It has to be the best, most fabulous bathroom in the world! I want you on your hands and knees all day cleaning it. And if I come back here and don't like what I see, you're fired!
VRRRRRR
VRRRRRRR

WRITER: DUCK EDWING ARTIST: PAUL COKER

HOW WWE'S LINDA MCMAHON IS CHANGING TRUMP'S ADMINISTRATION

Election Day will officially be renamed "The Red State-Blue State SmackDown"

Before every press conference, there will be 10 minutes of Trump cupping his ear to "gather" the crowd's cheers

---

Trump will study old Hulk Hogan promos, to learn how to soften and calm his own rhetoric

---

The Surgeon General will serve as the attending ringside physician at WrestleMania 33

Referees will oversee especially contentious Senate debates – but will always be distracted at crucial moments toward the end

---

Trump will now be able to use the vast military knowledge of Sgt. Slaughter

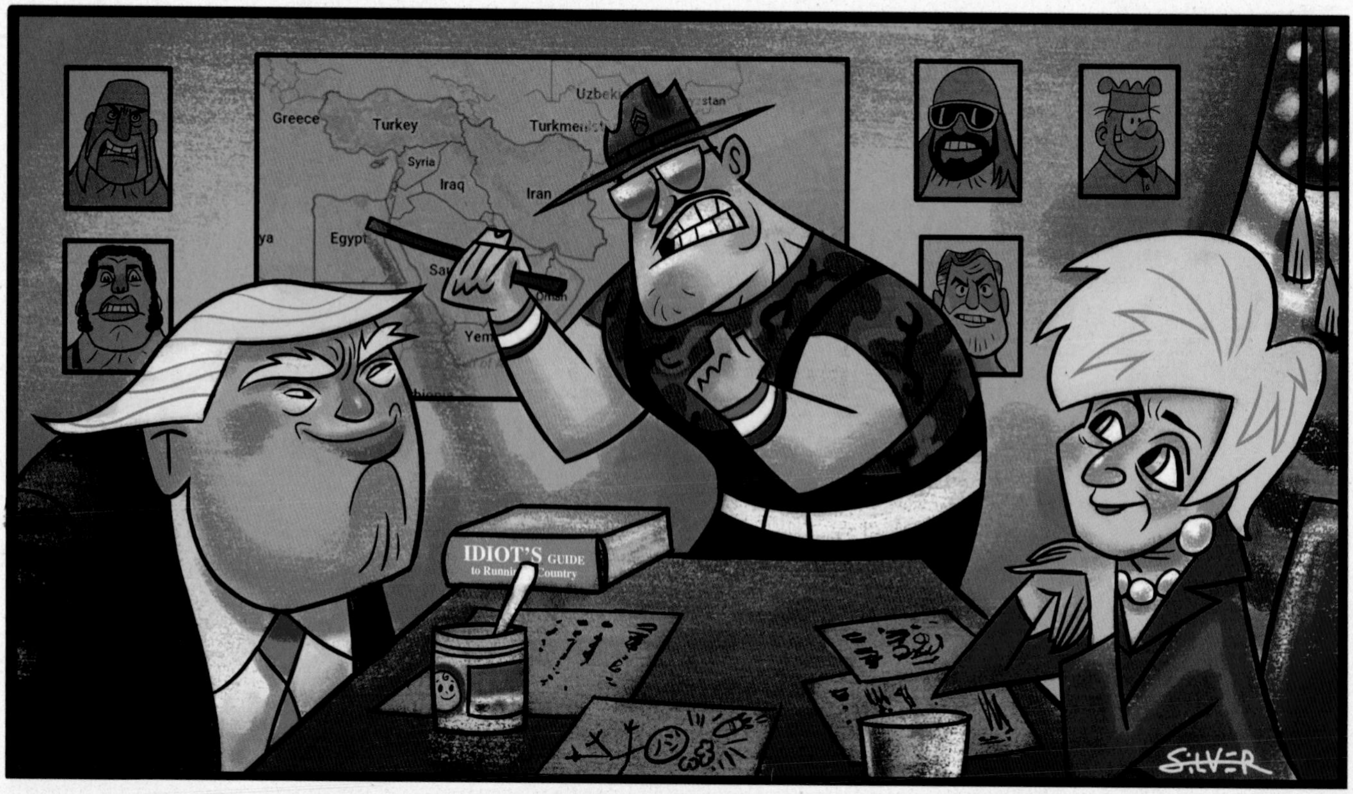
Greece
Turkey
Syria
Iraq
Iran
Egypt
IDIOT'S GUIDE
SILVER

ARTIST: STEPHEN SILVER

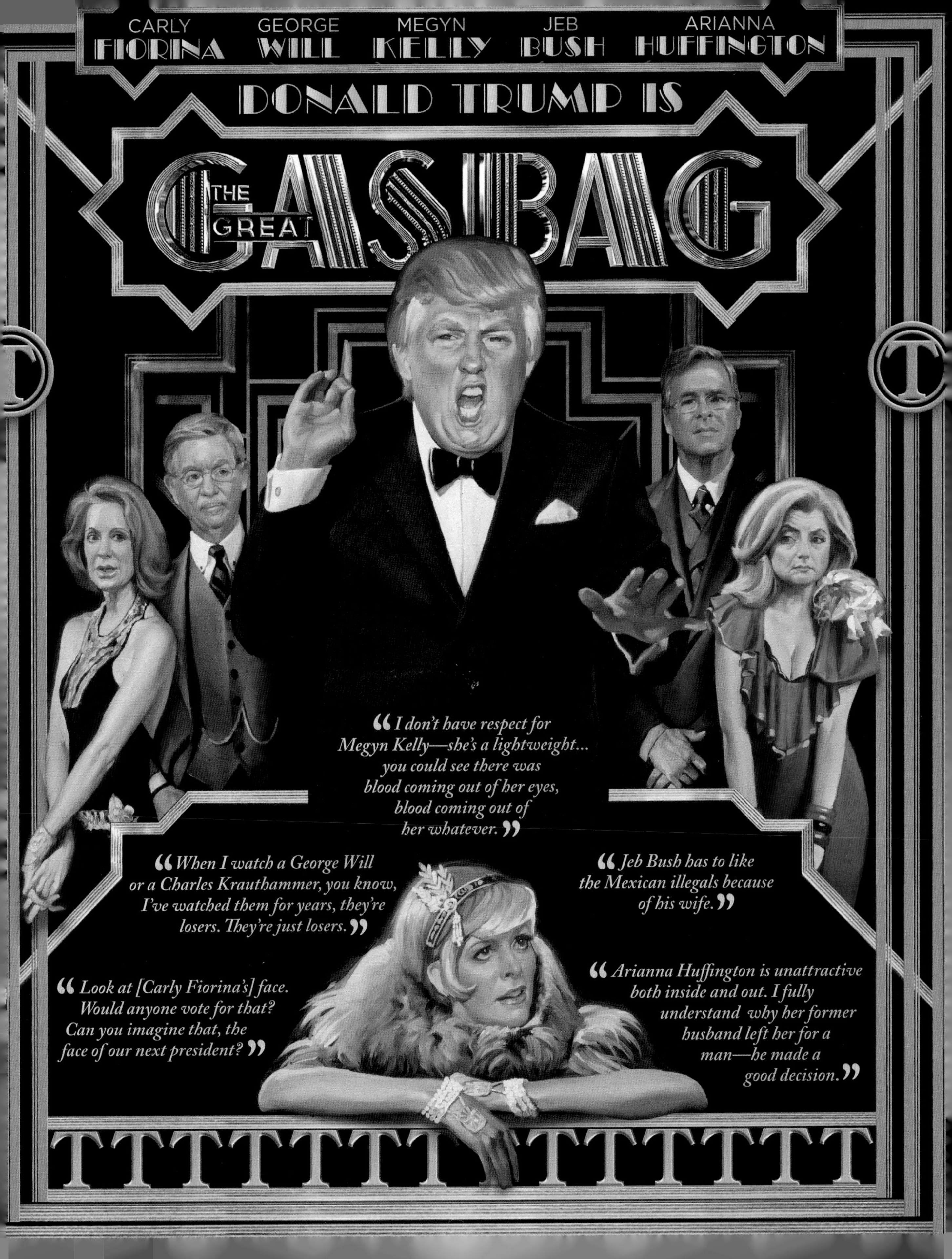
CARLY FIORINA
GEORGE WILL
MEGYN KELLY
JEB BUSH
ARIANNA HUFFINGTON
DONALD TRUMP IS
THE GREAT GASBAG
“I don’t have respect for Megyn Kelly—she’s a lightweight... you could see there was blood coming out of her eyes, blood coming out of her whatever.”
“When I watch a George Will or a Charles Krauthammer, you know, I’ve watched them for years, they’re losers. They’re just losers.”
“Jeb Bush has to like the Mexican illegals because of his wife.”
“Look at [Carly Fiorina’s] face. Would anyone vote for that? Can you imagine that, the face of our next president?”
“Arianna Huffington is unattractive both inside and out. I fully understand why her former husband left her for a man—he made a good decision.”

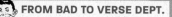

And lo, it came to pass that the carrot-hued man with hair of finely woven grain did say, "Nothing beats the Bible, not even *The Art of the Deal.*" And there was much rejoicing, and even more chortling. And the man spoke again, and he did say, "What's my favorite book?"

Donald vs. The

And he said to them, "Take care, and be on your guard against all covetousness, for one's life does not consist in the abundance of his possessions.

— Luke 12:15

It's hard for me to turn down money, because that's what I've done in my whole life. I grab and grab and grab. You know I get greedy. I want money, money.

— Donald 2/23/2016

When you give a feast, invite the poor, the crippled, the lame, the blind.

— Luke 14:13

I don't like losers.

— Donald 7/18/2015

When a sentence is not executed at once against a crime, the human heart is encouraged to do evil.

— Ecclesiastes 8:11

I could stand in the middle of Fifth Avenue and shoot somebody, and I wouldn't lose any voters, okay? It's, like, incredible.

— Donald 1/23/2016

And if any man will sue thee, and take away thy coat, let him have thy cloak also.

— Matthew 5:40

Throw them out. Throw them out into the cold. Don't give them their coat. No coats!

— Donald 1/7/2016

WRITER: DESMOND DEVLIN ARTIST: WARD SUTTON

The Bible!...We take the Bible all the way!" And there was great tumult, and the cable news did rend asunder. And the man spoke unto the masses for a third time, proclaiming, "The Bible means a lot to me, but I don't want to get into specifics." But we do!

Trump Bible

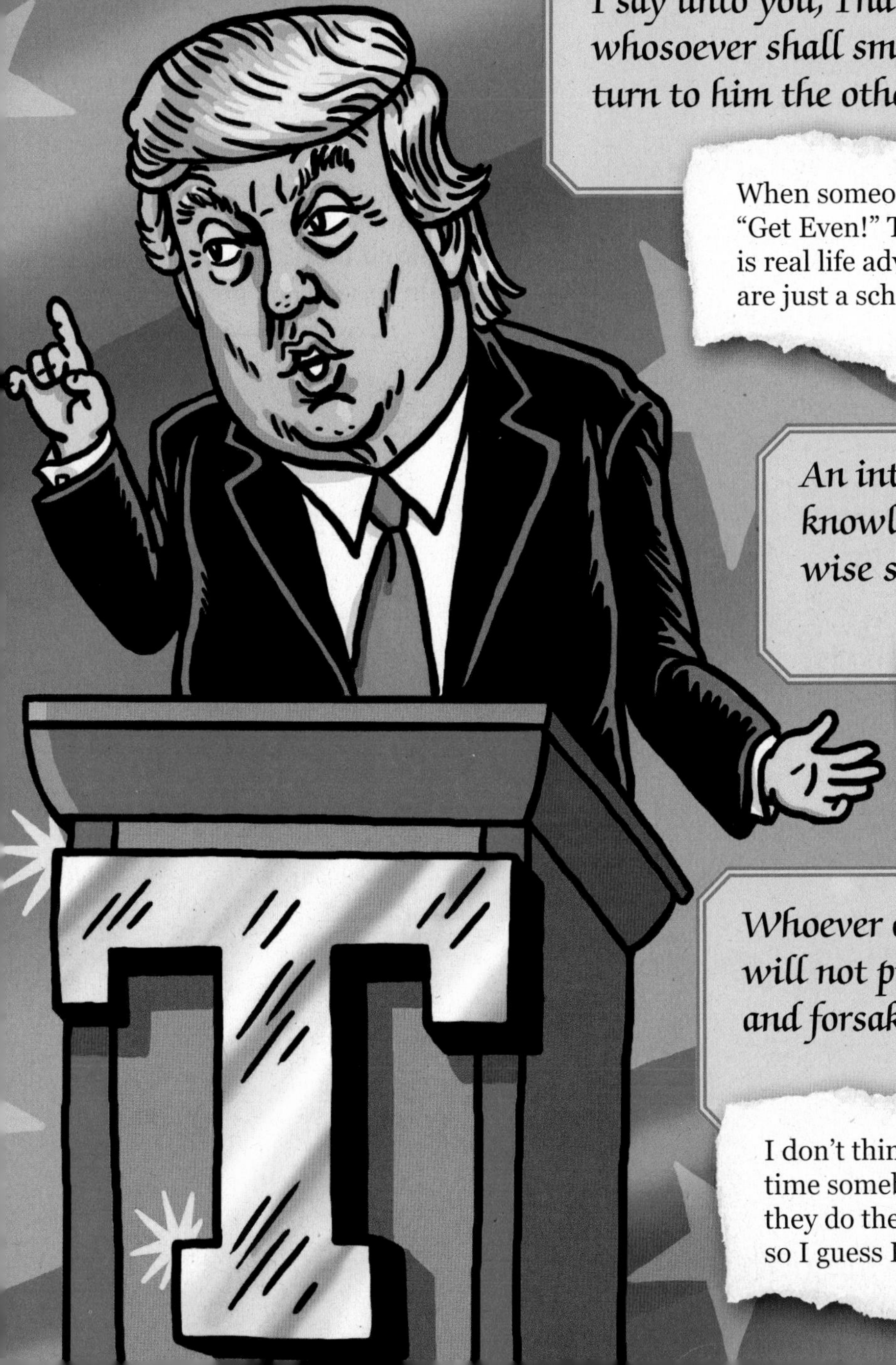

Do not have sexual relations with both a woman and her daughter...They are close relatives, and this would be a wicked act.

— Leviticus 18:16-17

She does have a very nice figure. I've said if Ivanka weren't my daughter, perhaps I'd be dating her.

— Donald 3/6/2006

I say unto you, That ye resist not evil: but whosoever shall smite thee on thy right cheek, turn to him the other also.

— Matthew 5:39

When someone crosses you, my advice is "Get Even!" That is not typical advice, but it is real life advice. If you do not get even, you are just a schmuck!... I love getting even.

— Donald 11/1/1987

An intelligent heart acquires knowledge, and the ear of the wise seeks knowledge.

— Proverbs 18:15

We won with poorly educated. I love the poorly educated.

— Donald 2/23/2016

Whoever conceals his transgressions will not prosper, but he who confesses and forsakes them will obtain mercy.

— Proverbs 28:13

I don't think I've made mistakes. Every time somebody said I made a mistake, they do the polls and my numbers go up, so I guess I haven't made any mistakes.

— Donald 8/15/2015

Thou shalt not bear false witness against thy neighbor.

— Exodus 20:16

An extremely credible source has called my office and told me that Barack Obama's birth certificate is a fraud.

— Donald 8/6/2012

Blessed are the meek, for they will inherit the earth.

— Matthew 5:5

Show me someone without an ego, and I'll show you a loser. Having a healthy ego, or high opinion of yourself, is a real positive in life!

— Donald 7/19/2012

Do not associate with a simple babbler.

— Proverbs 20:19

[Lincoln] was a man who was of great intelligence, which most presidents would be. But he was a man of great intelligence, but he was also a man who did something that was a very vital thing to do at that time. Ten years before or 20 years before, what he was doing would never have even been thought possible. So he did something that was a very important thing to do, and especially at that time.

— Donald 3/31/2016

Do not say, "I will repay evil." Wait for the Lord, and he will deliver you.

— Proverbs 20:22

If you see somebody getting ready to throw a tomato, knock the crap out of them, would you? Seriously. I will pay for the legal fees, I promise.

— Donald 2/1/2016

Who among you is wise and understanding? Let him show by his good behavior his deeds in the gentleness of wisdom.

— James 3:13

Sorry losers and haters, but my I.Q. is one of the highest—and you all know it! Please don't feel so stupid or insecure, it's not your fault.

— Donald 5/8/2013

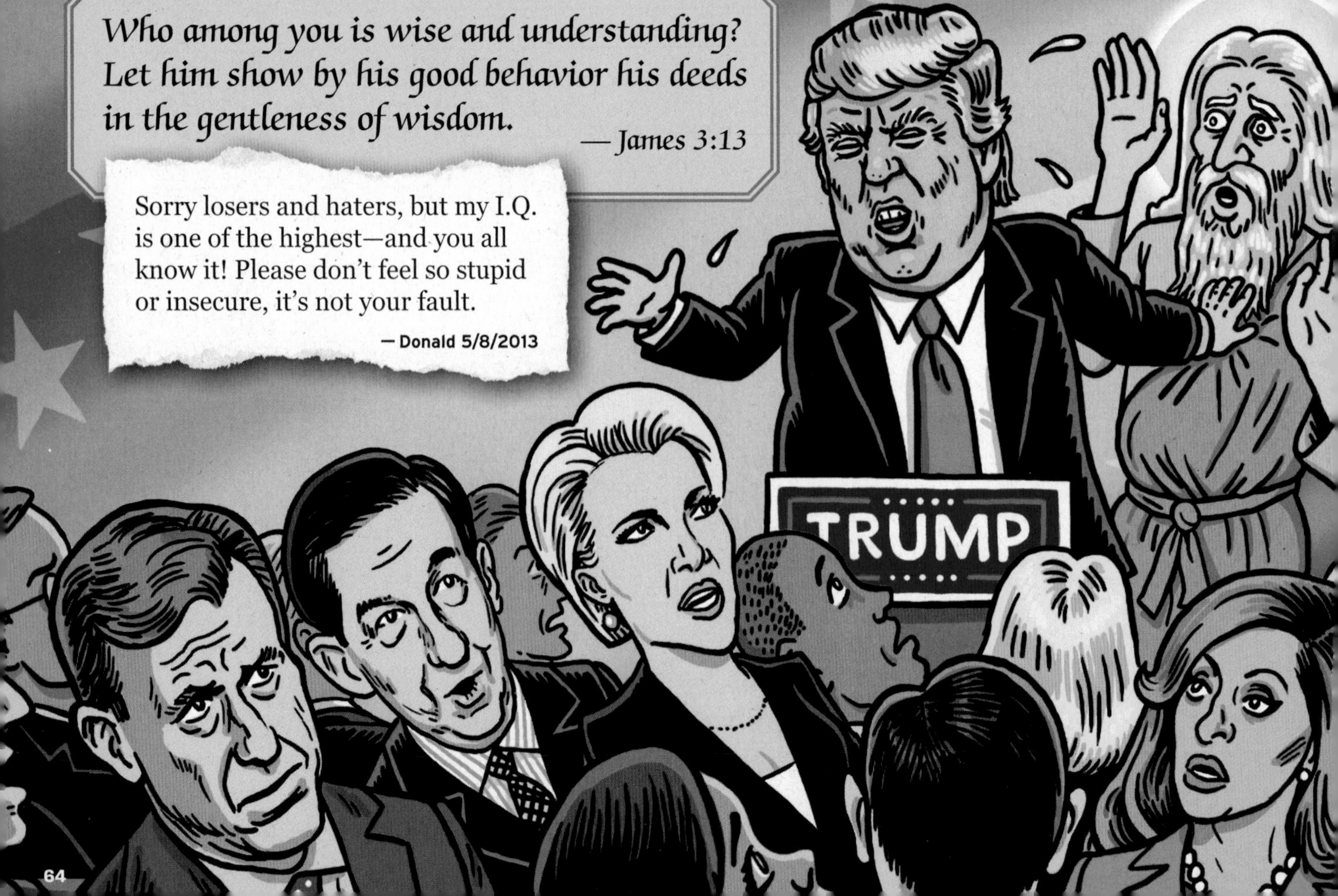
TRUMP

TRUMPTY DUMPTY
(A Nursery Rhyme Update)

Trumpty Dumpty
wanted a wall,

Lining the border,
20 feet tall.

The Mexican people
agreed with the lout,

"We'll pay for the thing,
if it keeps Trumpty out!"

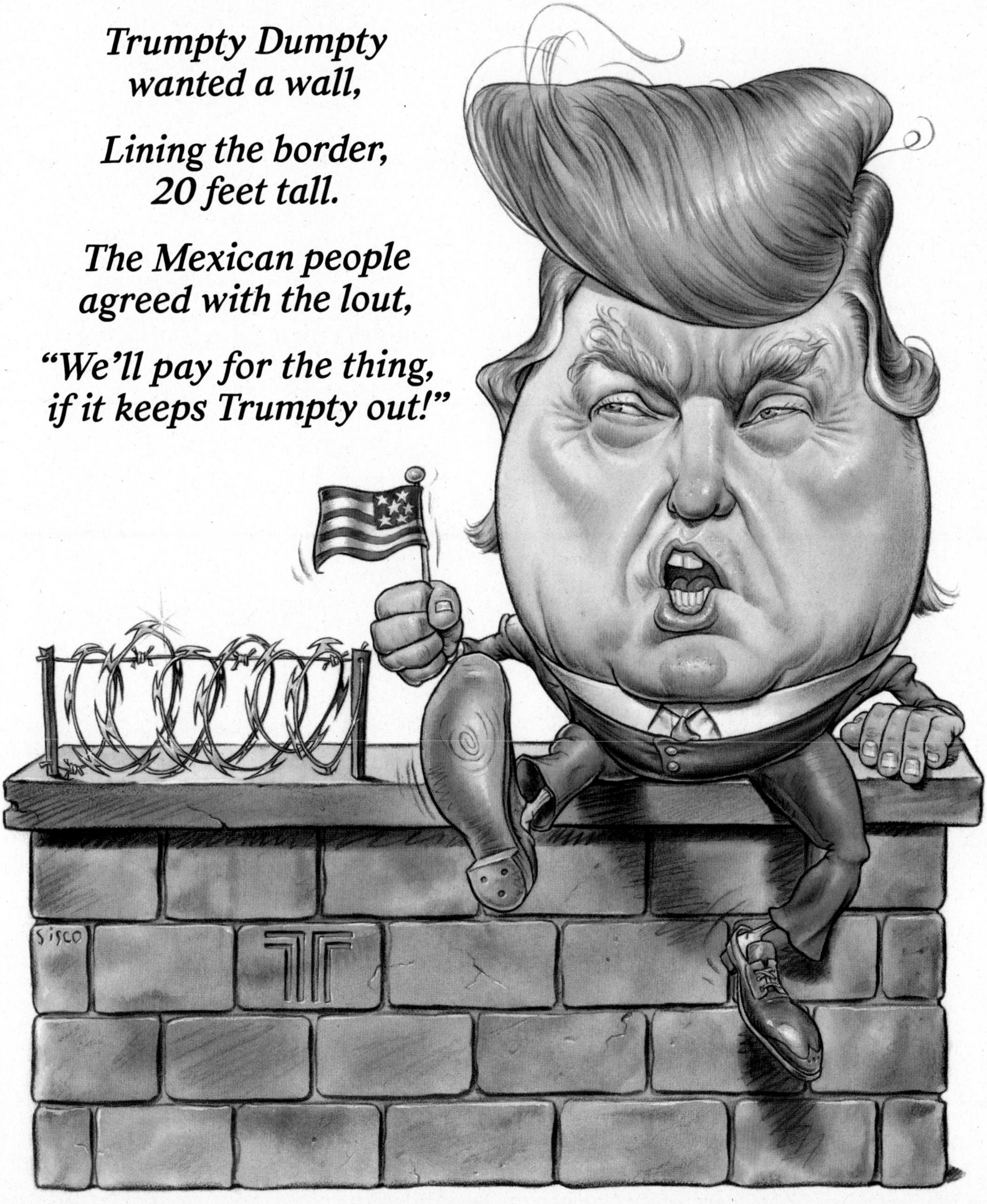
SISCO

WRITER: PATRICK MERRELL ARTIST: SAM SISCO

One of the most inspirational songs of all time is John Lennon's "Imagine," in which the ex-Beatle visualized a world of peace, love and non-materialism. In other words, he never imagined Donald Trump! In his Presidential campaign, Trump has asked America to imagine a somewhat different world than Lennon did, which led *us* to imagine...

"imagine" rewritten by donald trump

Imagine there's no Muslims
It's really great to do
No blacks or lib'rals
And no Hispanics, too.
Imagine just one country
white like me and you...*whoo hoo-oo!*

Imagine no more gun laws
"Yuge" tax cuts for the rich
No reason to be P.C.
Call every woman "bitch"
Imagine no more free press
Hillary in jail...*whoo hoo-oo!*

You might say I'm a fascist
A mad demagogue time-bomb
Like tyrants I admire
Stalin, Putin and Saddam

Imagine there's a big wall
For all the world to see
No one can leave or enter
Unless approved by me
Imagine the next world war
Started by my tweet...*whoo hoo-oo!*

You might say I'm a racist
Who cares only for white men
You now know what I mean by
"Make America Great Again"

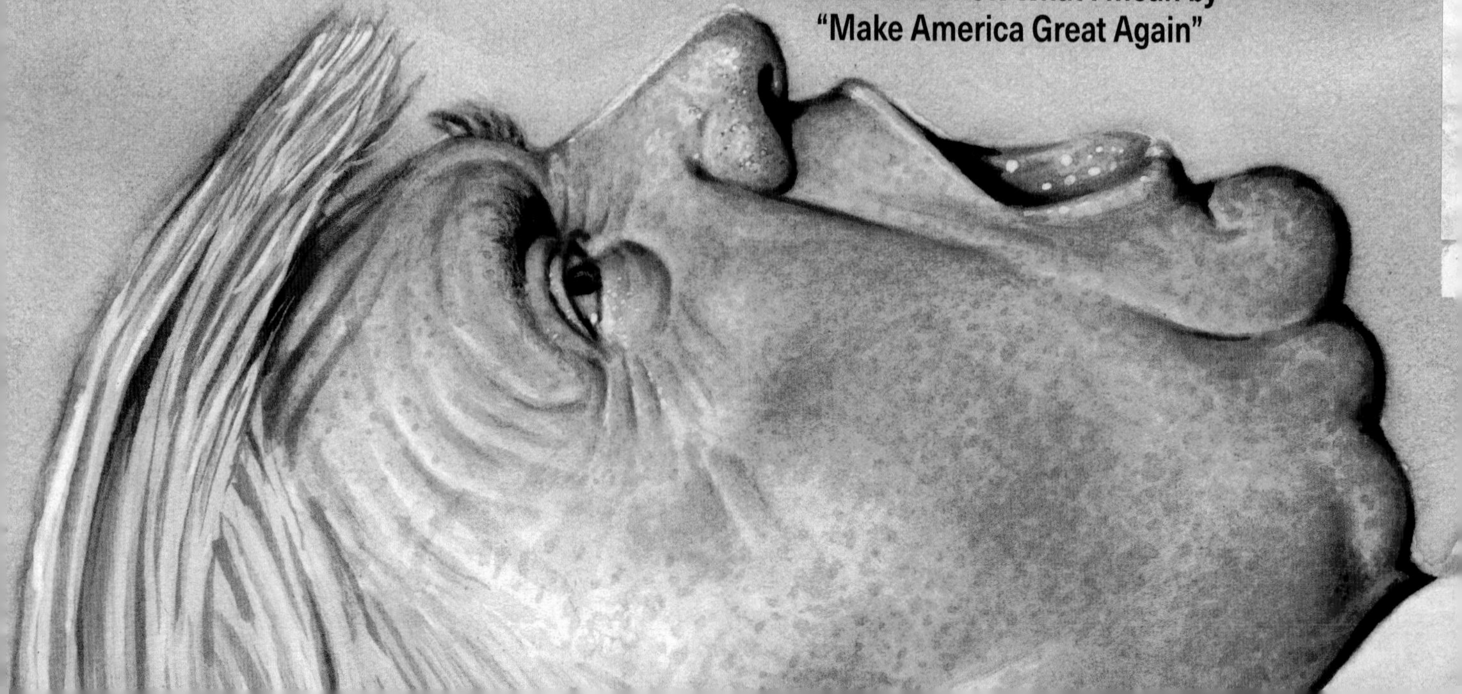

A HIP HOP ALBUM WE'D LIKE TO SEE

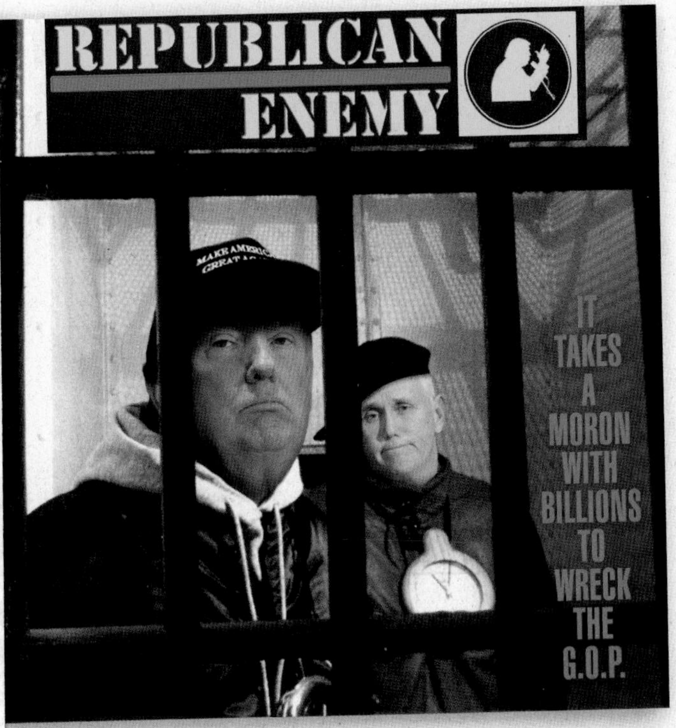
REPUBLICAN ENEMY
IT TAKES A MORON WITH BILLIONS TO WRECK THE G.O.P.

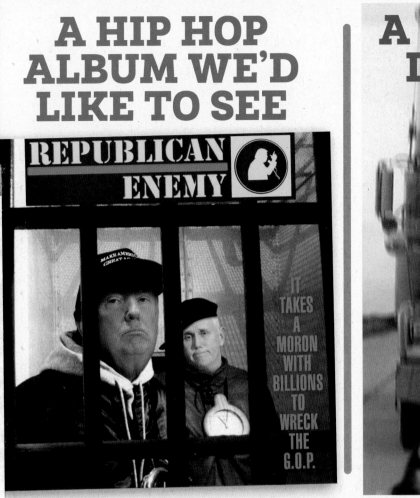

A SELFIE WE'D LIKE TO SEE

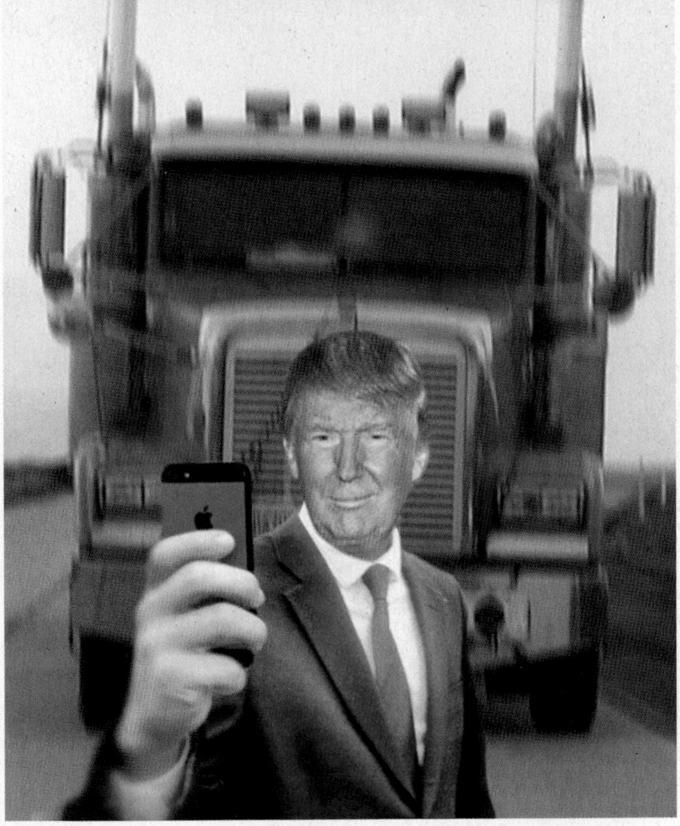

6 SIGNS THAT THE ELECTION IS RIGGED

- Hillary will appear on the ballot without "Crooked" printed in front of her name
- Trump is losing, even though he's *repeatedly* stated that he's the best, greatest, smartest person for the job
- Whenever a video surfaces of Trump bragging of sexual assault, the media acts like it's a big deal
- Hillary hasn't yet been tossed in jail, despite Trump's legally sound, brilliantly argued pleas
- Debate moderators insist on asking Trump about things besides his beautiful buildings and impressive wang
- WikiLeaks just published Hillary's drapery order for the Oval Office

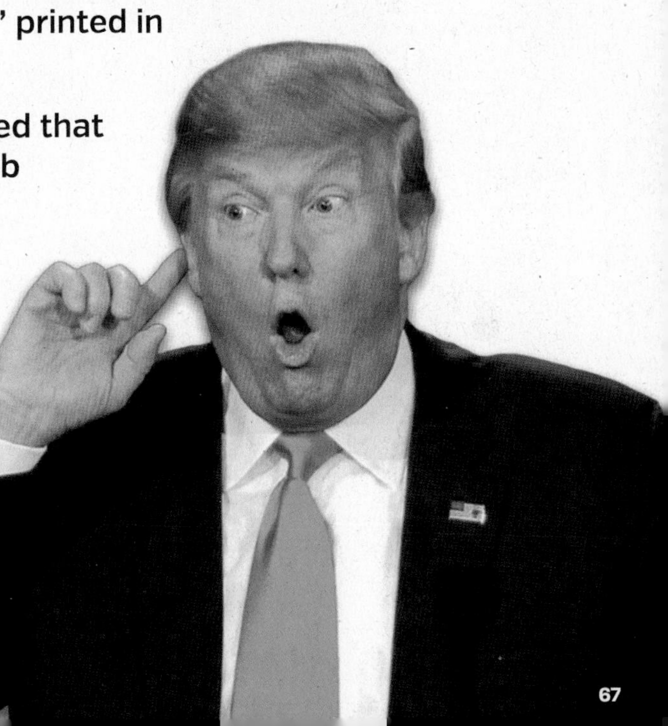

TRUMP UNIVERSITY'S NEW POSTER

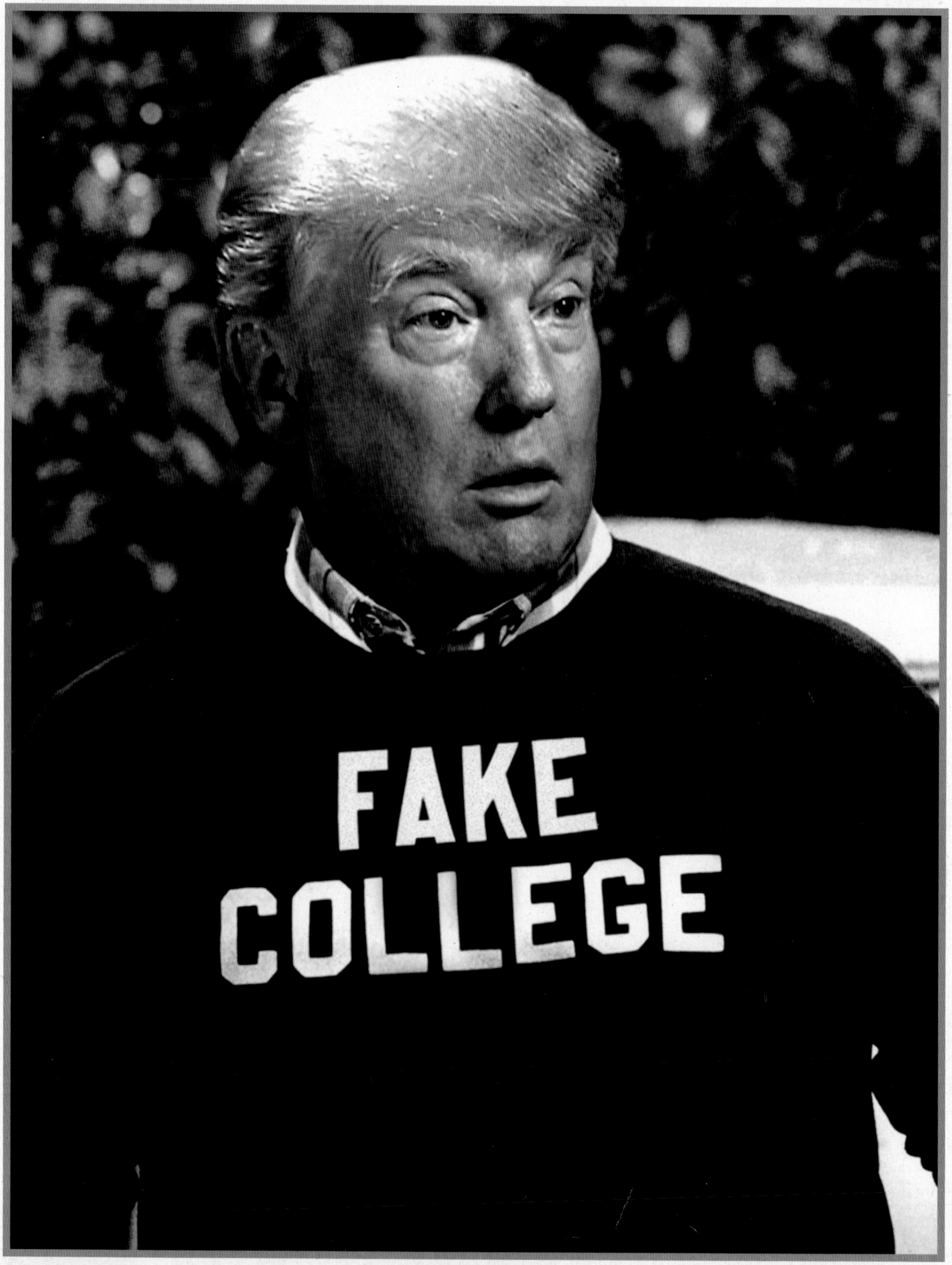
FAKE
COLLEGE

Trump University

BE IT KNOWN UPON THIS DAY THAT BY VIRTUE OF
HAVING COMPLETELY MAXED OUT THEIR CREDIT CARDS IN ORDER TO
PAY FOR A SHADY, UNINFORMATIVE AND DUBIOUS COURSE OF STUDY, AND WITH
ALL THE HONORS AND PRIVILEGES PERTAINING THERETO (SO FAR, NONE),

---

IS HEREBY AWARDED THE FABULOUS, FLASHY, ELITE
AND EXCLUSIVE TRUMP DEGREE OF

B.S. — Been Suckered

THE ABOVE MENTIONED IS NOW FULLY QUALIFIED AT IDENTIFYING SLEAZY SCAMS PERPETRATED BY LOW-LIFE,
POMPOUS HUCKSTERS MASQUERADING AS SKILLED BUSINESSMEN, HAVING JUST BEEN THE VICTIM OF ONE

Donald Trump
Undisputed Master of B.S.
President, Trump University

DONALD TRUMP
UNIVERSITY

FIRST HE HIT SYRIA. THEN HE HIT THE LINKS.
WHAT'S HIS NEXT PLAY?
DONALD TRUMP
Titleist
Titleist
WORLD WAR
T

The Startling Similarities and Differences Between
DONALD TRUMP
and
BURGER KING'S NEW "MAC N' CHEETOS"

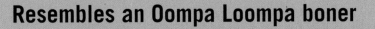

	Trump	Mac N' Cheetos
Resembles an Oompa Loompa boner	✓	✓
Is a revolting combination of oranges, yellows and fat	✓	✓
Known for its gross, crispy skin and glue-like, rubbery center	✓	✓
Is beloved by Melania Trump	—	✓
Is a disgusting thing to discuss at the dinner table	✓	✓
Seems concocted by Satan himself	✓	✓
May cause runny, greasy stool	✓	✓
Is really, really cheesy	✓	✓

SHOCKING REVELATIONS FROM OBAMA'S TRUMP TOWER WIRETAPS

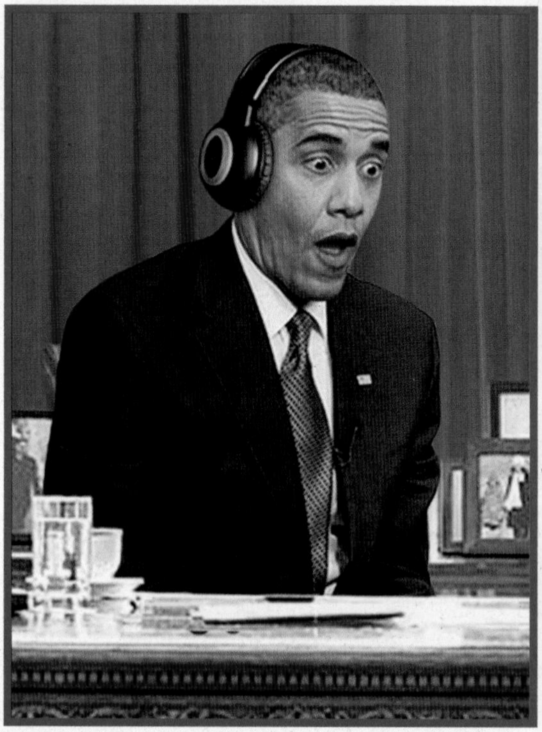

- Trump once spent six hours on the phone with Reince Priebus in a game of "You Hang Up First, No, You Hang Up First!"
- Last February, Trump ordered Melania the $19.95 Russel Stover milk chocolate Valentine's heart, but balked at the $34 assortment that included truffles
- A week doesn't go by without Trump prank calling Chris Christie and offering him the ambassadorship to McDonaldland
- Trump has spent countless hours arguing with Dial-A-Mattress customer service over their policy of not exchanging urine-stained boxsprings
- Trump once put House Speaker Paul Ryan on hold, then went out to dinner, came back, said "Paul, are you still there? Good. It will be just a few more minutes!" Then went to bed

HOW DONALD TRUMP IS SPENDING ST. PATRICK'S DAY

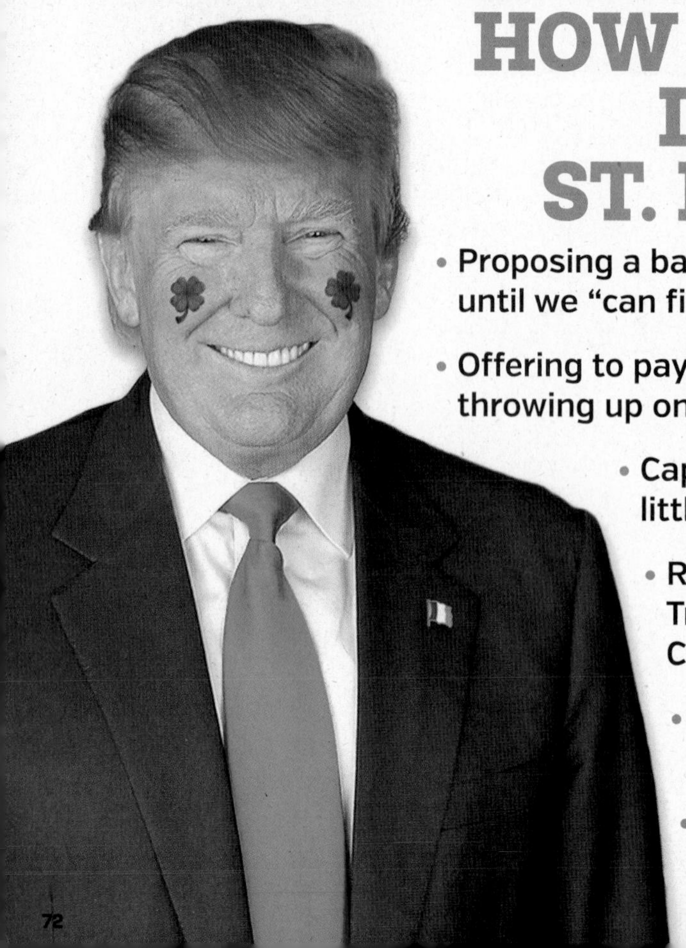

- Proposing a ban on all Leprechauns from entering the country until we "can figure out what the hell is going on"
- Offering to pay the legal fees of any parade-goer caught throwing up on Ted Cruz
- Capping off his usual hateful diatribe with a jaunty little jig
- Regretting inviting Chris Christie to the annual Trump "All-You-Can-Eat Corned Beef and Cabbage Buffet"
- Blaming Hillary Clinton for the Great Potato Famine of 1845
- Making dangerously uninformed blanket statements about Muslims (Hey, it's not going to be *all* play today!)

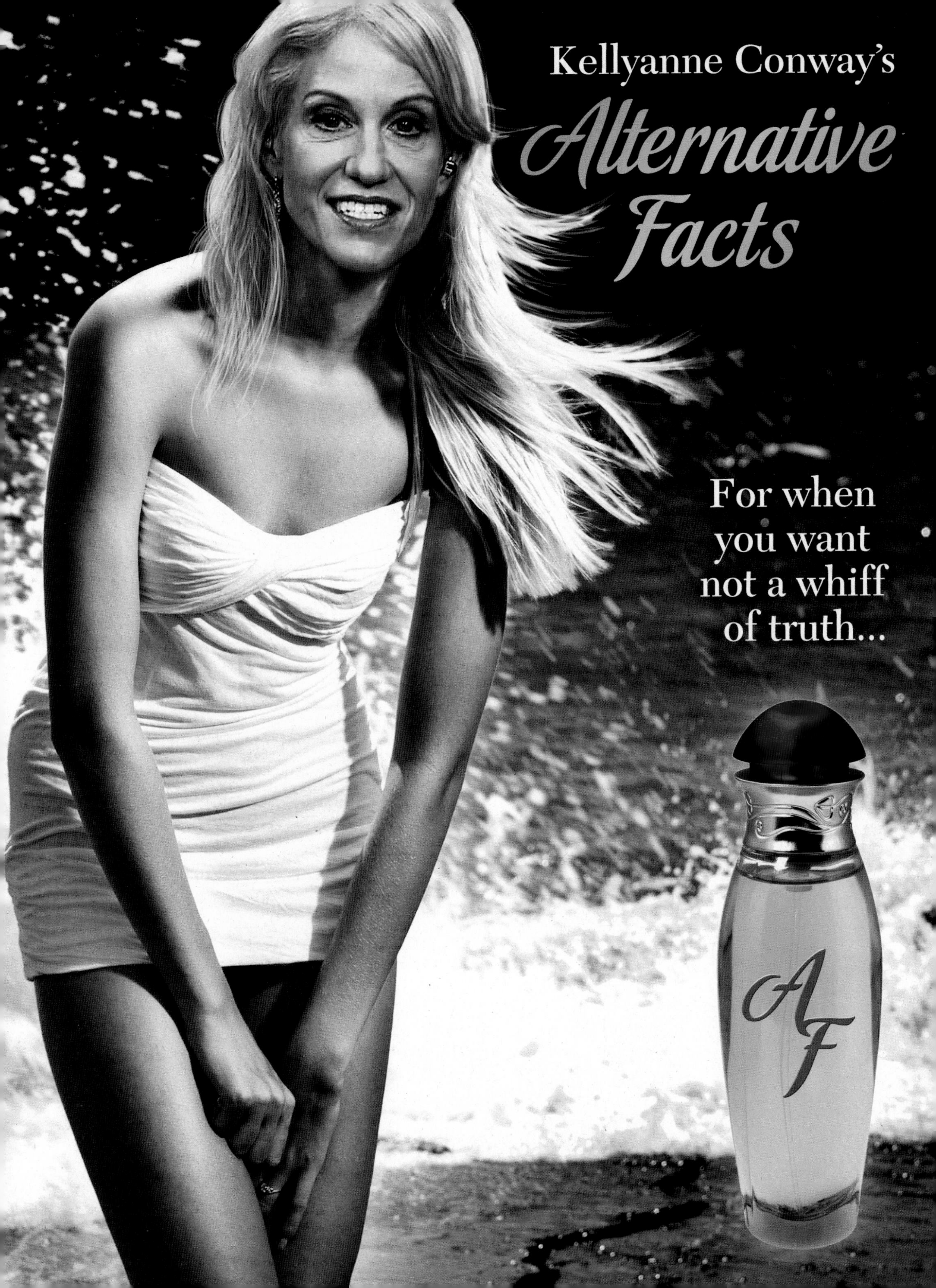

Kellyanne Conway's
Alternative
Facts
For when
you want
not a whiff
of truth...
AF

THINGS YOU NEED TO KNOW ABOUT MIKE PENCE

Hit for the cycle off Elizabeth Warren in the
annual Republicans vs. Democrats softball game

Once suggested that, if schoolteachers are so smart, they should earn
extra cash on *Jeopardy!* rather than grubbing for more taxpayer money

---

As a congressman, he voted to defund
NASA because of all the aborted missions

Is considered by many to be a friend of the common man,
as his policies often favor multi-millionaires over billionaires

---

Gives speeches at grade schools encouraging kids that anyone can
grow up to deny basic constitutional rights to certain Americans

---

He was "Mikey" from those Life cereal ads in the '70s

WRITER: JEFF KRUSE
ARTIST: ANTON EMDIN

PUTIN'S INFLUENCE OVER TRUMP CONTINUES TO GROW

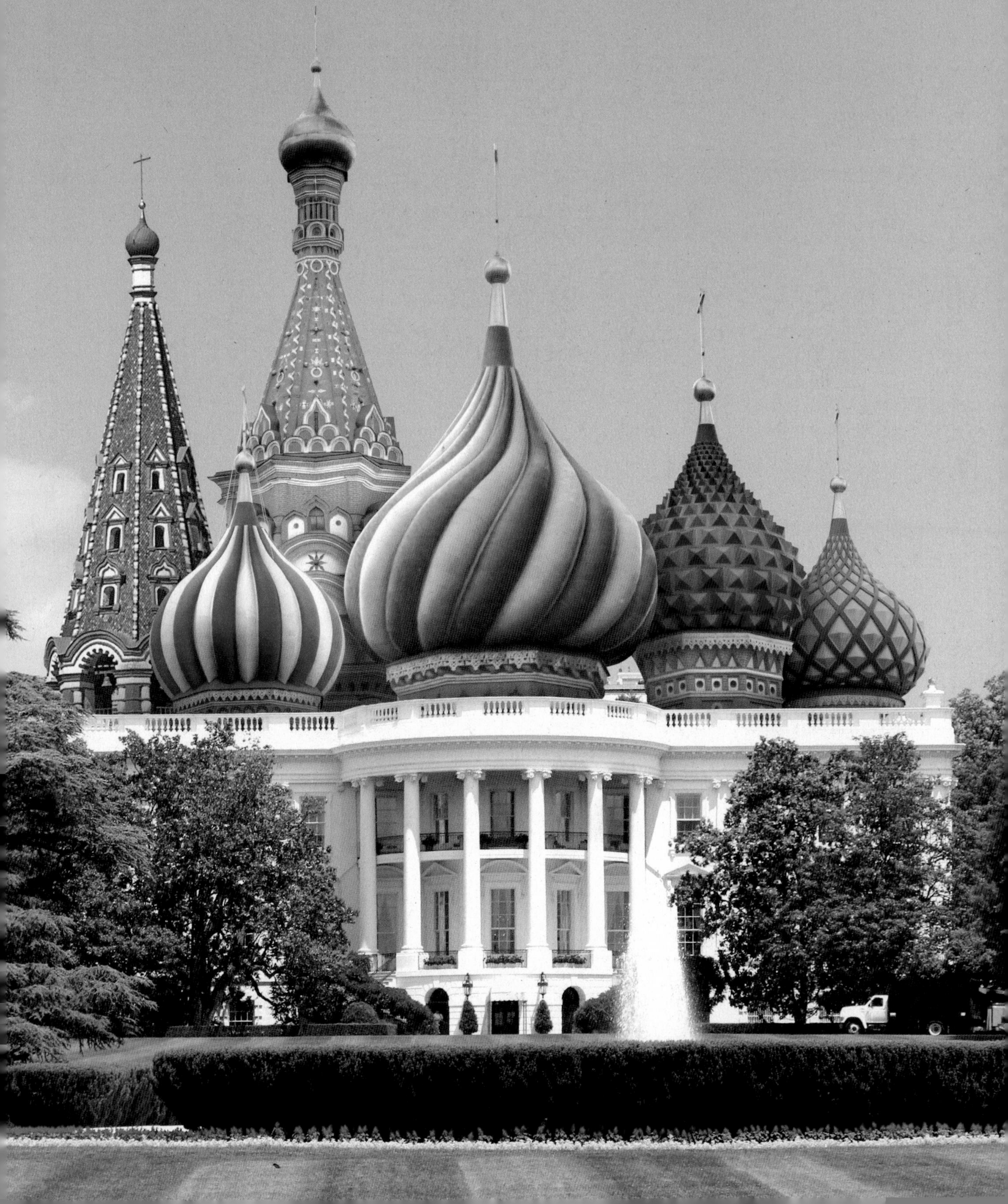

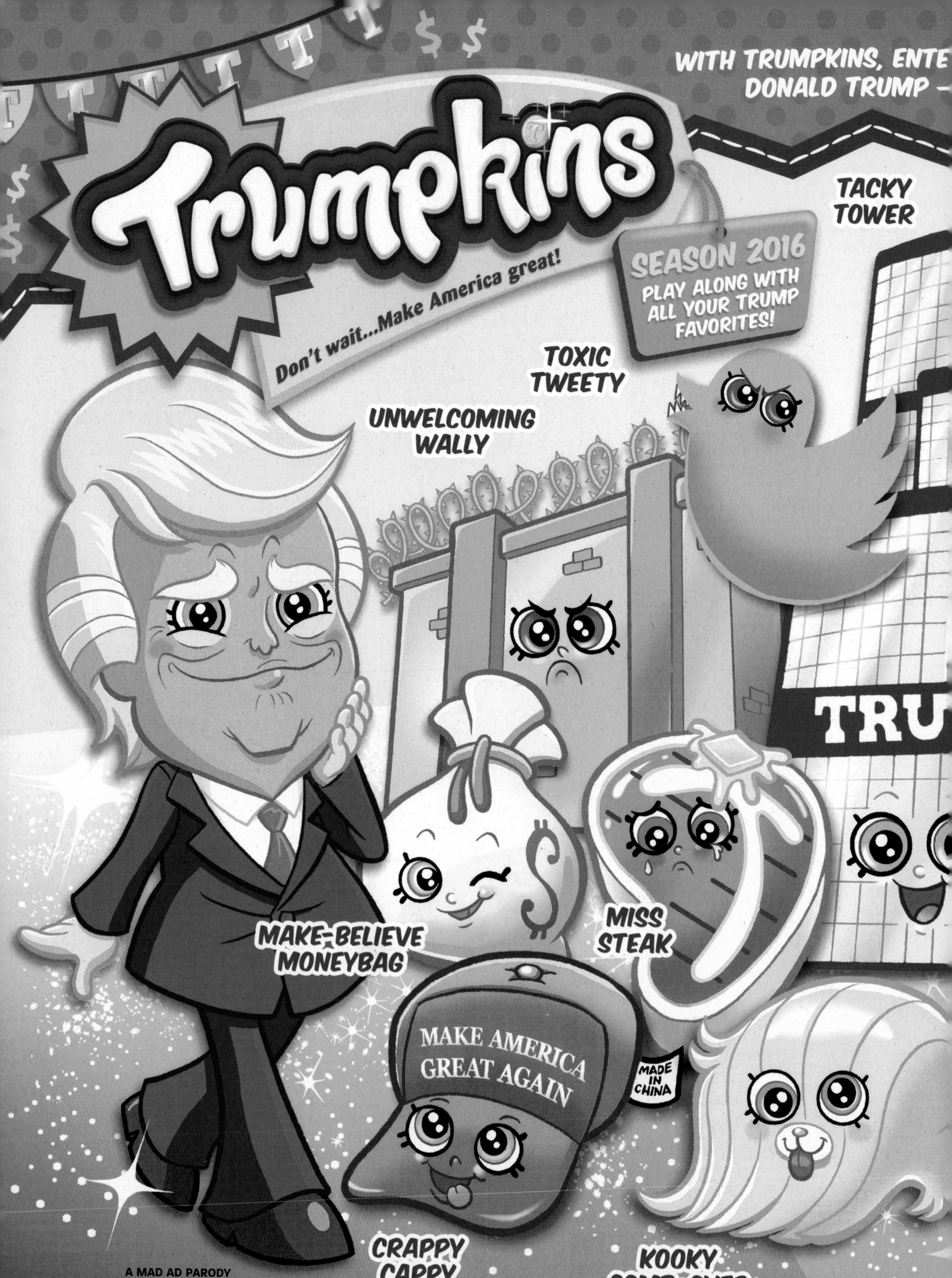
WITH TRUMPKINS, ENTE
DONALD TRUMP –
Trumpkins
Don't wait...Make America great!
SEASON 2016
PLAY ALONG WITH ALL YOUR TRUMP FAVORITES!
TACKY TOWER
TOXIC TWEETY
UNWELCOMING WALLY
TRU
MAKE-BELIEVE MONEYBAG
MISS STEAK
MAKE AMERICA GREAT AGAIN
MADE IN CHINA
CRAPPY CAPPY
KOOKY COMB-OVER

A MAD AD PARODY
WRITER: JACOB LAMBERT ARTIST: JACOB CHABOT

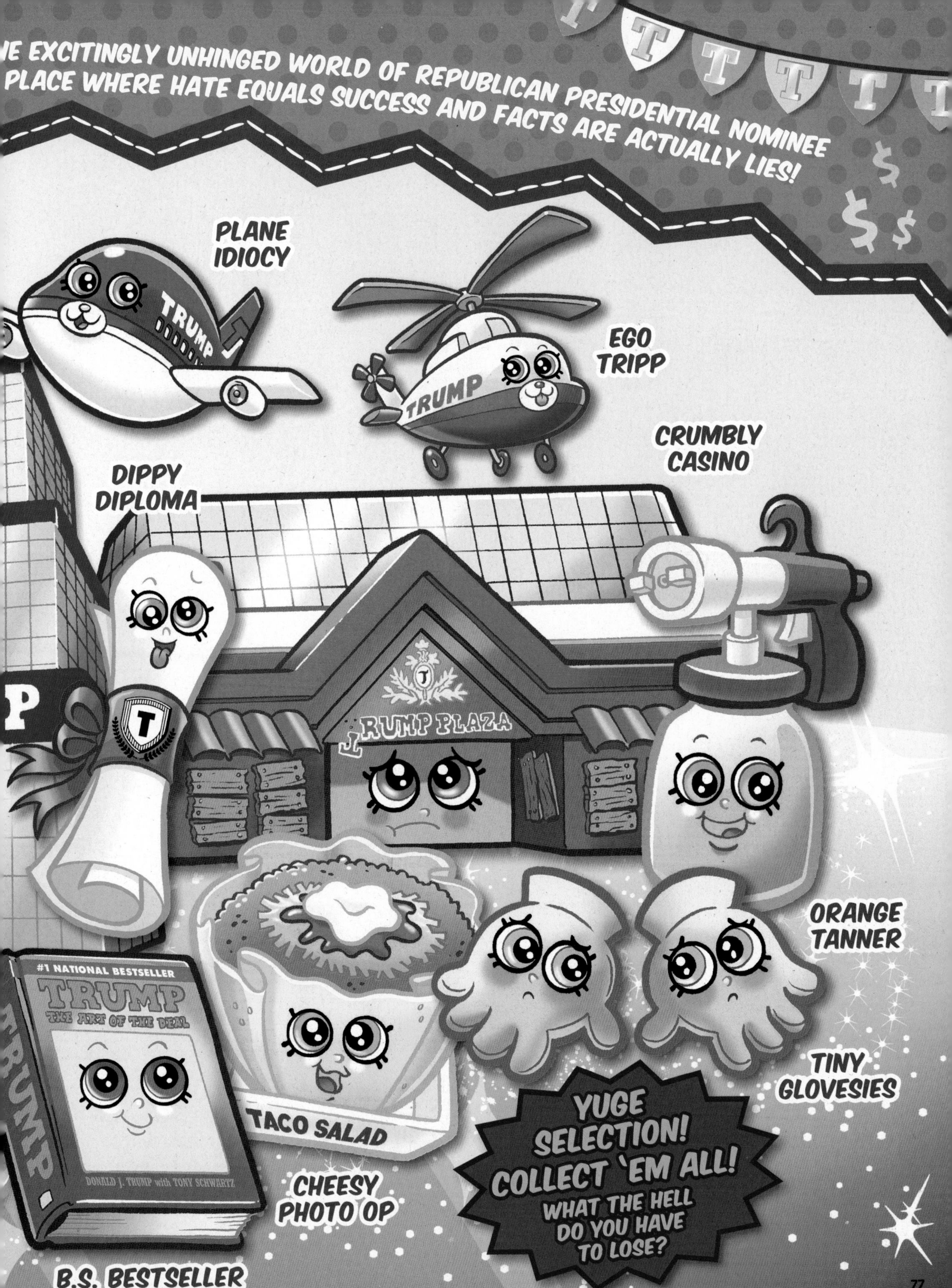

E EXCITINGLY UNHINGED WORLD OF REPUBLICAN PRESIDENTIAL NOMINEE
PLACE WHERE HATE EQUALS SUCCESS AND FACTS ARE ACTUALLY LIES!
PLANE IDIOCY
TRUMP
EGO TRIPP
TRUMP
CRUMBLY CASINO
DIPPY DIPLOMA
TRUMP PLAZA
ORANGE TANNER
#1 NATIONAL BESTSELLER
TRUMP
THE ART OF THE DEAL
DONALD J. TRUMP with TONY SCHWARTZ
TRUMP
TACO SALAD
TINY GLOVESIES
YUGE SELECTION! COLLECT 'EM ALL!
WHAT THE HELL DO YOU HAVE TO LOSE?
CHEESY PHOTO OP
B.S. BESTSELLER

OUCH! This year's election is going to be a CAT-ASTROPHE of personal MOUSE-CONDUCT!

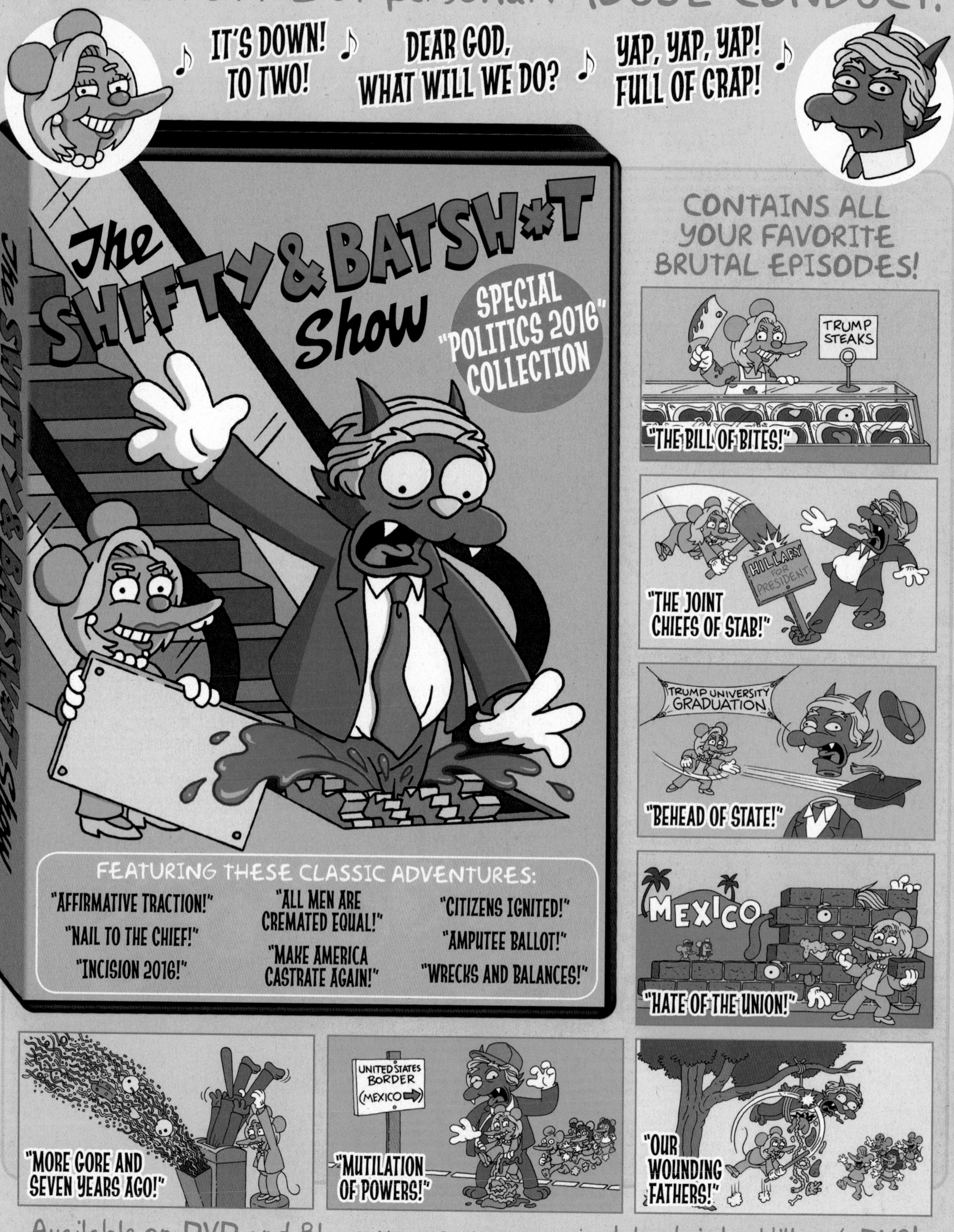

♪ IT'S DOWN! TO TWO! ♪
DEAR GOD, WHAT WILL WE DO? ♪
YAP, YAP, YAP! FULL OF CRAP! ♪
The SHIFTY & BATSH*T Show
SPECIAL "POLITICS 2016" COLLECTION
The SHIFTY & BATSH*T Show
FEATURING THESE CLASSIC ADVENTURES:
"AFFIRMATIVE TRACTION!"
"NAIL TO THE CHIEF!"
"INCISION 2016!"
"ALL MEN ARE CREMATED EQUAL!"
"MAKE AMERICA CASTRATE AGAIN!"
"CITIZENS IGNITED!"
"AMPUTEE BALLOT!"
"WRECKS AND BALANCES!"
CONTAINS ALL YOUR FAVORITE BRUTAL EPISODES!
TRUMP STEAKS
"THE BILL OF BITES!"
HILLARY FOR PRESIDENT
"THE JOINT CHIEFS OF STAB!"
TRUMP UNIVERSITY GRADUATION
"BEHEAD OF STATE!"
MEXICO
"HATE OF THE UNION!"
"MORE GORE AND SEVEN YEARS AGO!"
UNITED STATES BORDER (MEXICO ➡)
"MUTILATION OF POWERS!"
"OUR WOUNDING FATHERS!"

Available on DVD and Blu-ray — or you can just hack into Hillary's DVR!

Our Guarantee: It's the only battle that somehow manages to be more painful, mindless and cartoonish than the actual election!

WRITER: DESMOND DEVLIN ARTIST: BILL MORRISON COLORIST: ROBERT STANLEY A MAD AD PARODY

SIGNS THAT THE "GOLDEN SHOWER" REPORT IS FALSE

Trump says that it didn't happen, and he *always* tells the truth

His campaign slogan was "Make America Great Again," not "Make America #1 Again"

Everyone knows that his real fetish is s#!tting on the Constitution

Experts agree: for something like this, you get a much bigger bang for your buck in Thailand

He's more of a Rusty Trombone sort of guy

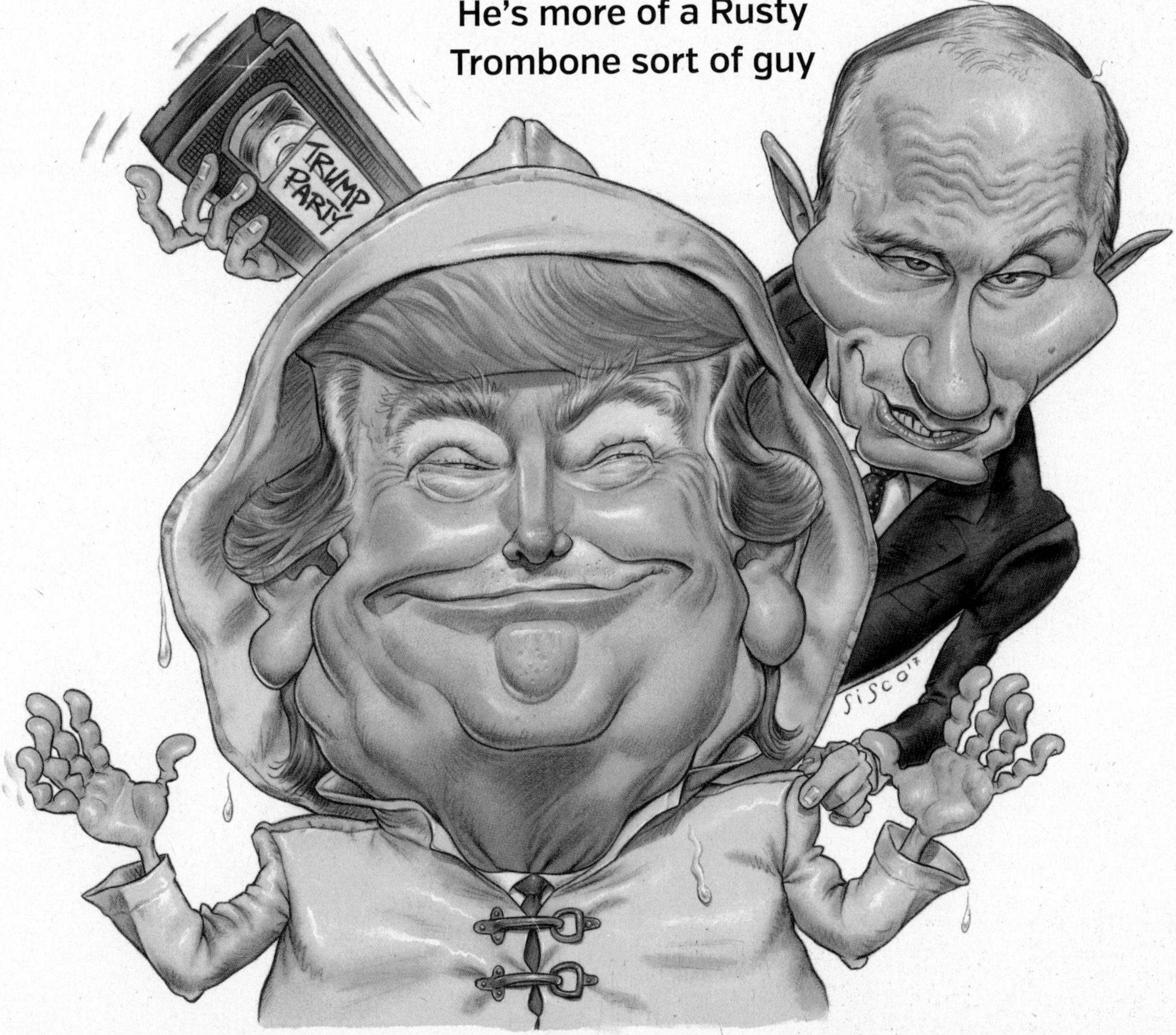
TRUMP PARTY
SISCO'17

ARTIST: SAM SISCO

Donald Trump's Proposed Change to the Statue of Liberty

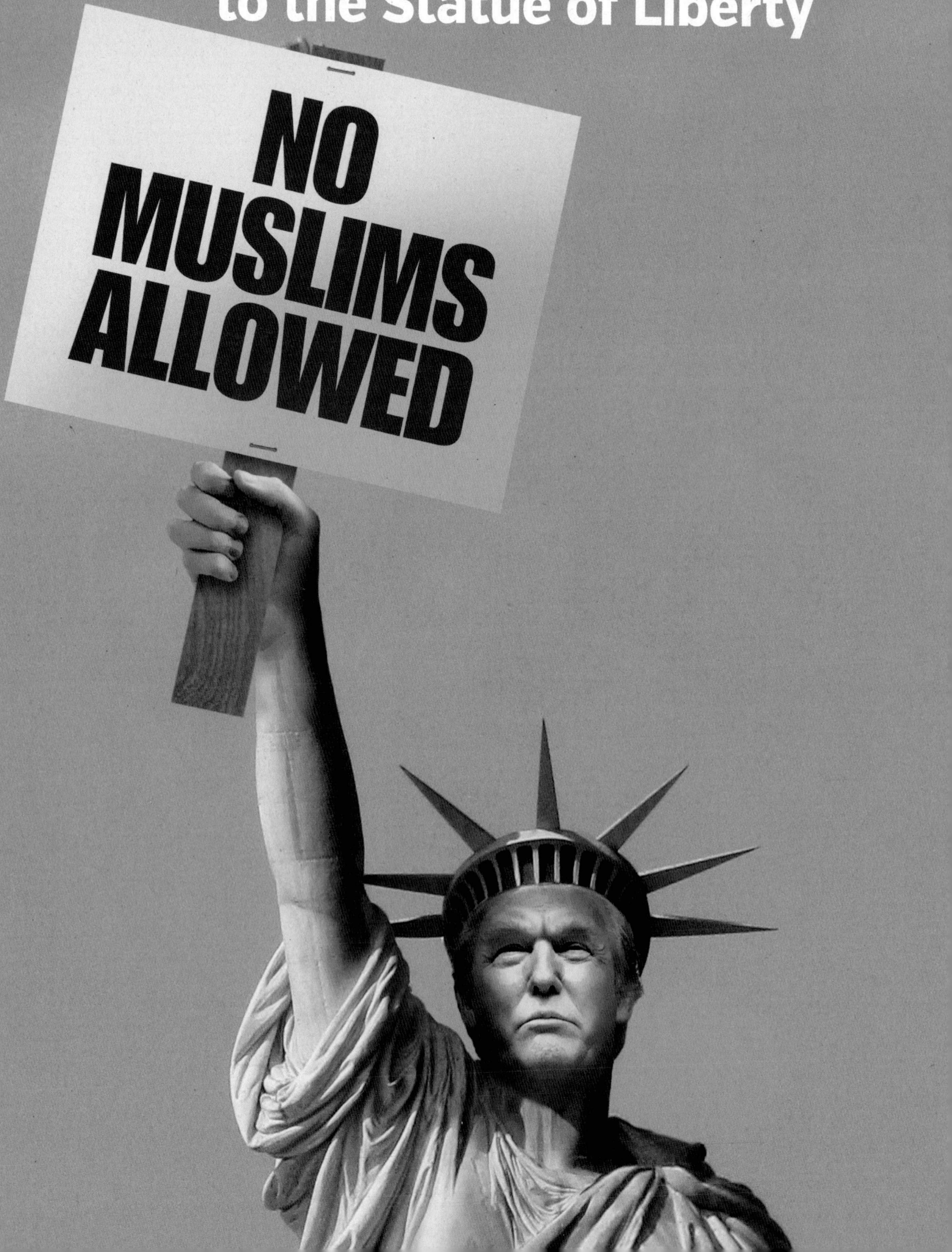
NO
MUSLIMS
ALLOWED

TRUMP CANDY HEARTS

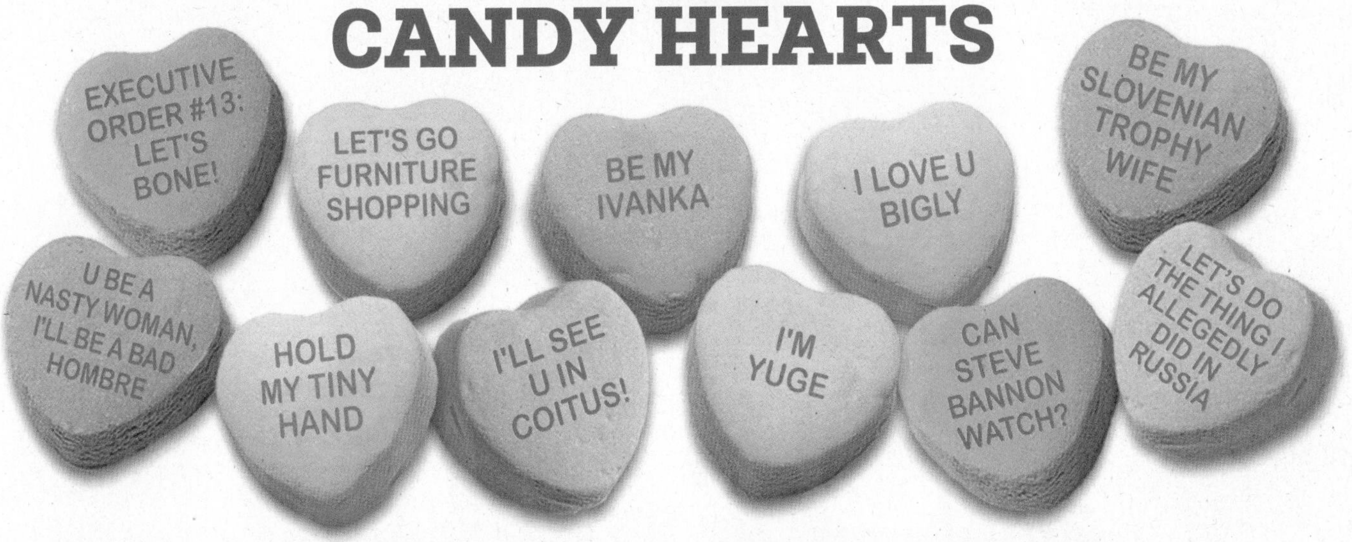
EXECUTIVE ORDER #13: LET'S BONE!
LET'S GO FURNITURE SHOPPING
BE MY IVANKA
I LOVE U BIGLY
BE MY SLOVENIAN TROPHY WIFE
U BE A NASTY WOMAN, I'LL BE A BAD HOMBRE
HOLD MY TINY HAND
I'LL SEE U IN COITUS!
I'M YUGE
CAN STEVE BANNON WATCH?
LET'S DO THE THING I ALLEGEDLY DID IN RUSSIA

TRUMP'S LATEST FAMILY APPOINTMENTS

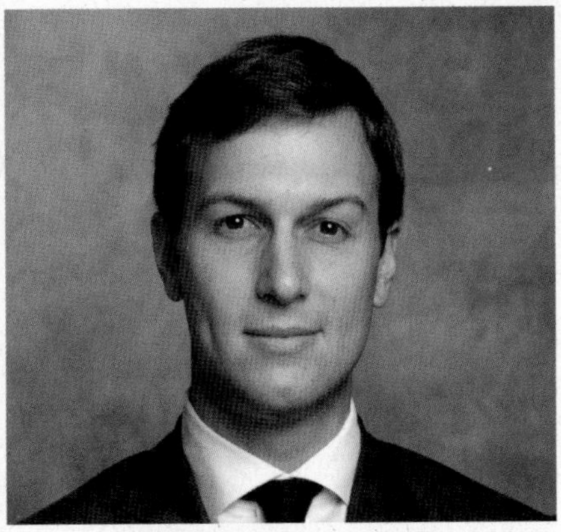

JARED KUSHNER
Chairman of
Inexperienced Advisors

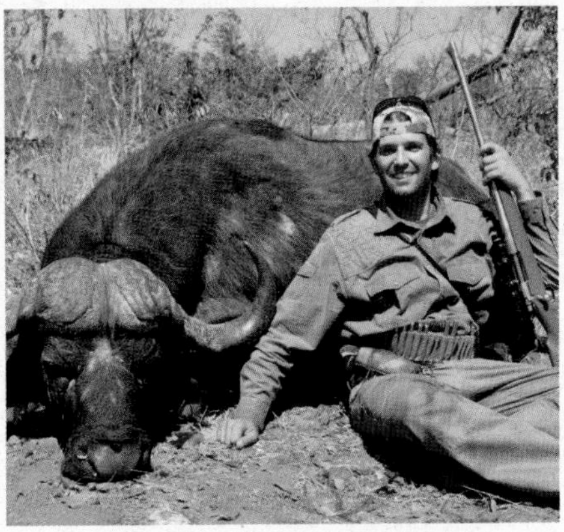

DONALD TRUMP, JR.
Director of
Wildlife Extinction

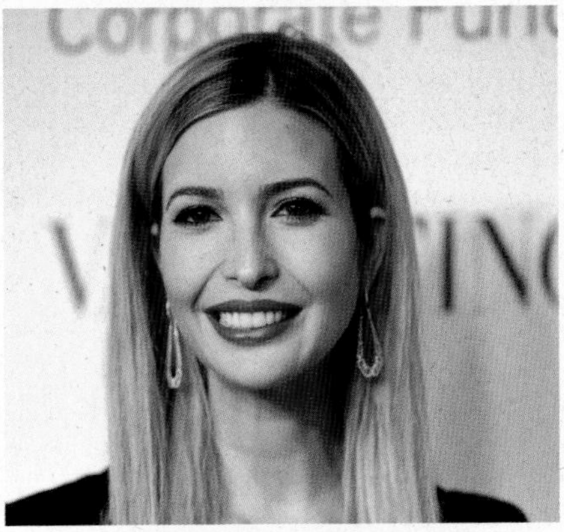

IVANKA TRUMP
Secretary of Defense
of Her Father

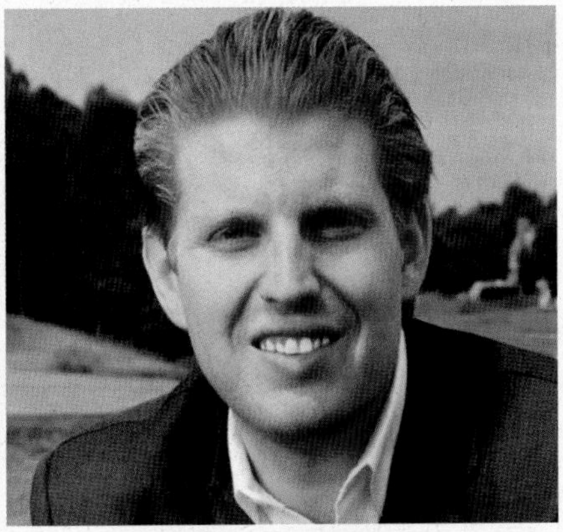

ERIC TRUMP
Gary Busey
Lookalike Liaison

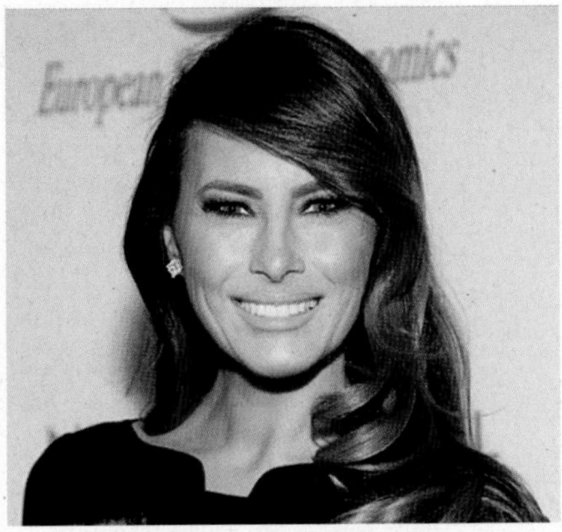

MELANIA TRUMP
Plastic
Surgeon General

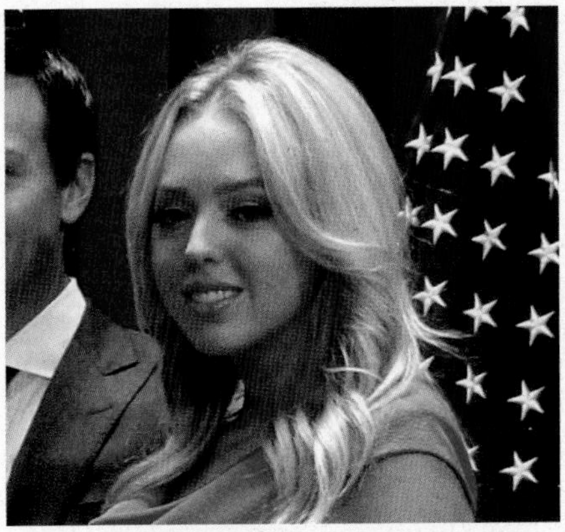

TIFFANY TRUMP
Secretary of Standing
Quietly for Photo-Ops

THE TRUMP FOUNDATION SCAM I AM

When most people think of a charity, they think of something like the Bill and Melinda Gates Foundation – an organization set up to help others in need. But Donald Trump's "charity" seems to have been set up only for his own "need" – specifically, garish oil portraits of himself, a possible bribe to Florida's attorney general and paying legal settlements from other wings of his shady empire. Maybe Trump isn't as generous as he claims he is because he isn't as rich as he claims. Whatever. When the truth about the Trump Foundation emerged in 2016, leading to its shutdown in New York State, nobody seemed surprised – it was clear to all that Donald Trump believes charity begins in the tacky Manhattan tower he calls home.

Every year Donald Trump's "charity" operated like his own personal piggy bank. In 2016, he got found out.

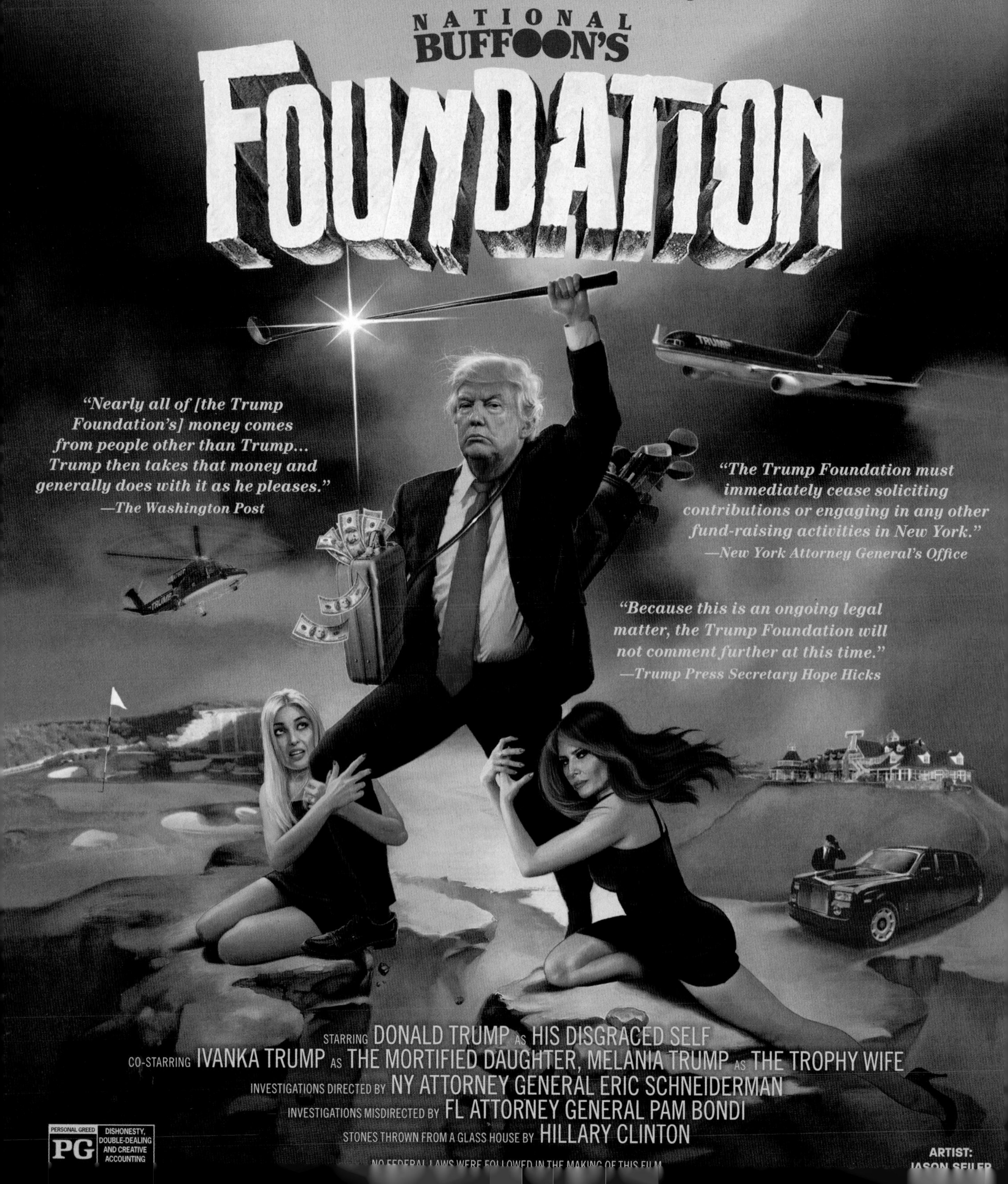
NATIONAL BUFFOON'S
FOUNDATION
TRUMP
"Nearly all of [the Trump Foundation's] money comes from people other than Trump... Trump then takes that money and generally does with it as he pleases."
—The Washington Post
"The Trump Foundation must immediately cease soliciting contributions or engaging in any other fund-raising activities in New York."
—New York Attorney General's Office
"Because this is an ongoing legal matter, the Trump Foundation will not comment further at this time."
—Trump Press Secretary Hope Hicks
STARRING DONALD TRUMP AS HIS DISGRACED SELF
CO-STARRING IVANKA TRUMP AS THE MORTIFIED DAUGHTER, MELANIA TRUMP AS THE TROPHY WIFE
INVESTIGATIONS DIRECTED BY NY ATTORNEY GENERAL ERIC SCHNEIDERMAN
INVESTIGATIONS MISDIRECTED BY FL ATTORNEY GENERAL PAM BONDI
STONES THROWN FROM A GLASS HOUSE BY HILLARY CLINTON
PERSONAL GREED
PG
DISHONESTY, DOUBLE-DEALING AND CREATIVE ACCOUNTING
NO FEDERAL LAWS WERE FOLLOWED IN THE MAKING OF THIS FILM
ARTIST:
JASON SEILER

ABOUT A BOYCOTT DEPT.

THINGS TRUMP DID WHEN HE SKIPPED THE FOX DEBATE

Binge-watched *House of Cards* to pick up a few governing tips

Prank-called Bobby Jindal to ask if he'd be his running mate

Stripped down to a wife-beater and jeans, then sought out Des Moines' most violent fight club

Caught up on six months of scrapbooking

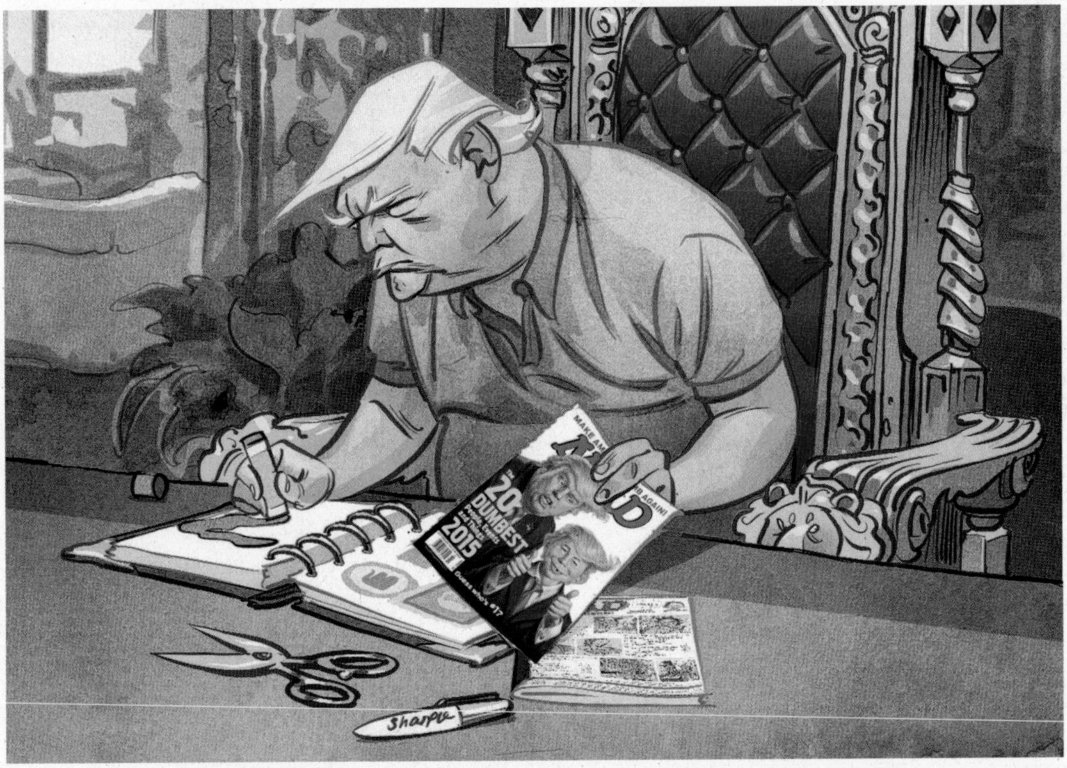
DUMBEST
2015

Prepped for a softball interview on the next day's *Morning Joe*

Reviewed "Re-elect Trump in 2020" bumper sticker designs

Played pinochle with Shatner, Oprah and Cosby

Gave his hair a much-needed night off

Spouted empty rhetoric and lowest-common-denominator insults from the comfort of his own home

MAD ASKS: WHAT'S IN A SLOGAN?

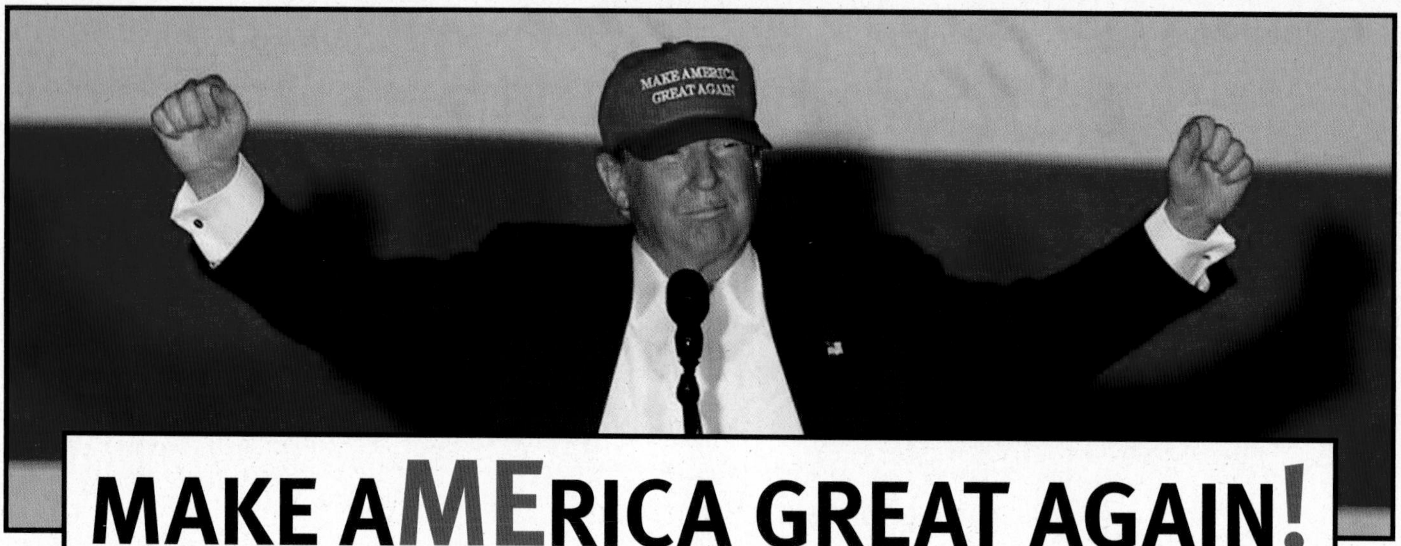
MAKE AMERICA
GREAT AGAIN

MAKE AMERICA GREAT AGAIN!

OVERHEARD IN THE COURTHOUSE WHERE DONALD TRUMP IS SERVING JURY DUTY

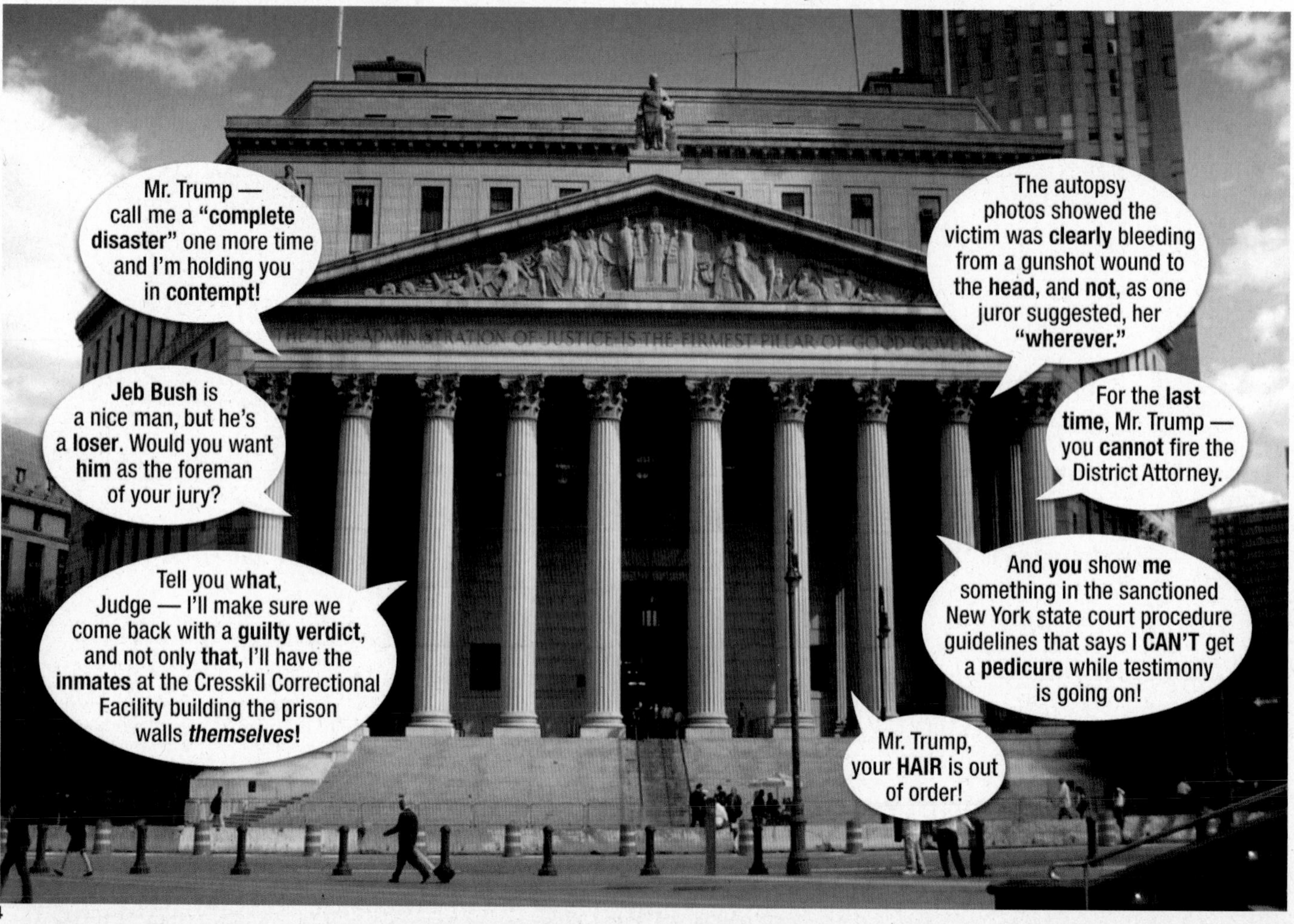
Mr. Trump — call me a **"complete disaster"** one more time and I'm holding you in **contempt**!
The autopsy photos showed the victim was **clearly** bleeding from a gunshot wound to the **head**, and **not**, as one juror suggested, her **"wherever."**
Jeb Bush is a nice man, but he's a **loser**. Would you want **him** as the foreman of your jury?
For the **last time**, Mr. Trump — you **cannot** fire the District Attorney.
Tell you **what**, Judge — I'll make sure we come back with a **guilty verdict**, and not only **that**, I'll have the **inmates** at the Cresskil Correctional Facility building the prison walls ***themselves***!
And **you** show **me** something in the sanctioned New York state court procedure guidelines that says I **CAN'T** get a **pedicure** while testimony is going on!
Mr. Trump, your **HAIR** is out of order!

A Betsy DeVos Poster We'd Like to See

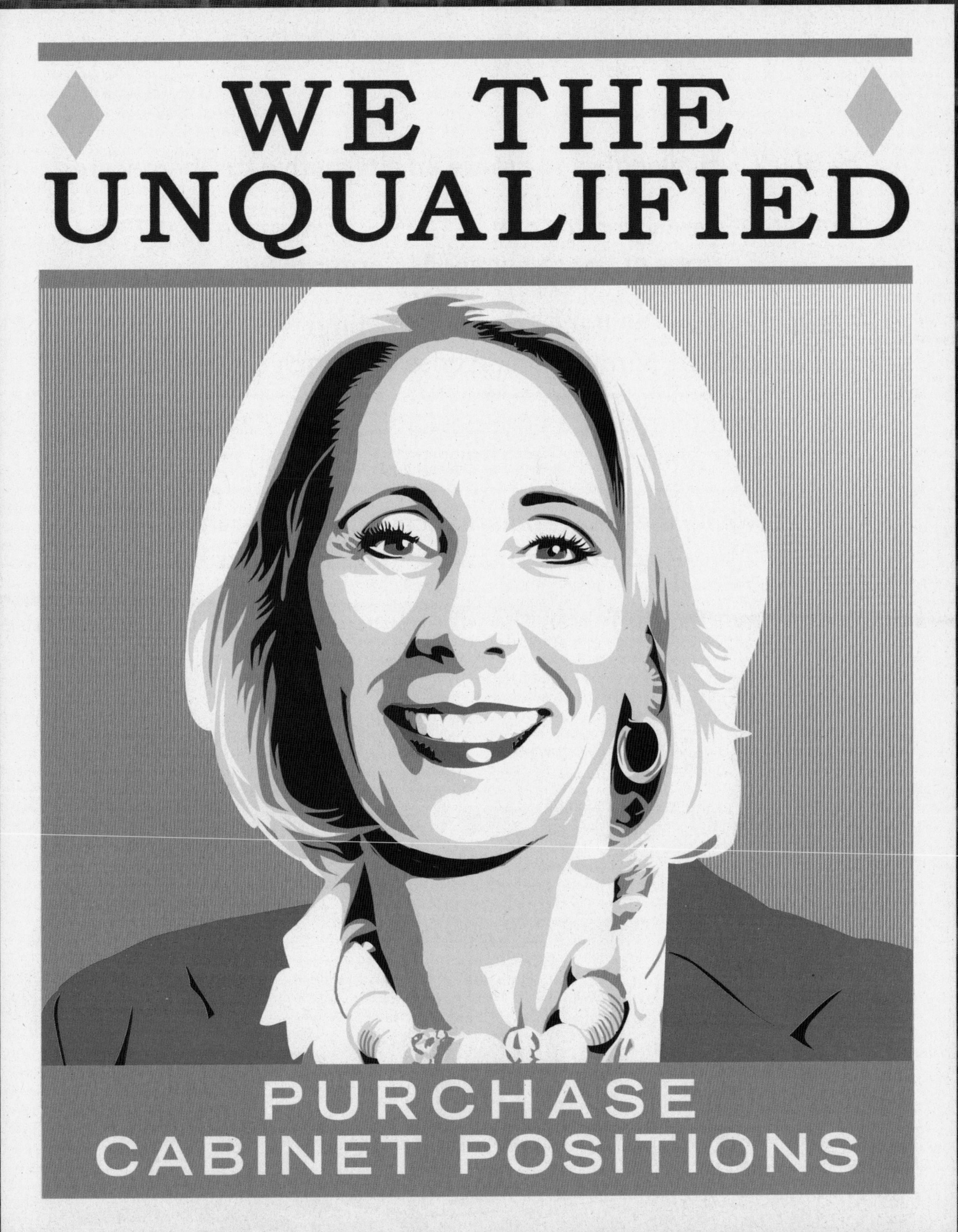
WE THE
UNQUALIFIED
PURCHASE
CABINET POSITIONS

PRESIDENT TRUMP'S CHANGES TO THE CELEBRITY APPRENTICE

The Week 3 challenge is to create an alternative to Obamacare

Contestants are vying for one of 1,100 – wait, make that 730 – jobs at the Indianapolis Carrier plant

Production may be halted whenever Trump is called away to tweet about SNL, berate a union boss or launch a nuclear attack

Due to his commitments as our new ambassador to North Korea, Dennis Rodman only sporadically appears on the show

It will be the first regularly-scheduled program to pre-empt the State of the Union Address

When losers leave Trump Tower, the limousine's chauffeur is Chris Christie

ARTIST:
PAUL COKER

LET'S DO PUNCH DEPT.

TONIGHT!

"THE TUSSLE IN TINSELTOWN"

TALE OF THE TAPE

MERYL "THE ACTIN' ASSASSIN" STREEP VS DONALD "KID LOUDMOUTH" TRUMP

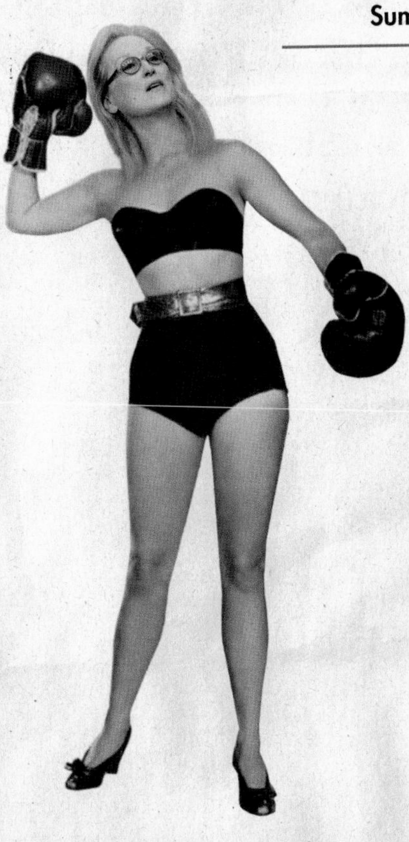

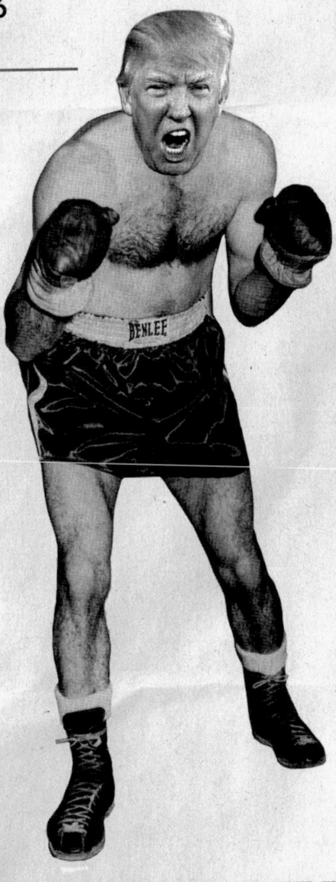

BENLEE

MERYL STREEP June 22, 1949 Summit, NJ		DONALD TRUMP June 14, 1946 Queens, NY
1	ELOQUENT POLITICAL SPEECHES GIVEN	0
YES	HAS SUPPORTED HILLARY IN THE PAST	YES
0	RANTS DIRECTED AT CRITICS	1,427,844
YES	PREPARES TIRELESSLY FOR LEAD ROLES	NO
1	MOVIES APPEARED IN WITH A CULKIN	1
YES	WAS IN "THE MANCHURIAN CANDIDATE"	NO
NO	WAS A MANCHURIAN CANDIDATE	YES

WHY WE LIKE THE IDEA OF MELANIA TRUMP AS FIRST LADY

Well, there's the whole "former swimsuit model" thing

It would mean that none of the Religious-Right
nut job Republicans became President

She's a great example to girls that a super-hot woman can
accomplish anything her gazillionaire husband puts his mind to

---

Anyone who has a skin care product line called
"Caviar Complexe C6" *has* to be a woman of the people

The press will inevitably run puff pieces on what Marla Maples
has been up to, which is always valuable information to have

She's still young enough to have more children, which will produce the
kind of delightful media frenzy so beloved by the British Royal Family

---

Her April 26 birthday is shared by both William Shakespeare
and Jet Li. Try telling us *that's* a coincidence!

WRITER: JEFF KRUSE   ARTIST: HERMANN MEJIA

WORKERS' CONDESCENSION DEPT.

Public distrust of wealthy CEOs is nothing compared to CEOs' distrust of their workforce! In order to find out what's really going on in their companies, a new show follows bosses as they go undercover. You'll get to see what crappy conditions underpaid workers have to put up with. But more importantly, you'll see how a fat-cat, pompous CEO becomes an...

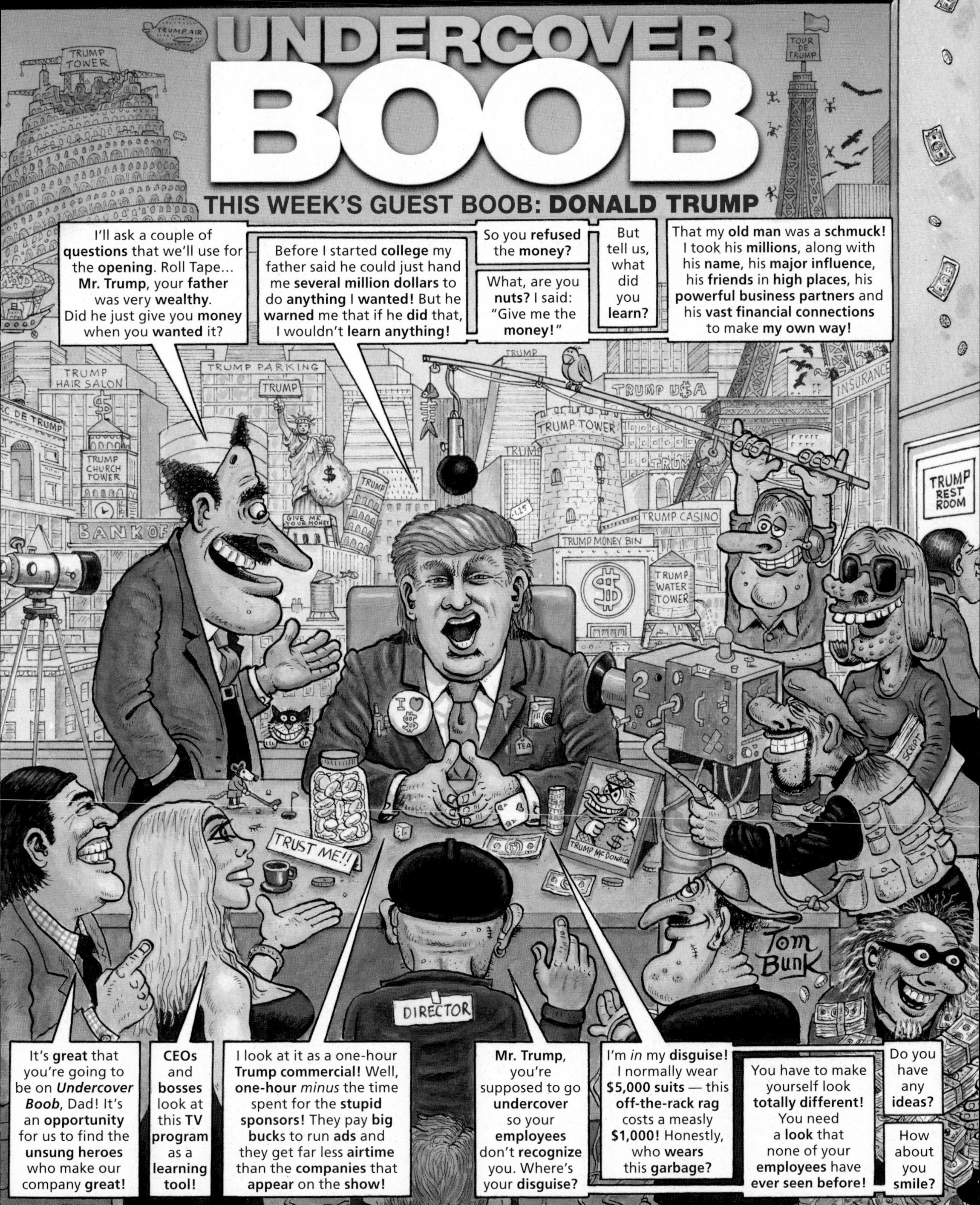

UNDERCOVER BOOB
THIS WEEK'S GUEST BOOB: DONALD TRUMP
I'll ask a couple of questions that we'll use for the opening. Roll Tape... Mr. Trump, your father was very wealthy. Did he just give you money when you wanted it?
Before I started college my father said he could just hand me several million dollars to do anything I wanted! But he warned me that if he did that, I wouldn't learn anything!
So you refused the money?
What, are you nuts? I said: "Give me the money!"
But tell us, what did you learn?
That my old man was a schmuck! I took his millions, along with his name, his major influence, his friends in high places, his powerful business partners and his vast financial connections to make my own way!
It's great that you're going to be on Undercover Boob, Dad! It's an opportunity for us to find the unsung heroes who make our company great!
CEOs and bosses look at this TV program as a learning tool!
I look at it as a one-hour Trump commercial! Well, one-hour minus the time spent for the stupid sponsors! They pay big bucks to run ads and they get far less airtime than the companies that appear on the show!
Mr. Trump, you're supposed to go undercover so your employees don't recognize you. Where's your disguise?
I'm in my disguise! I normally wear $5,000 suits — this off-the-rack rag costs a measly $1,000! Honestly, who wears this garbage?
You have to make yourself look totally different! You need a look that none of your employees have ever seen before!
Do you have any ideas?
How about you smile?
TRUMP AIR
TRUMP TOWER
TOUR DE TRUMP
TRUMP PARKING
TRUMP HAIR SALON
TRUMP CHURCH TOWER
BANK OF
TRUMP U$A
TRUMP CASINO
TRUMP MONEY BIN
TRUMP WATER TOWER
TRUMP REST ROOM
INSURANCE
TRUST ME!!
TRUMP McDONALD
DIRECTOR
SCRIPT
Tom Bunk

WRITER: DICK DEBARTOLO ARTIST: TOM BUNK

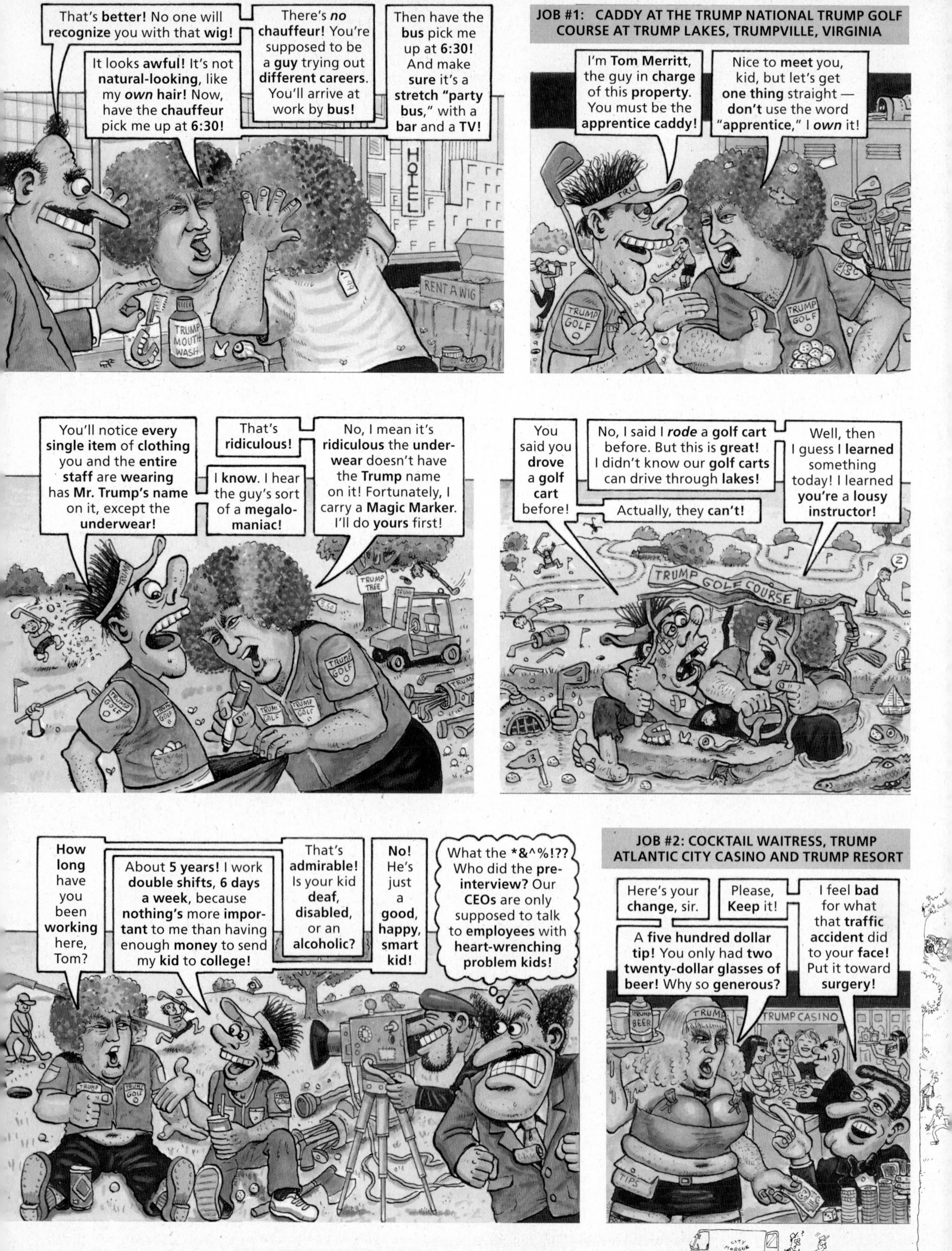
That's **better!** No one will **recognize** you with that **wig!**
It looks **awful!** It's not **natural-looking**, like my ***own* hair!** Now, have the **chauffeur** pick me up at **6:30!**
There's ***no* chauffeur!** You're supposed to be a **guy** trying out **different careers**. You'll arrive at work by **bus!**
Then have the **bus** pick me up at **6:30!** And make **sure** it's a **stretch "party bus,"** with a **bar** and a **TV!**
HOTEL
RENT A WIG
TRUMP MOUTH WASH
JOB #1: CADDY AT THE TRUMP NATIONAL TRUMP GOLF COURSE AT TRUMP LAKES, TRUMPVILLE, VIRGINIA
I'm **Tom Merritt**, the guy in **charge** of this **property**. You must be the **apprentice caddy!**
Nice to **meet** you, kid, but let's get **one thing** straight — **don't** use the word **"apprentice,"** I ***own*** it!
TRUMP GOLF
You'll notice **every single item** of **clothing** you and the **entire staff** are **wearing** has **Mr. Trump's name** on it, except the **underwear!**
That's **ridiculous!**
I **know**. I hear the guy's sort of a **megalo-maniac!**
No, I mean it's **ridiculous** the **under-wear** doesn't have the **Trump** name on it! Fortunately, I carry a **Magic Marker**. I'll do **yours** first!
TRUMP TREE
You said you **drove** a **golf cart** before!
No, I said I ***rode*** a **golf cart** before. But this is **great!** I didn't know our **golf carts** can drive through **lakes!**
Actually, they **can't!**
Well, then I guess I **learned** something today! I learned **you're a lousy instructor!**
TRUMP GOLF COURSE
How long have you been **working** here, Tom?
About **5 years!** I work **double shifts, 6 days a week**, because **nothing's** more **impor-tant** to me than having enough **money** to send my **kid** to **college!**
That's **admirable!** Is your kid **deaf**, **disabled**, or an **alcoholic?**
No! He's just a **good**, **happy**, **smart kid!**
What the ***&^%!??** Who did the **pre-interview?** Our **CEOs** are only supposed to talk to **employees** with **heart-wrenching problem kids!**
JOB #2: COCKTAIL WAITRESS, TRUMP ATLANTIC CITY CASINO AND TRUMP RESORT
Here's your **change**, sir.
Please, **Keep** it!
A **five hundred dollar tip!** You only had **two twenty-dollar glasses of beer!** Why so **generous?**
I feel **bad** for what that **traffic accident** did to your **face!** Put it toward **surgery!**
TRUMP BEER
TRUMP CASINO
TIPS
CITY MORGUE

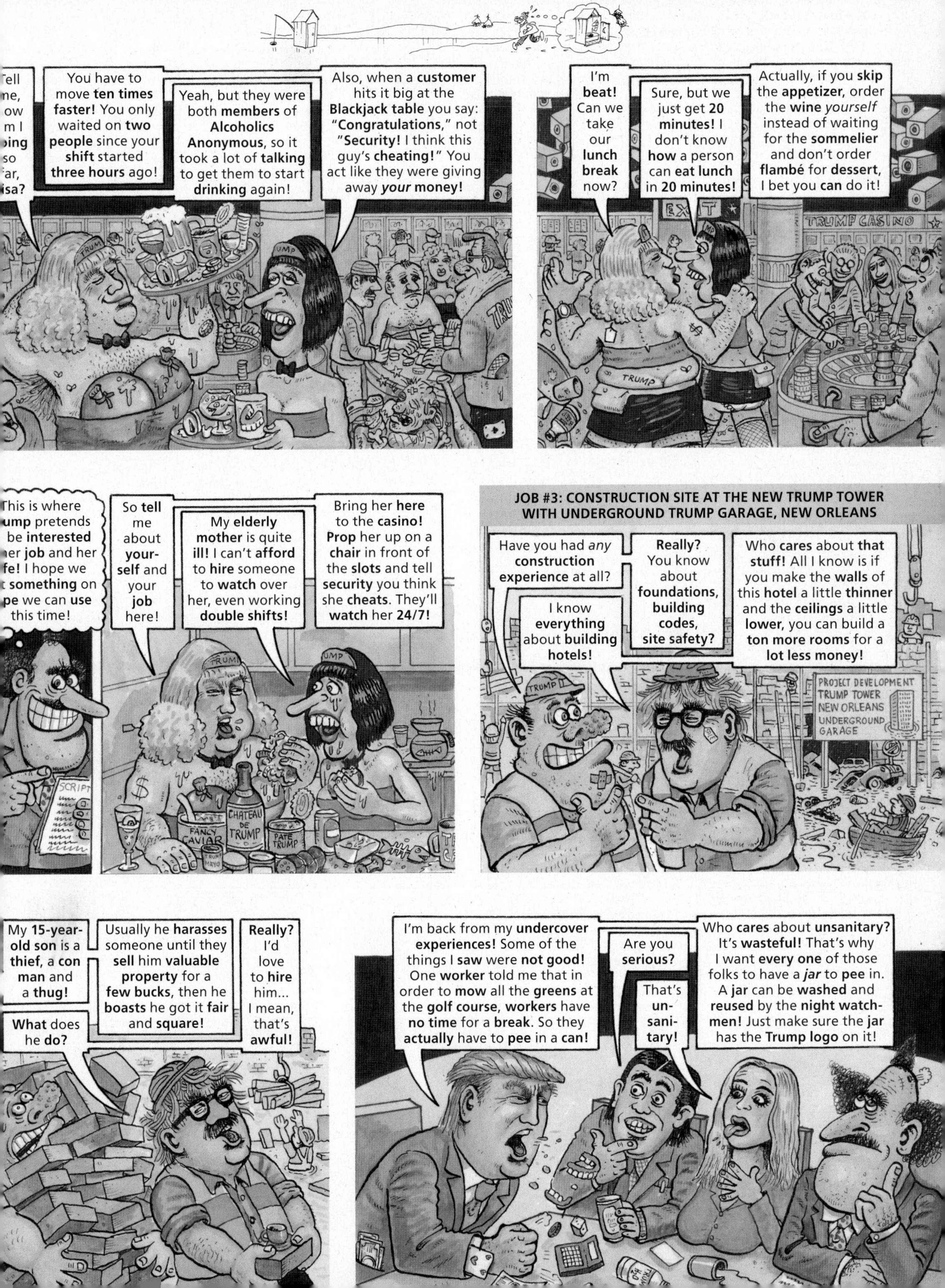

ell ne, ow m I oing so ar, isa?
You have to move ten times faster! You only waited on two people since your shift started three hours ago!
Yeah, but they were both members of Alcoholics Anonymous, so it took a lot of talking to get them to start drinking again!
Also, when a customer hits it big at the Blackjack table you say: "Congratulations," not "Security! I think this guy's cheating!" You act like they were giving away your money!
TRUMP
I'm beat! Can we take our lunch break now?
Sure, but we just get 20 minutes! I don't know how a person can eat lunch in 20 minutes!
Actually, if you skip the appetizer, order the wine yourself instead of waiting for the sommelier and don't order flambé for dessert, I bet you can do it!
EXIT
TRUMP CASINO
TRUMP
This is where ump pretends be interested er job and her fe! I hope we something on pe we can use this time!
SCRIPT
So tell me about yourself and your job here!
My elderly mother is quite ill! I can't afford to hire someone to watch over her, even working double shifts!
Bring her here to the casino! Prop her up on a chair in front of the slots and tell security you think she cheats. They'll watch her 24/7!
FANCY CAVIAR
CHATEAU DE TRUMP
PATE TRUMP
JOB #3: CONSTRUCTION SITE AT THE NEW TRUMP TOWER WITH UNDERGROUND TRUMP GARAGE, NEW ORLEANS
Have you had any construction experience at all?
I know everything about building hotels!
Really? You know about foundations, building codes, site safety?
Who cares about that stuff! All I know is if you make the walls of this hotel a little thinner and the ceilings a little lower, you can build a ton more rooms for a lot less money!
TRUMP
PROJECT DEVELOPMENT TRUMP TOWER NEW ORLEANS UNDERGROUND GARAGE
My 15-year-old son is a thief, a con man and a thug!
What does he do?
Usually he harasses someone until they sell him valuable property for a few bucks, then he boasts he got it fair and square!
Really? I'd love to hire him... I mean, that's awful!
I'm back from my undercover experiences! Some of the things I saw were not good! One worker told me that in order to mow all the greens at the golf course, workers have no time for a break. So they actually have to pee in a can!
Are you serious?
That's un-sani-tary!
Who cares about unsanitary? It's wasteful! That's why I want every one of those folks to have a jar to pee in. A jar can be washed and reused by the night watchmen! Just make sure the jar has the Trump logo on it!

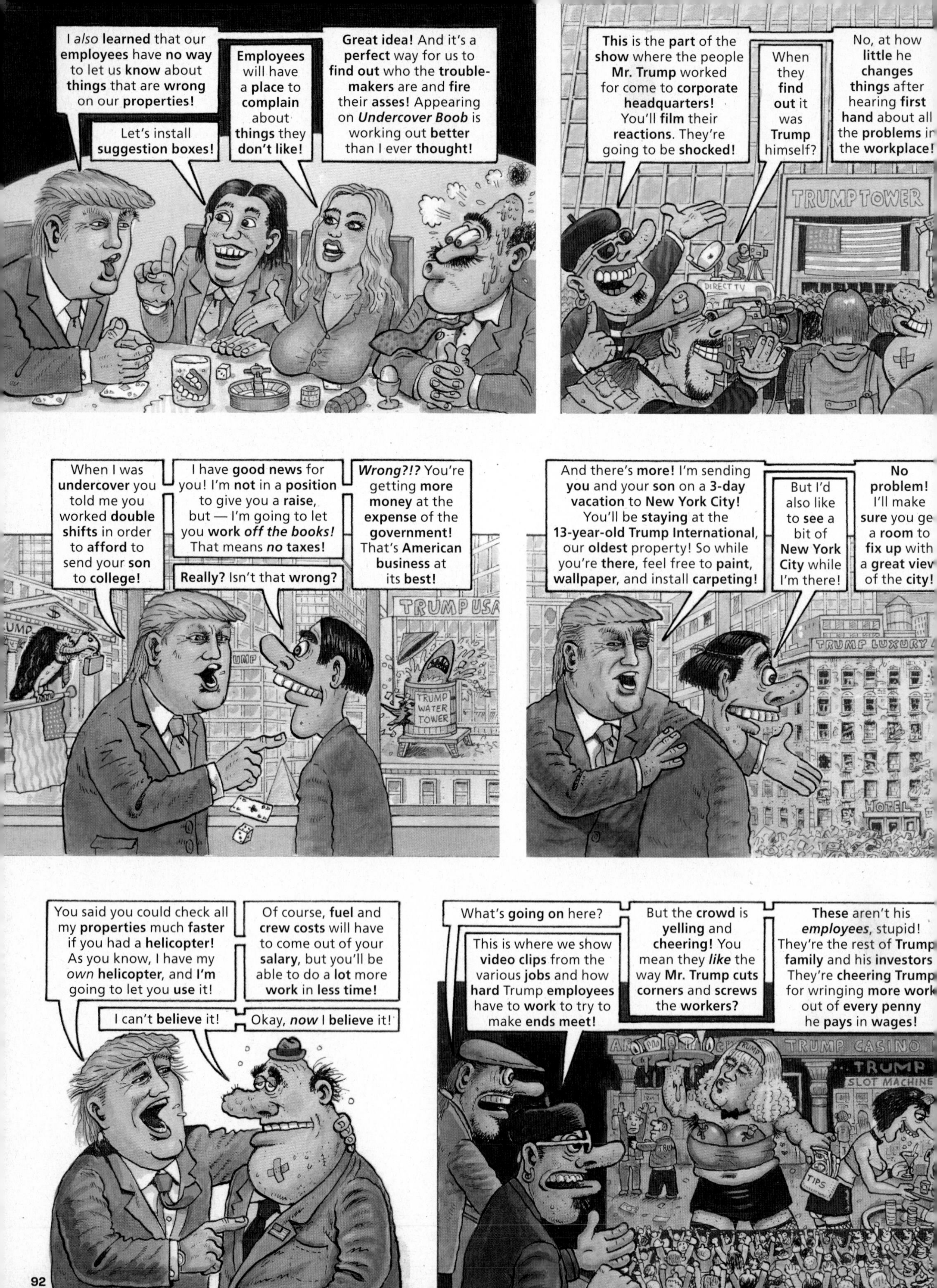
I *also* **learned** that our **employees** have **no way** to let us **know** about **things** that are **wrong** on our **properties!**
Let's install **suggestion boxes!**
Employees will have a **place** to **complain** about **things** they **don't like!**
Great idea! And it's a **perfect** way for us to **find out** who the **trouble-makers** are and **fire** their **asses!** Appearing on ***Undercover Boob*** is working out **better** than I ever **thought!**
This is the **part** of the **show** where the people **Mr. Trump** worked for come to **corporate headquarters!** You'll **film** their **reactions.** They're going to be **shocked!**
When they **find out** it was **Trump** himself?
No, at how **little** he **changes things** after hearing **first hand** about all the **problems** i the **workplace!**
TRUMP TOWER
DIRECT TV
When I was **undercover** you told me you worked **double shifts** in order to **afford** to send your **son** to **college!**
I have **good news** for you! I'm **not** in a **position** to give you a **raise,** but — I'm going to let you **work *off the books!*** That means ***no*** **taxes!**
Really? Isn't that **wrong?**
Wrong?!? You're getting **more money** at the **expense** of the **government!** That's **American business** at its **best!**
TRUMP USA
TRUMP WATER TOWER
And there's **more!** I'm sending **you** and your **son** on a **3-day vacation** to **New York City!** You'll be **staying** at the **13-year-old Trump International,** our **oldest** property! So while you're **there,** feel free to **paint, wallpaper,** and install **carpeting!**
But I'd also like to **see** a bit of **New York City** while I'm there!
No problem! I'll make **sure** you ge a **room** to **fix up** with a **great viev** of the **city!**
TRUMP LUXURY
HOTEL
You said you could check all my **properties** much **faster** if you had a **helicopter!** As you know, I have my *own* **helicopter,** and **I'm** going to let you **use** it!
Of course, **fuel** and **crew costs** will have to come out of your **salary,** but you'll be able to do a **lot** more **work** in **less time!**
I can't **believe** it!
Okay, ***now*** I **believe** it!
What's **going on** here?
This is where we show **video clips** from the various **jobs** and how **hard** Trump **employees** have to **work** to try to make **ends meet!**
But the **crowd** is **yelling** and **cheering!** You mean they ***like*** the way **Mr. Trump cuts corners** and **screws** the **workers?**
These aren't his ***employees,*** stupid! They're the rest of **Trump family** and his **investors** They're **cheering Trump** for wringing **more work** out of **every penny** he **pays** in **wages!**
TRUMP CASINO
TRUMP SLOT MACHINE
TIPS

STOP HEARTBURN BIGLY!

Presidential executive orders THROWING YOUR BELLY INTO DISORDER?

Continual abuses of power CAUSING YOUR STOMACH TO GO SOUR?

SAD! TRY TRUMS!

TRUMS is the only antacid specifically designed to fight heartburn brought on by the Presidency of Donald Trump. Whether it's his racial and religious intolerance or his persistent gloating that's giving you gas, indigestion and bloating, orange-flavored **TRUMS** will make sure that the President's next unconstitutional action won't set off your chronic gastritis.

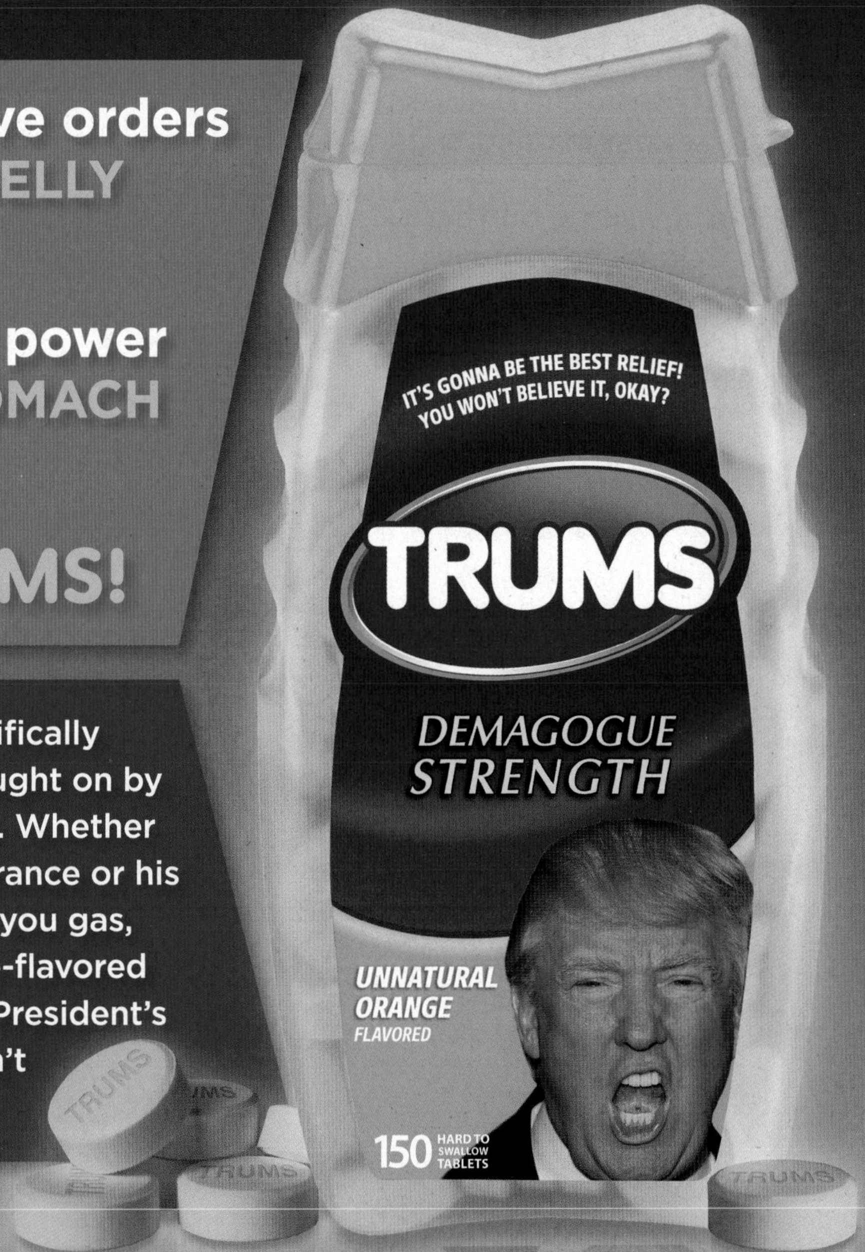
IT'S GONNA BE THE BEST RELIEF!
YOU WON'T BELIEVE IT, OKAY?
TRUMS
DEMAGOGUE STRENGTH
UNNATURAL ORANGE
FLAVORED
150 HARD TO SWALLOW TABLETS
TRUMS

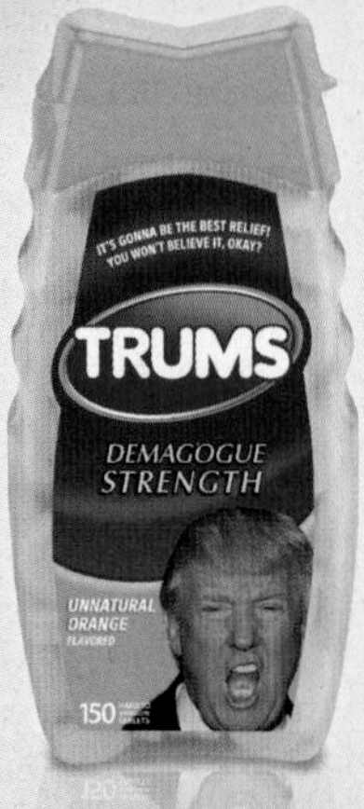
TRUMS
DEMAGOGUE STRENGTH

REDEEM FOR (1) FREE* BOTTLE OF TRUMS

*PAY FOR TRUMS NOW & MEXICO WILL REIMBURSE YOU FOR THEM LATER

Vendor's Note: While it did not win the popular vote of the best antacids on the market, TRUMS were voted "most bitter" and "most unpredictable" of all major antacids — and still, for some reason, many, many people continue to put their trust in TRUMS.

WRITER: CHRISTIAN ALSIS

A MAD AD PARODY

PROS AND CONS OF TRUMP BEING ALLOWED IN THE U.K.

PROS

If he's in the U.K., he's not in the U.S.

When visiting Northern Ireland, he'd surely ease its tensions with his soothing oratory

Finally, America gets its payback for the Stamp Act of 1756

Since he passed away, Britain's been longing for a replacement for Benny Hill

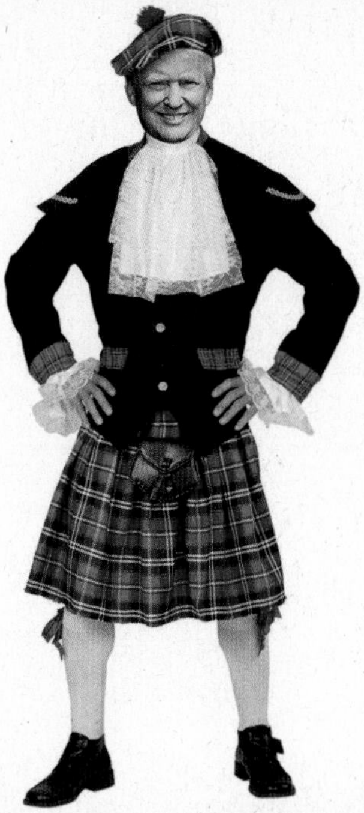

CONS

Upon meeting the Queen, he'd call her "a no-talent loser with zero business sense who deserves to get schlonged."

We'd witness the unsettling side-by-side comparison between his hair and a palace guard's hat

In Scotland, he'd insist on wearing kilts to air out his saggy, wizened Trump-nuts

He'd probably be wildly popular there, too

MAD REDESIGNS THE NORDSTROM LOGO

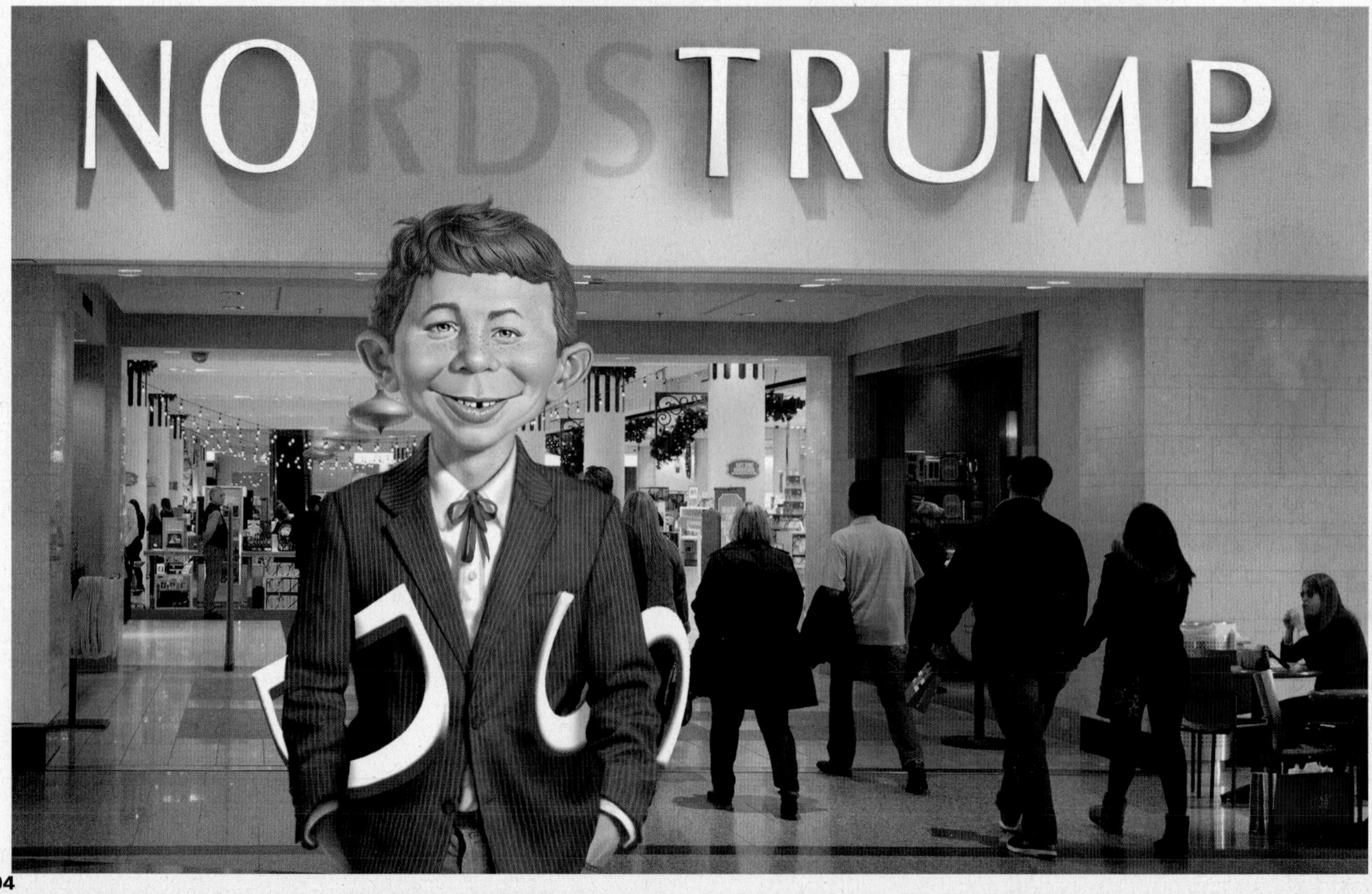
NO RDS TRUMP

A SCANDAL 20 YEARS IN THE MAKING!

"Maybe he is not as rich as he says he is. Maybe he is not as charitable as he claims to be... There is something he is hiding."
— Hillary Clinton

"Mr. Trump knows the tax code far better than anyone who has ever run for President and he is the only one that knows how to fix it."
— Trump Campaign Statement

"It makes me so angry that this country has gotten to this point that this fool, this bozo, has wound up where he has."
— Robert DeNiro

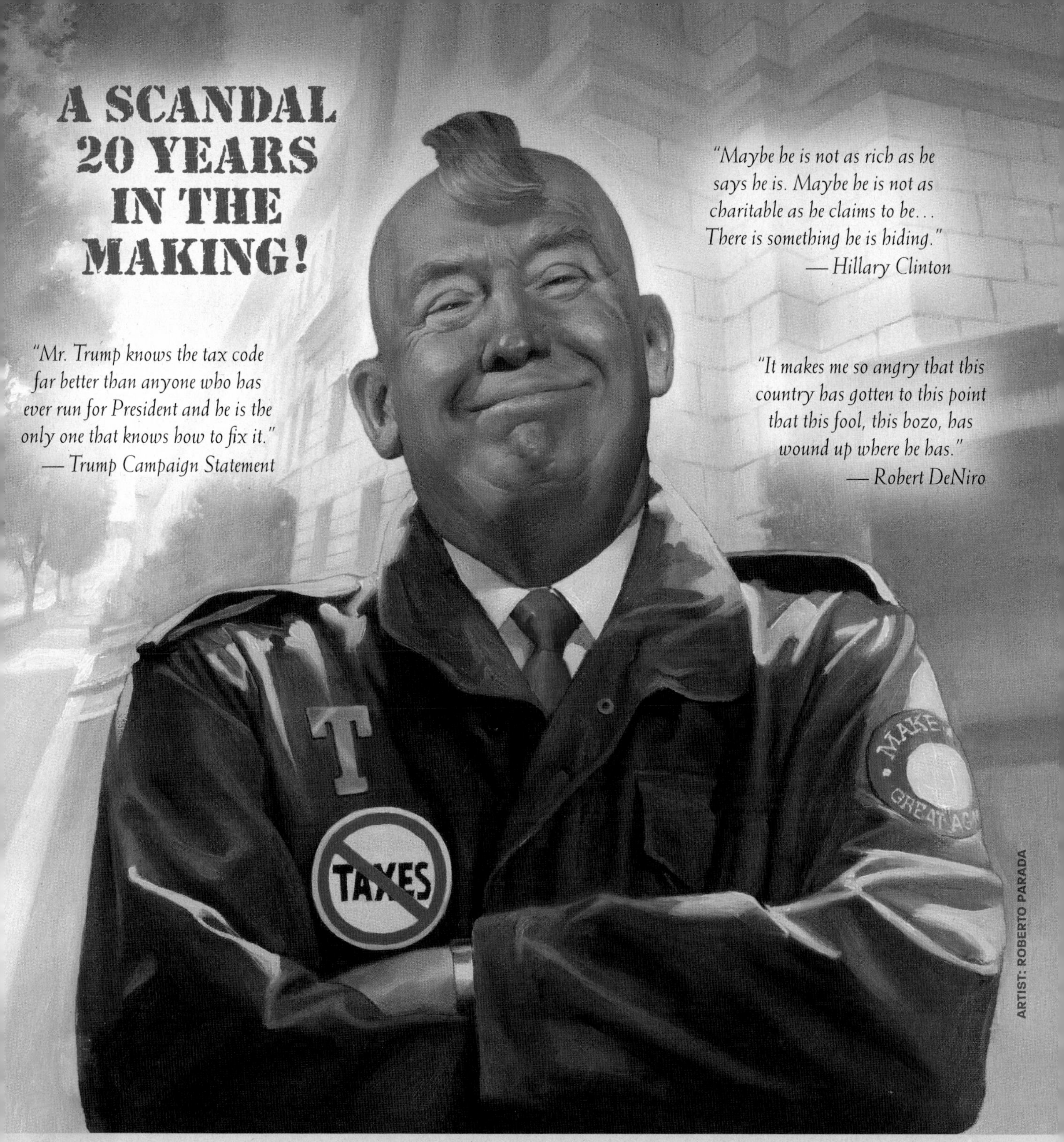
T
TAXES

ARTIST: ROBERTO PARADA

A New York Times Publication of Leaked Tax Returns

DONALD TRUMP
TAX EVADER

BASED ON MASSIVE TAX LOOPHOLES   CREATED BY "**THAT CROOKED HILLARY**"
PRODUCED FAR LESS OUTRAGE THAN YOU'D EXPECT   DIRECTED AT A PUBLIC THAT'S IMMUNE TO SHOCK AT THIS POINT
INSPIRED BY TRUE EVENTS THAT TRUMP IS WEIRDLY PROUD OF
SPECIAL APPEARANCE BY **WARREN BUFFET** AS THE ACTUAL BILLIONAIRE WHO ***DOES*** PAY HIS TAXES

RELEASED NATIONWIDE (UNLIKE TRUMP'S TAX RETURNS)

AN AD WE'D LIKE TO SEE

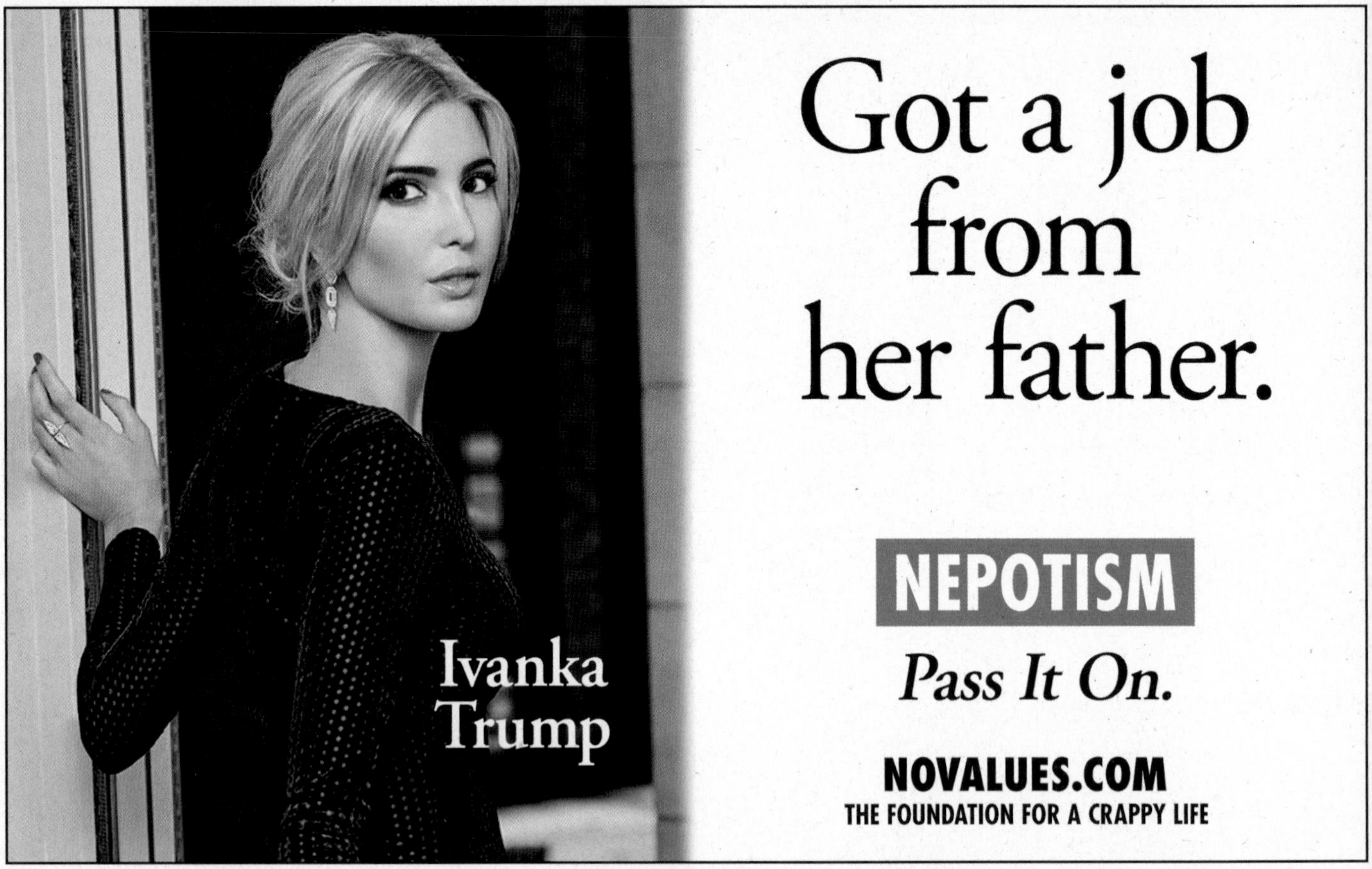
Got a job from her father.
Ivanka Trump
NEPOTISM
Pass It On.
NOVALUES.COM
THE FOUNDATION FOR A CRAPPY LIFE

WRITER: CAITLIN BITZEGAIO

A TRAVEL BAN WE'D LIKE TO SEE

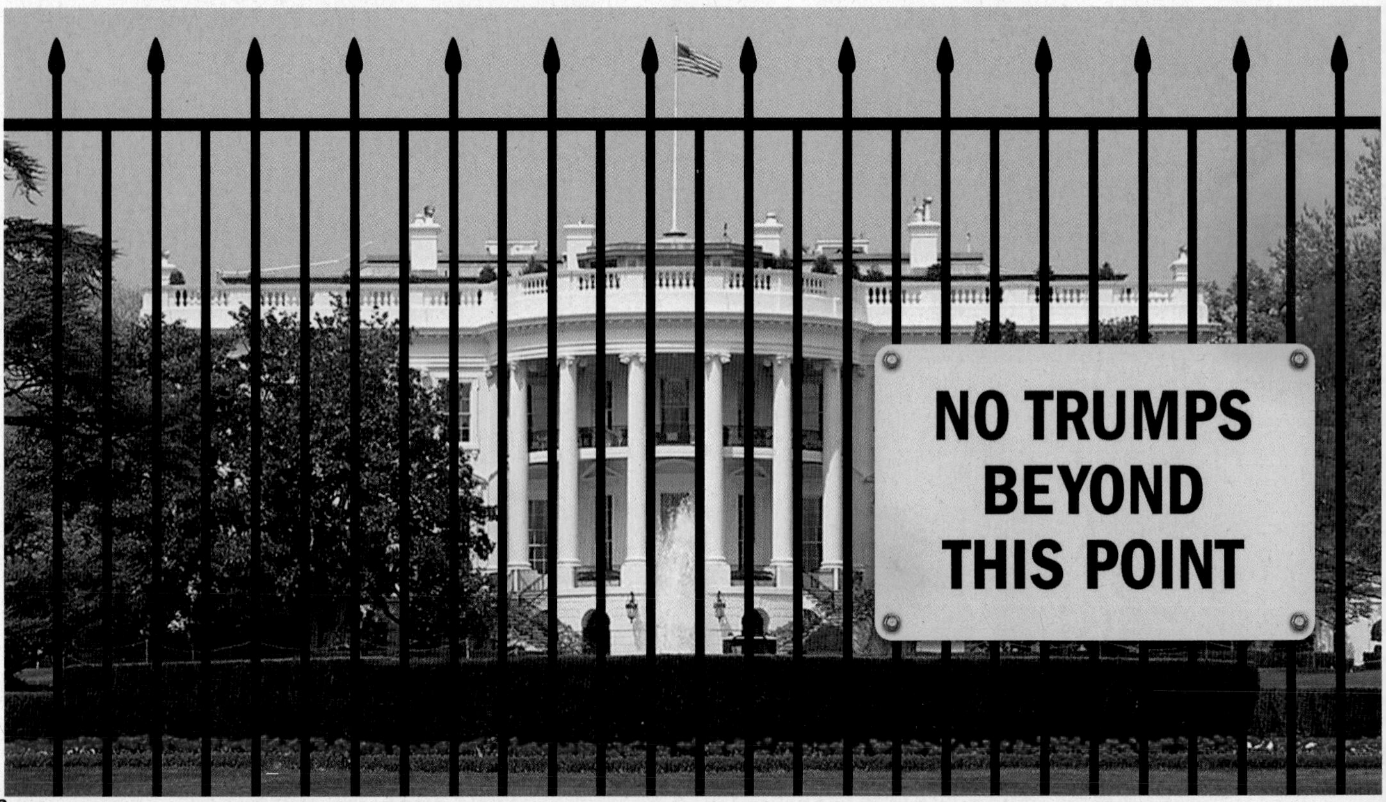
NO TRUMPS BEYOND THIS POINT

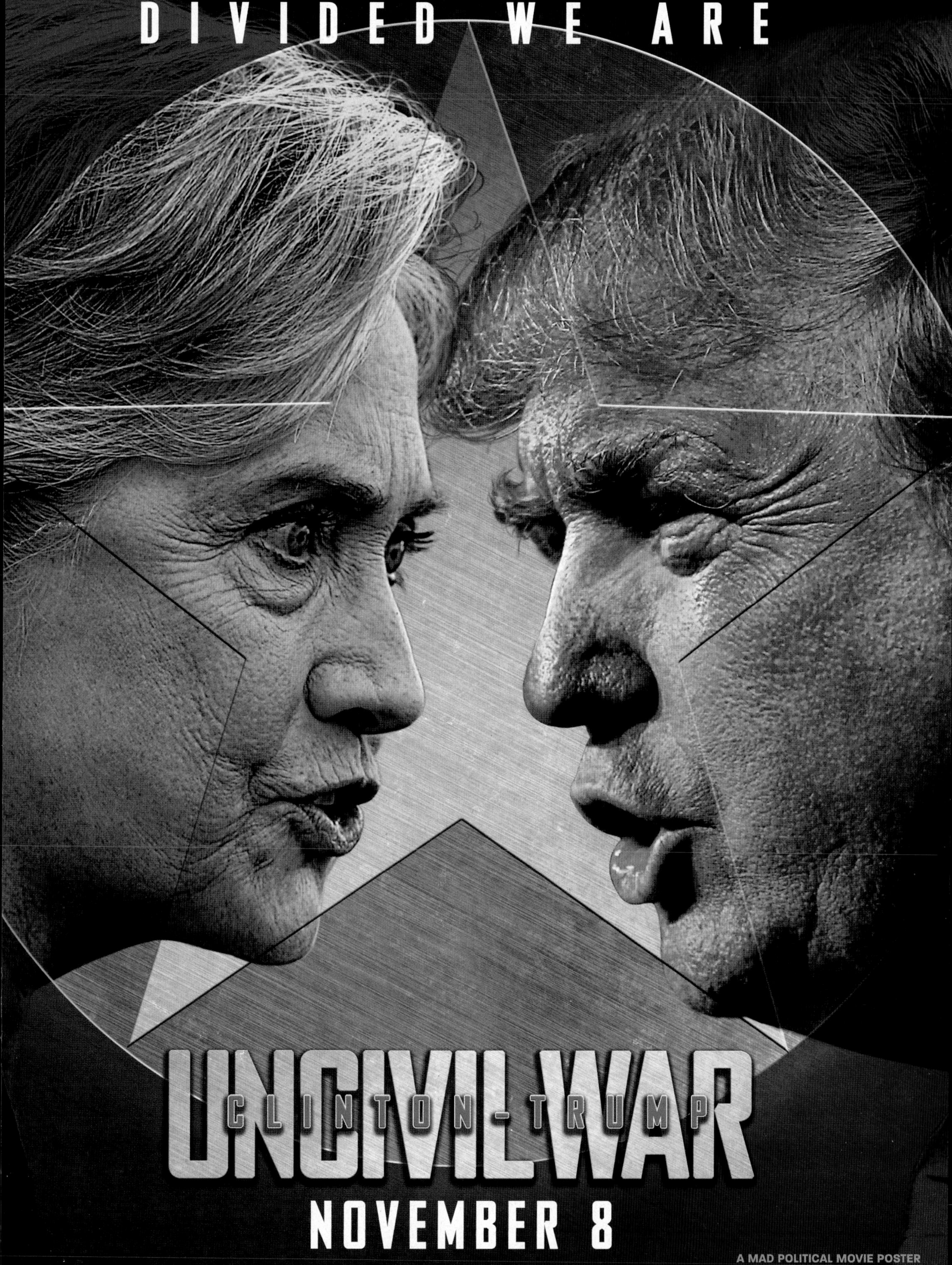
DIVIDED WE ARE
UNCIVIL WAR
CLINTON-TRUMP
NOVEMBER 8
A MAD POLITICAL MOVIE POSTER

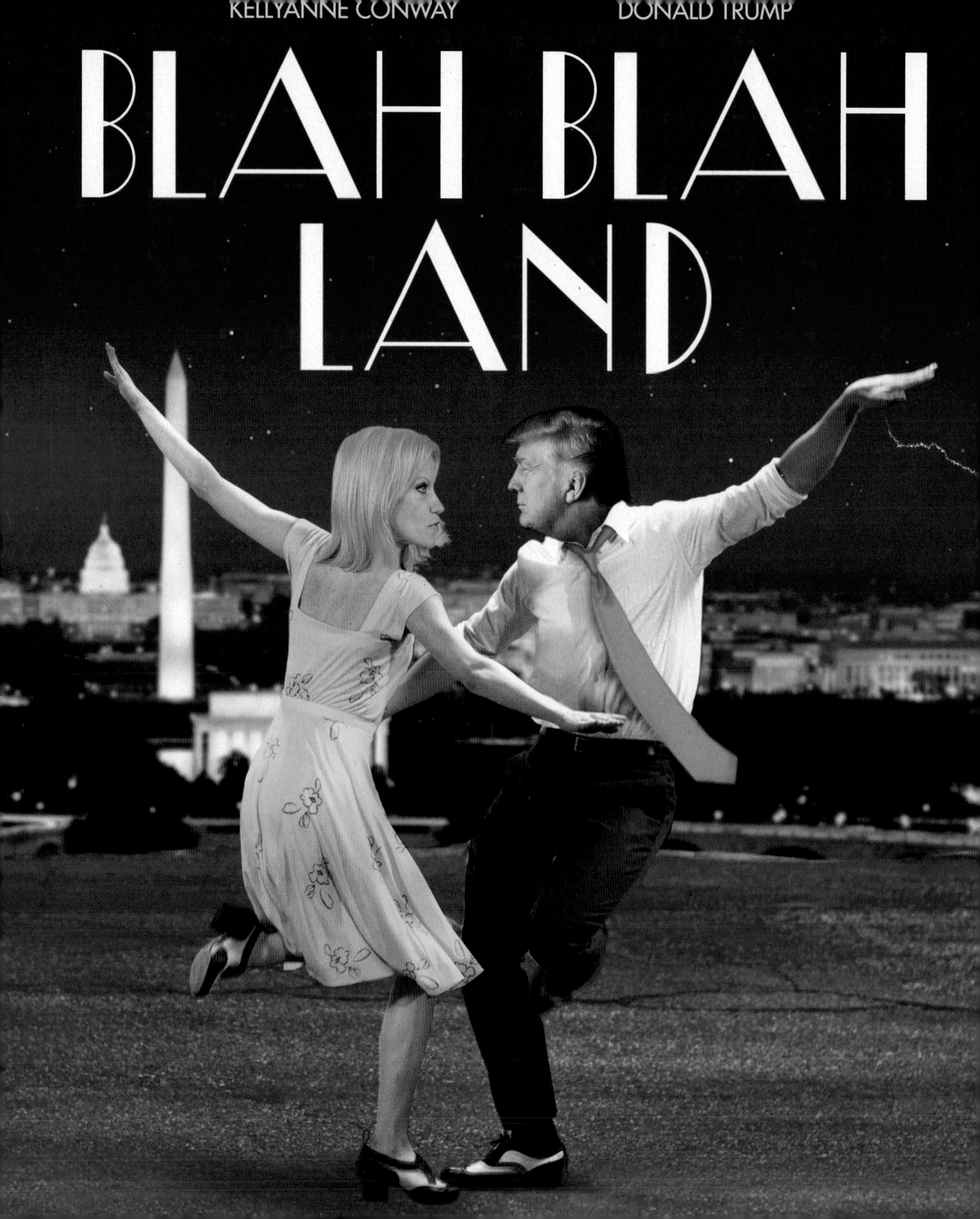
KELLYANNE CONWAY
DONALD TRUMP
BLAH BLAH
LAND

MINIONS OF DOLLARS DEPT.

ONE MORNING ON FIFTH AVENUE

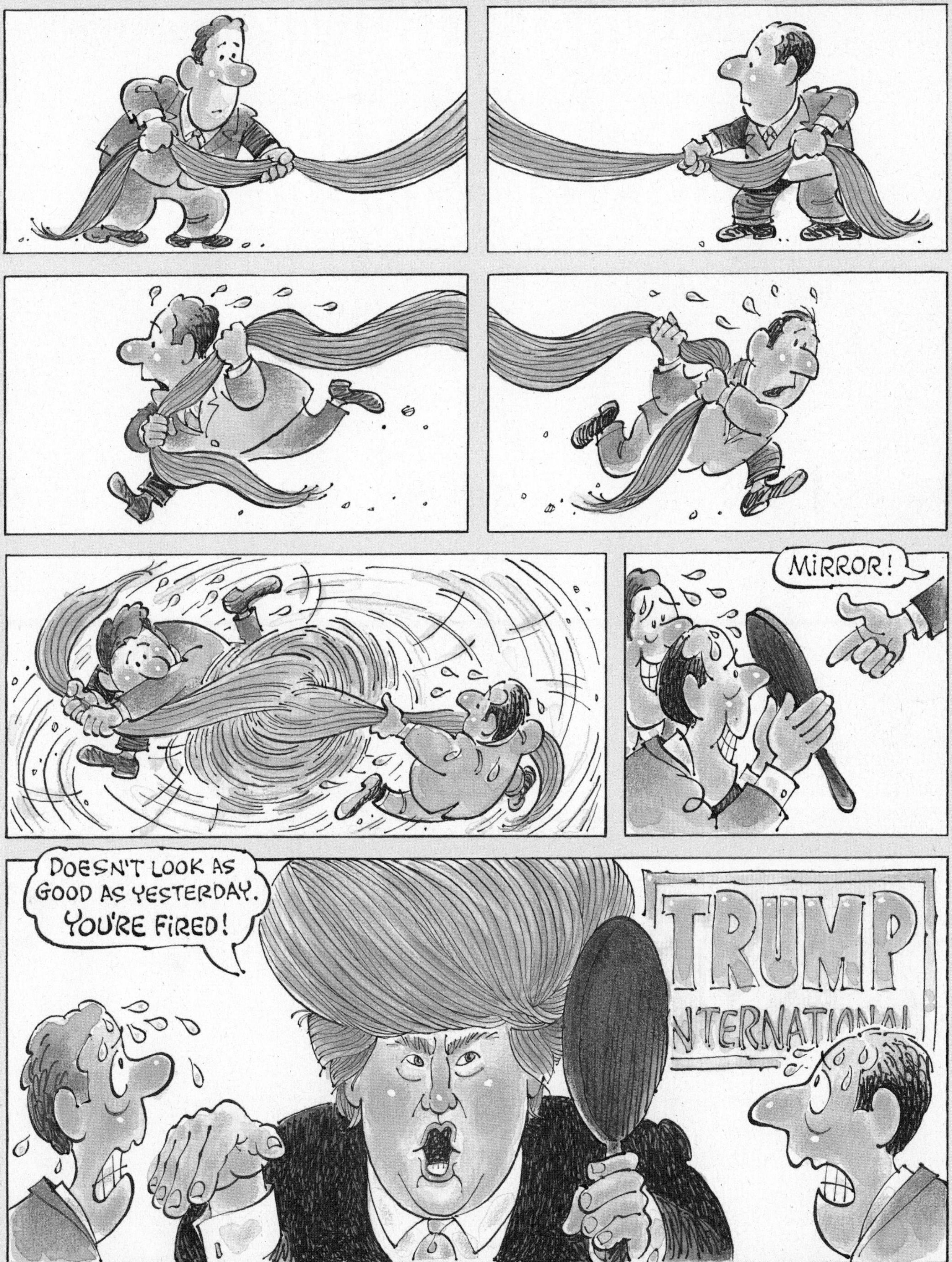
MIRROR!
DOESN'T LOOK AS GOOD AS YESTERDAY. YOU'RE FIRED!
TRUMP INTERNATIONAL

WRITER: DUCK EDWING ARTIST: PAUL COKER

HAIRY TALE DEPT.

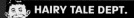

The Startling Similarities and Differences Between

DONALD TRUMP
and
THE BEAST FROM "BEAUTY AND THE BEAST"

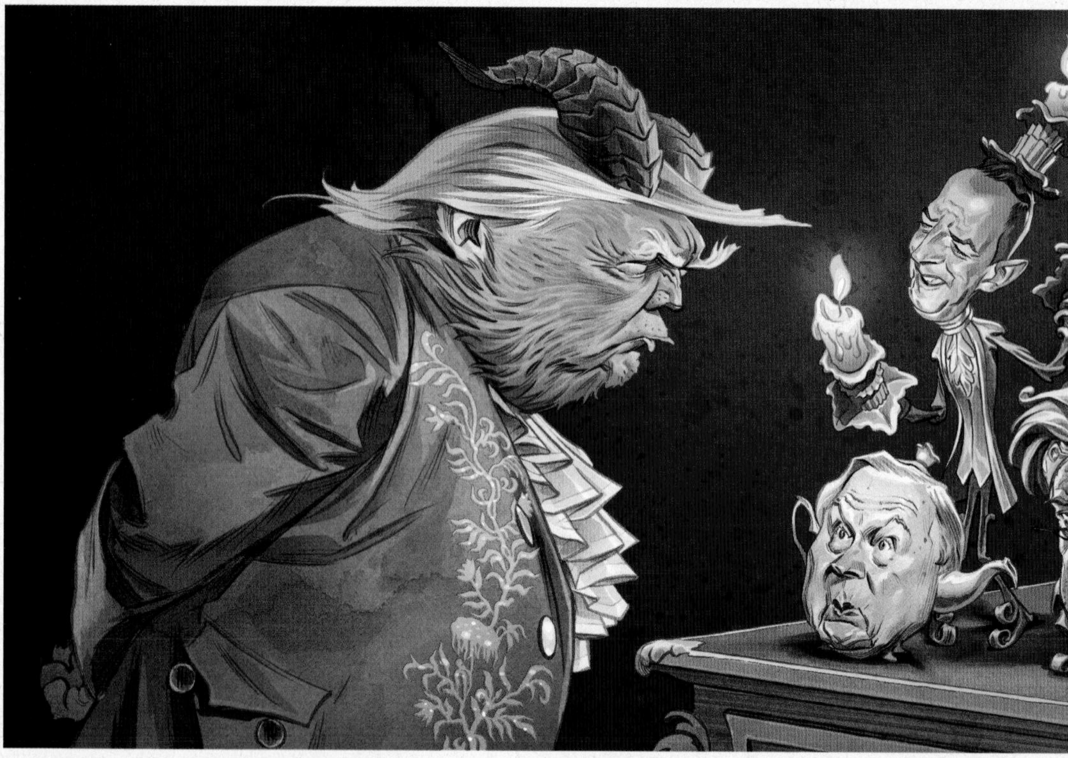

	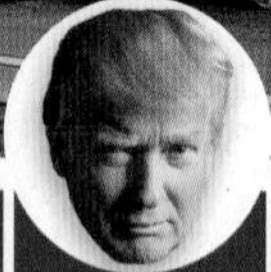	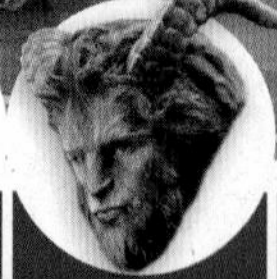
His short temper and erratic behavior tend to alienate others	✓	✓
Though physically hideous, he possesses a kind heart and a good soul	—	✓
His massive head is matted with an unruly tangle of fur	✓	✓
His only friends are members of his staff, who live in perpetual fear of him	✓	✓
He is on a quest for one true love to last a lifetime	—	✓
His very existence inspires angry mobs to take to the streets	✓	✓

 WRITER: CHRISTIAN ALSIS ARTIST: ALEJANDRO RIVAS WRITER: J. PRETE ARTIST: JACK SYRACUSE

THE FIRST SIGN OF SPRING

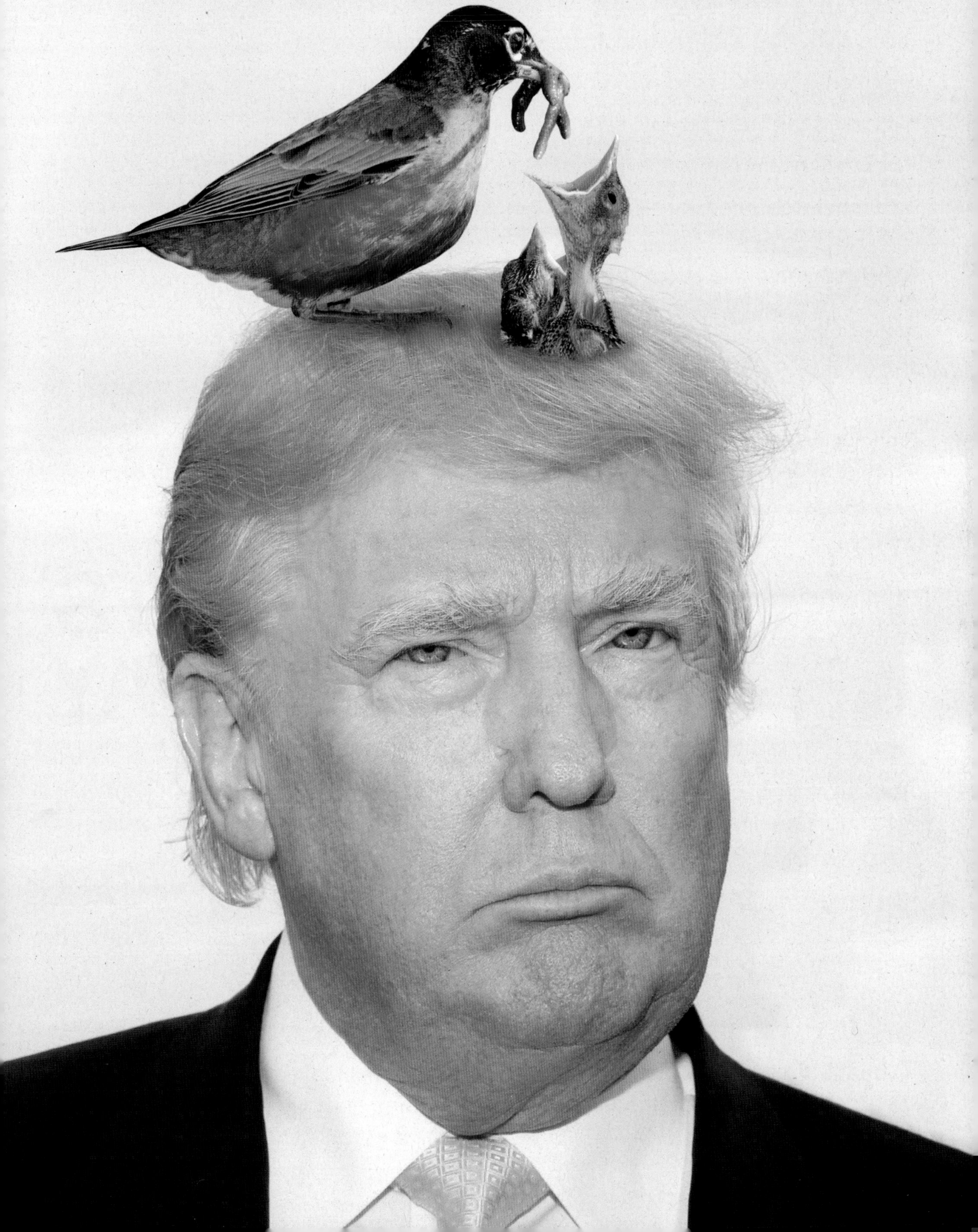

8 THINGS REVEALED BY TRUMP'S PHYSICAL

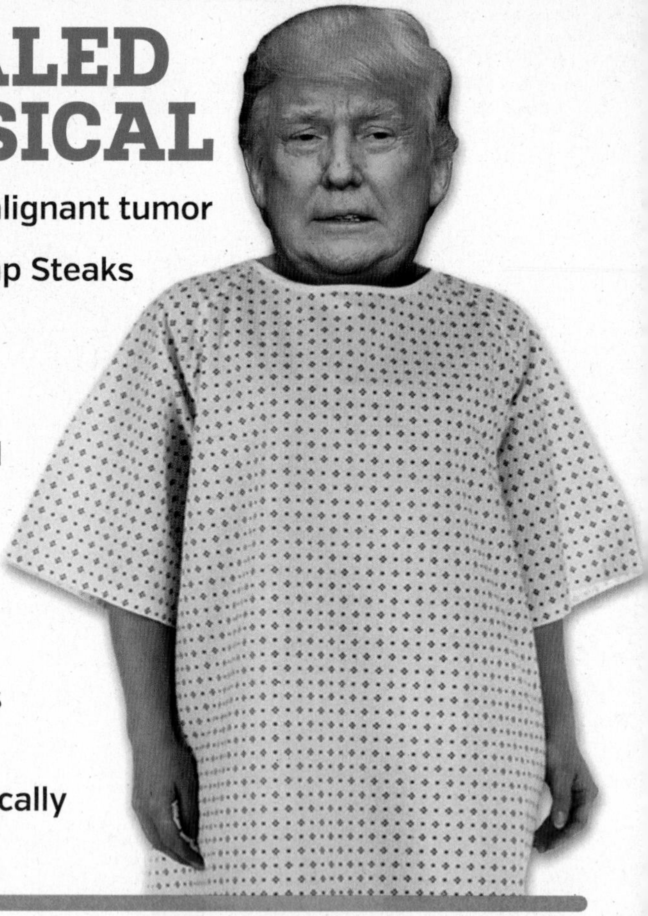

- Technically, he's a 267-pound, man-shaped malignant tumor
- His colon is packed solid with undigested Trump Steaks
- His forked tail has a terrible case of eczema
- He suffers from Terminal Thin Skin
- He desperately needs to "Make His Cholesterol Levels Great Again"
- Everything he's said about the size of his penis is true. Unfortunately, it's not attached to his body
- There's a large area of inflammation on his ass from all the times Sean Hannity has kissed it
- Technically, they're way too big to still be medically considered "man boobs"

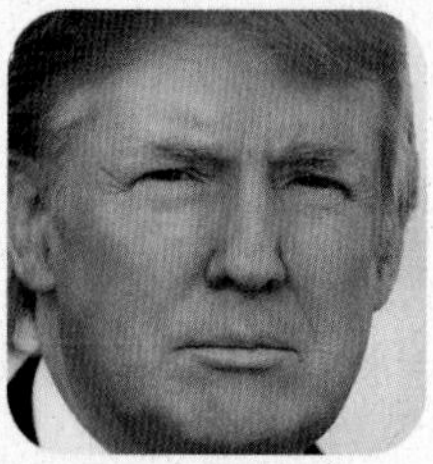

TRUMP TWEETS CYBER MONDAY

Retailers need to be vigilant — millions of people are illegally shopping today!

If you're trying to cheat on your wife, today's a great day to take a woman "furniture shopping"!

I'm president-elect of the freakin' United States, and even I can't get my hands on one of those little Nintendos! Sad!

Many people have told me that Trump Steaks are HUGE on #CyberMonday. True!

Who has time for online shopping when there are pot-stirring, dangerously uninformed tweets to write while you're taking a dump?

Don't tell @MelaniaTrump — but I'm getting her that "four years of freedom in New York" she keeps asking for!

BAD TO THE STONE DEPT.

ONE MISERABLE DAY IN SOUTH DAKOTA

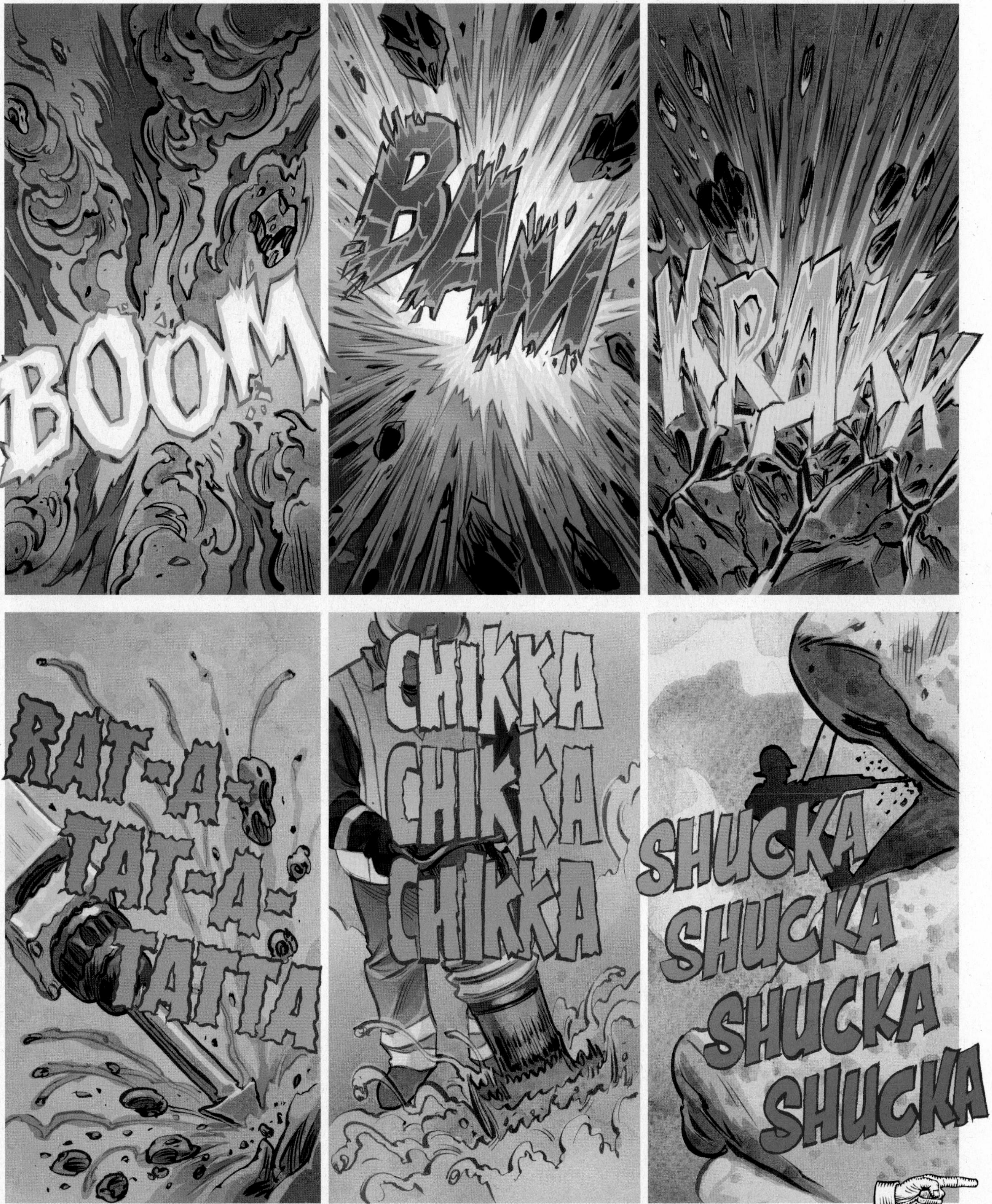
BOOM
BAM
KRAKK
RAT-A-TAT-A-TATTA
CHIKKA
CHIKKA
CHIKKA
SHUCKA
SHUCKA
SHUCKA
SHUCKA

WRITER: NICK NOMAD ARTIST: ALEJANDRO RIVAS

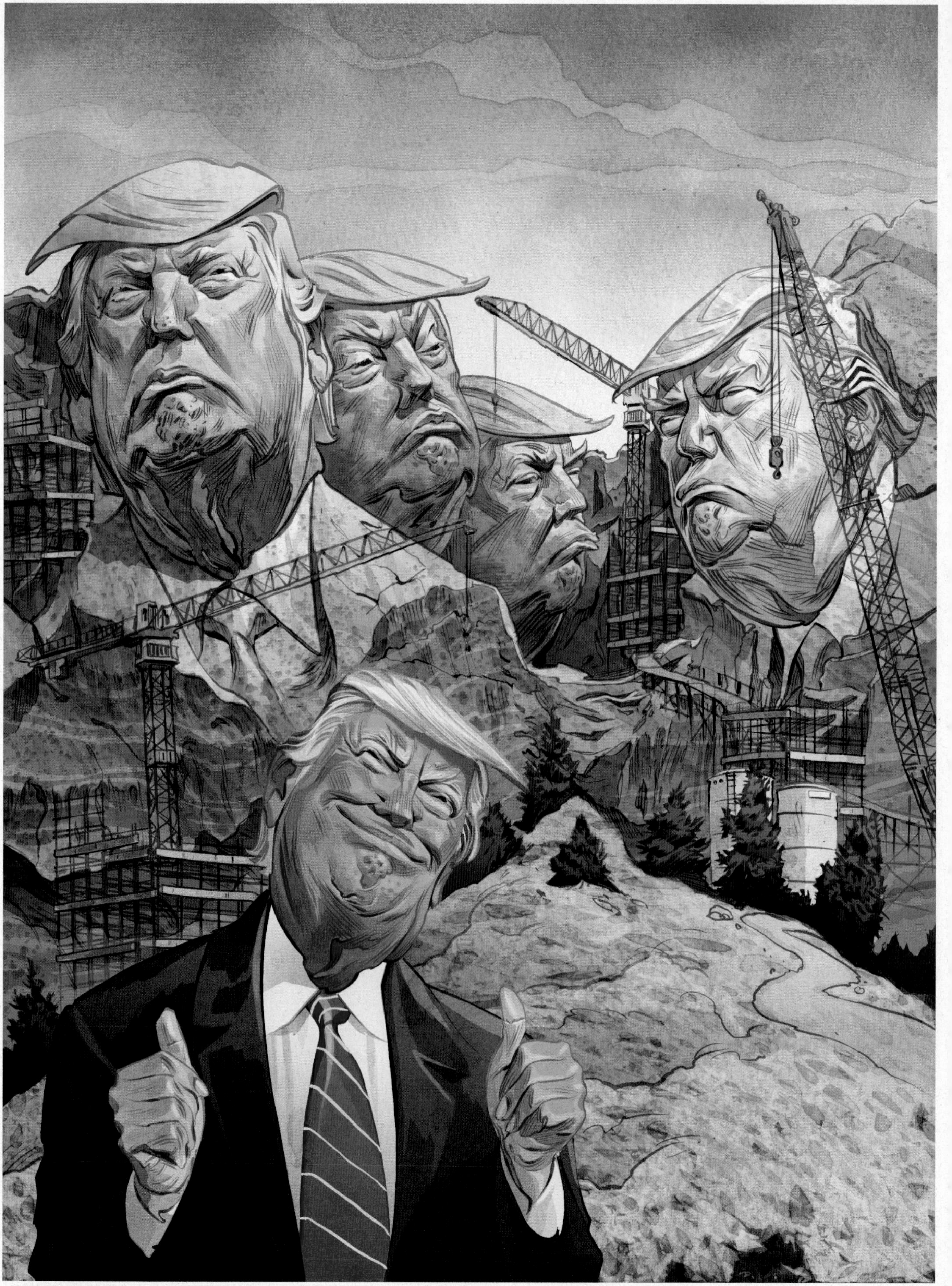

HISTORY DEADBEATS ITSELF DEPT.

Trump Recalls Other TRAGEDIES

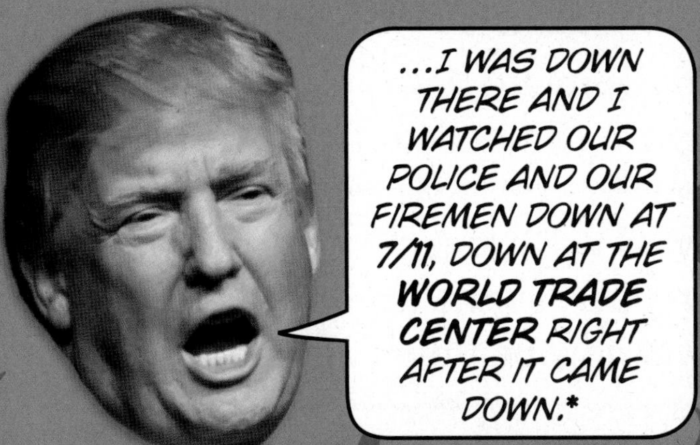
...I WAS DOWN THERE AND I WATCHED OUR POLICE AND OUR FIREMEN DOWN AT 7/11, DOWN AT THE WORLD TRADE CENTER RIGHT AFTER IT CAME DOWN.*

*actual quote from April 18, 2016

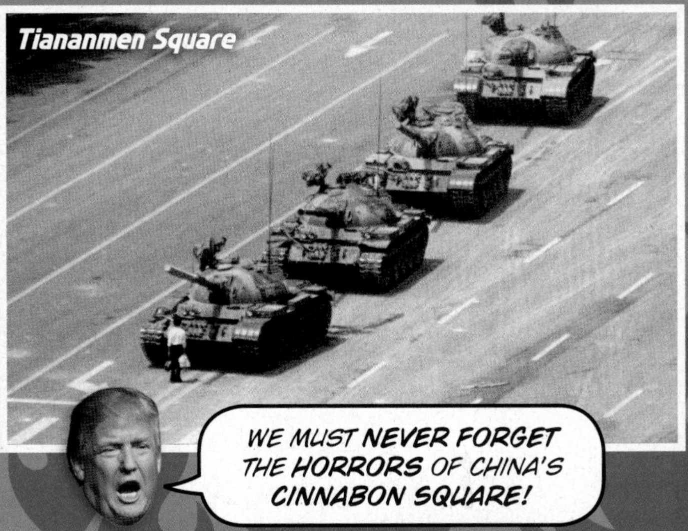
Tiananmen Square
WE MUST NEVER FORGET THE HORRORS OF CHINA'S CINNABON SQUARE!

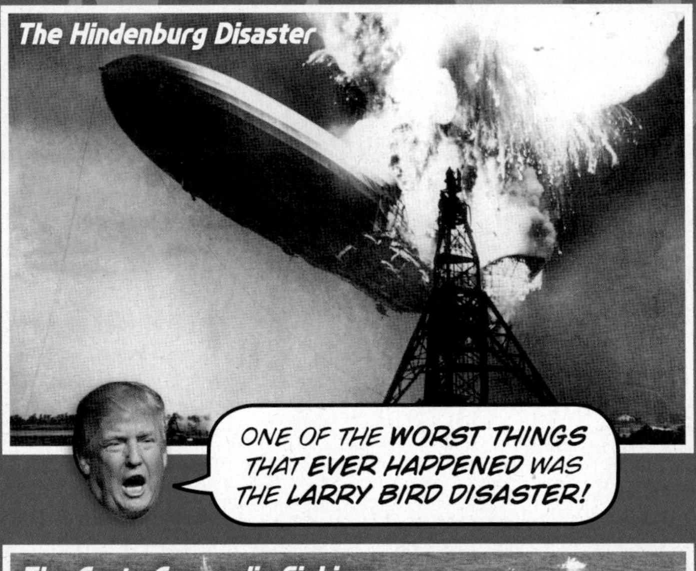
The Hindenburg Disaster
ONE OF THE WORST THINGS THAT EVER HAPPENED WAS THE LARRY BIRD DISASTER!

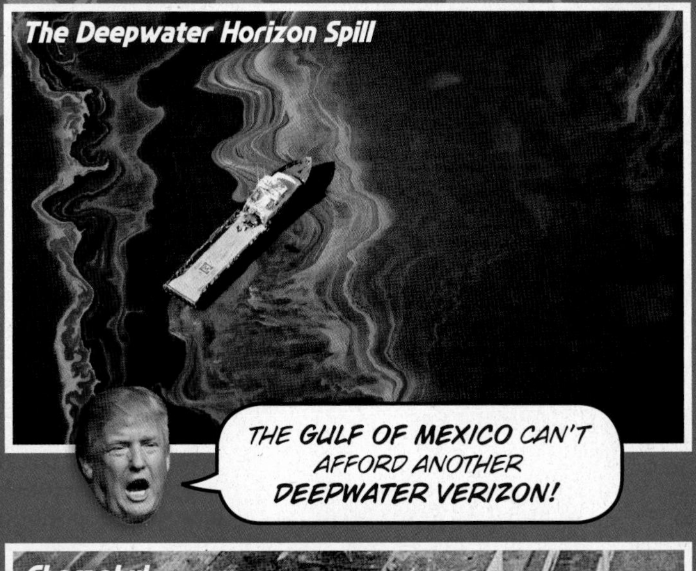
The Deepwater Horizon Spill
THE GULF OF MEXICO CAN'T AFFORD ANOTHER DEEPWATER VERIZON!

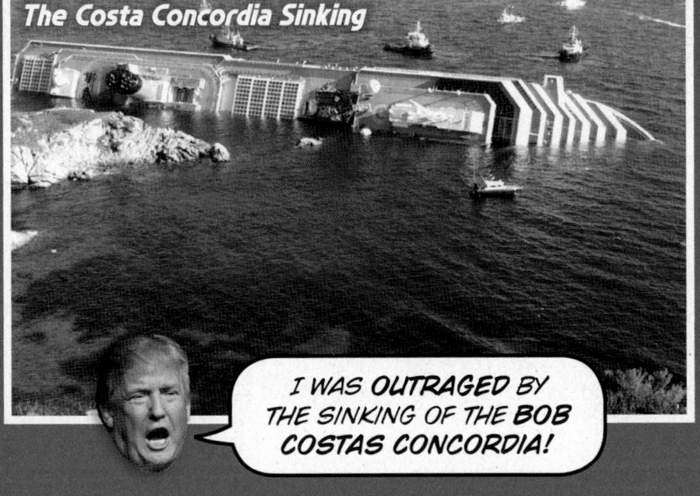
The Costa Concordia Sinking
I WAS OUTRAGED BY THE SINKING OF THE BOB COSTAS CONCORDIA!

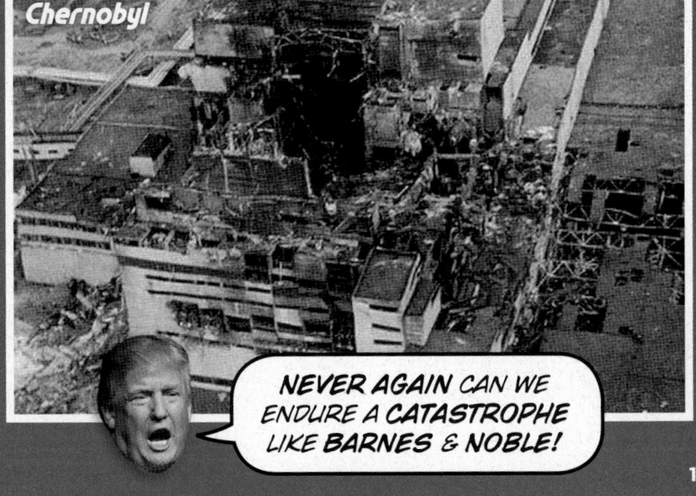
Chernobyl
NEVER AGAIN CAN WE ENDURE A CATASTROPHE LIKE BARNES & NOBLE!

FUN FACTS ABOUT THE U.S./MEXICO BORDER WALL

While Mexico won't pay for any of it, China has agreed to loan us the money to build it

---

They're shooting to complete it on Cinco de Mayo for that extra symbolic touch

---

The DEA estimates that a wall will prevent nearly all illegal drugs from coming across the border – except for the 99% which will now be flown across

---

A section of the wall will be rerouted in order to knock down a Nordstrom in Phoenix

---

Because of a budget shortfall, it will only be two feet tall

WRITER: JEFF KRUSE   ARTIST: KEVIN POPE

ALT-WRITE DEPT.

No, David!, the classic children's book by David Shannon, recounts the author's childhood schemes, gross behavior and bad manners, all responded to by the adults in the room with an exasperated cry of "No, David!" Since it's clear we now have a spoiled, juvenile, bad-mannered little schemer in the White House, perhaps the only way to reach him and get him to behave is with a children's book similar to Shannon's. One we call…

No, Donald!

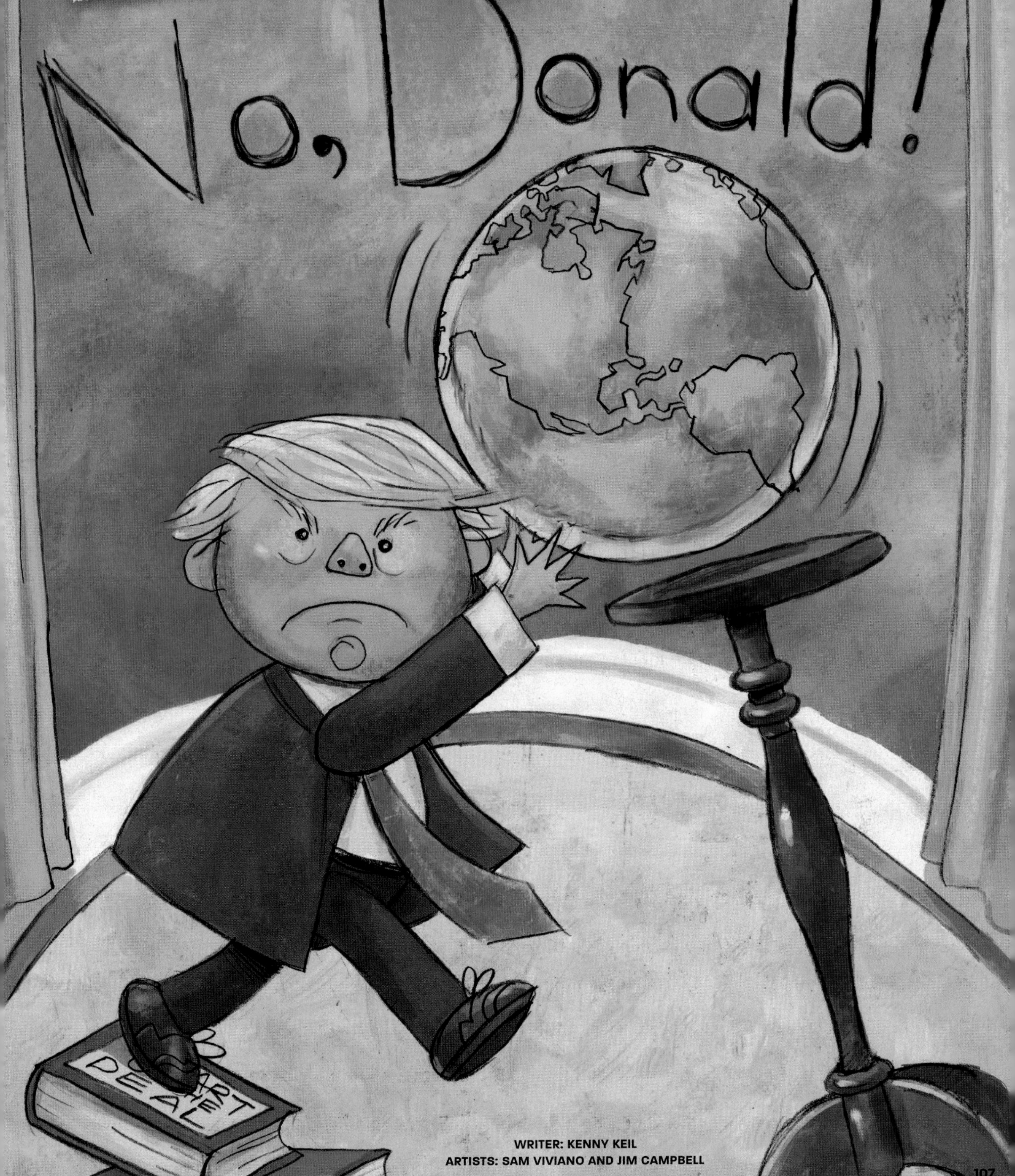

ART
DEAL

WRITER: KENNY KEIL
ARTISTS: SAM VIVIANO AND JIM CAMPBELL

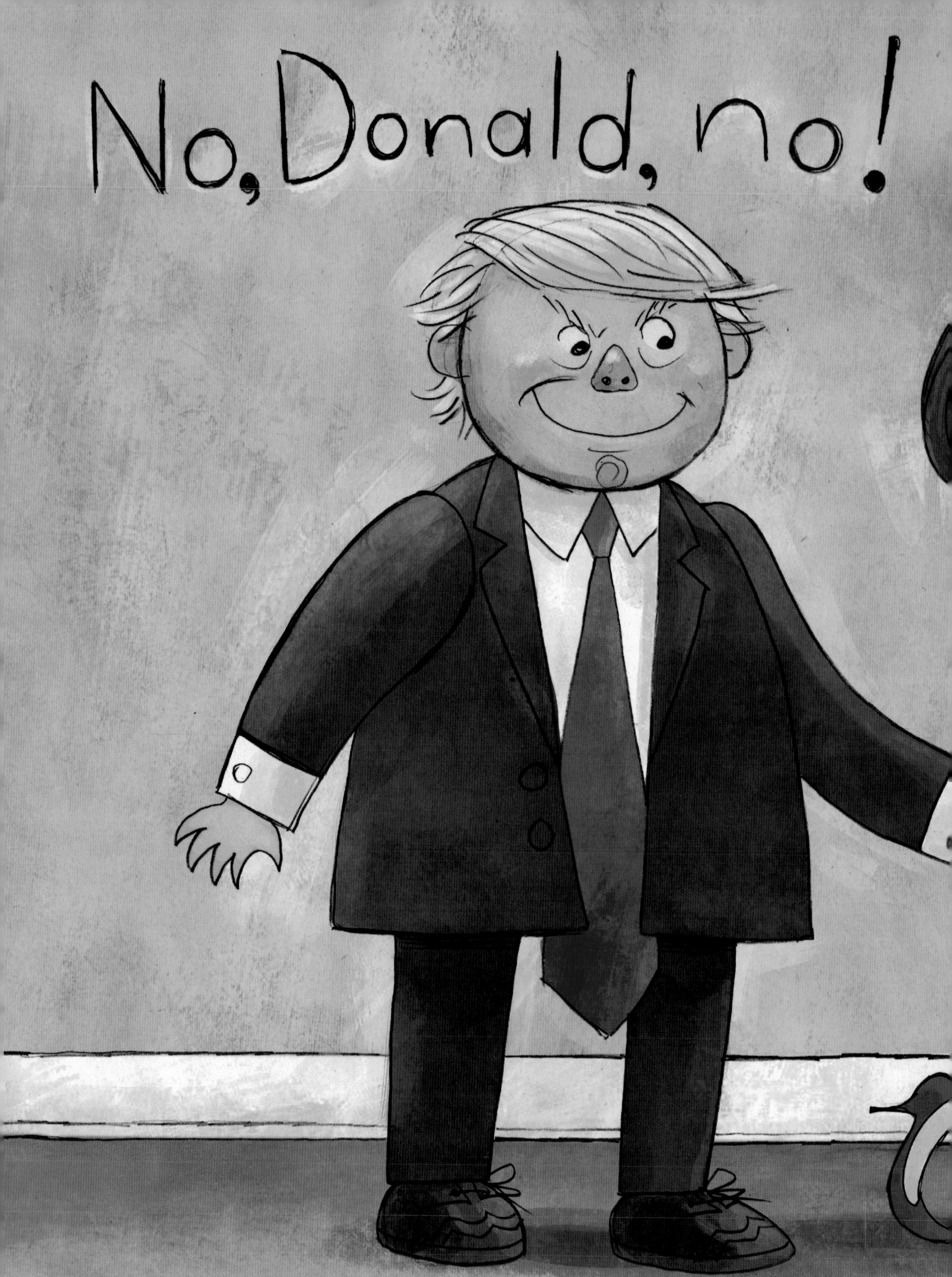
No, Donald, no!

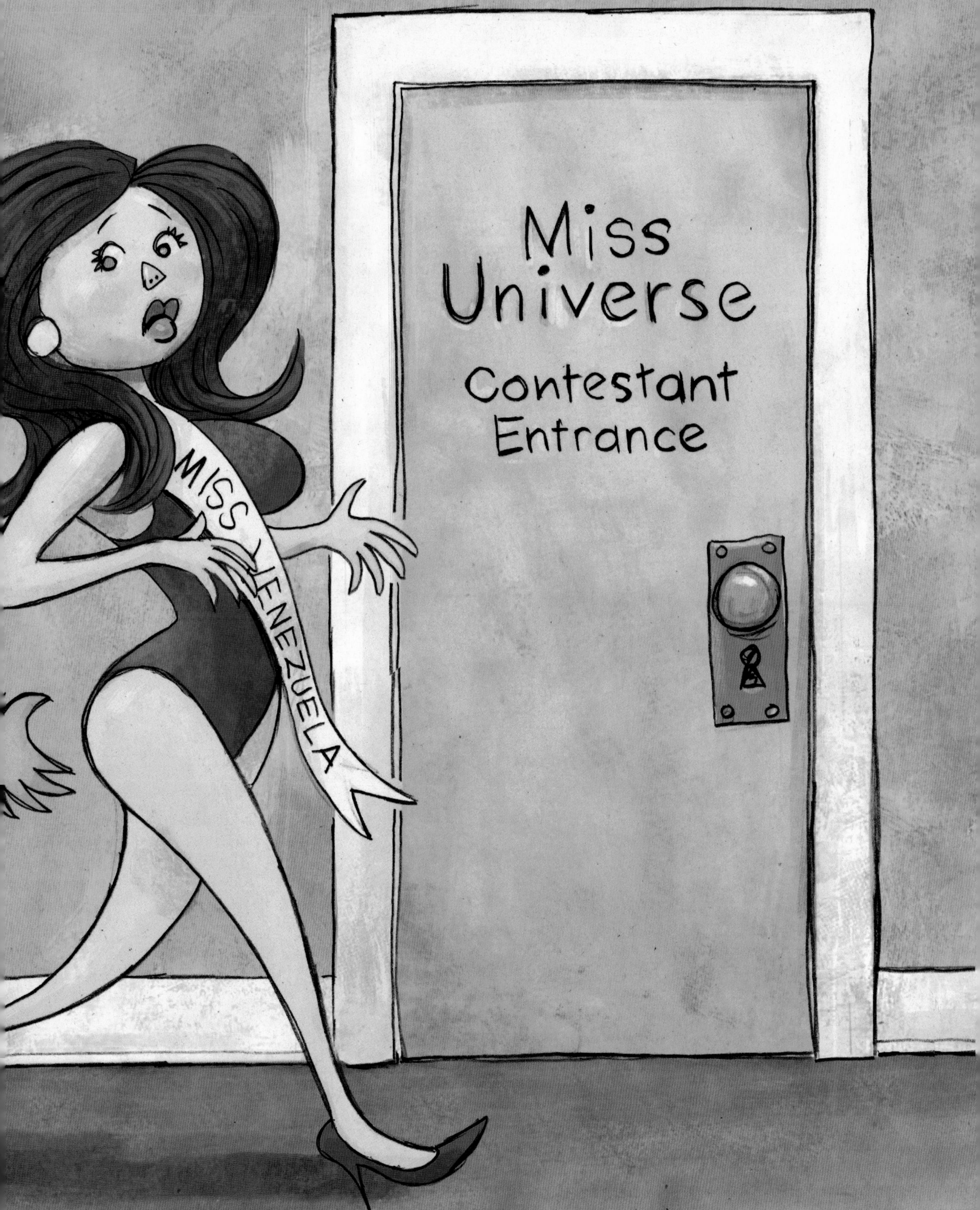
Miss Universe
Contestant Entrance
MISS VENEZUELA

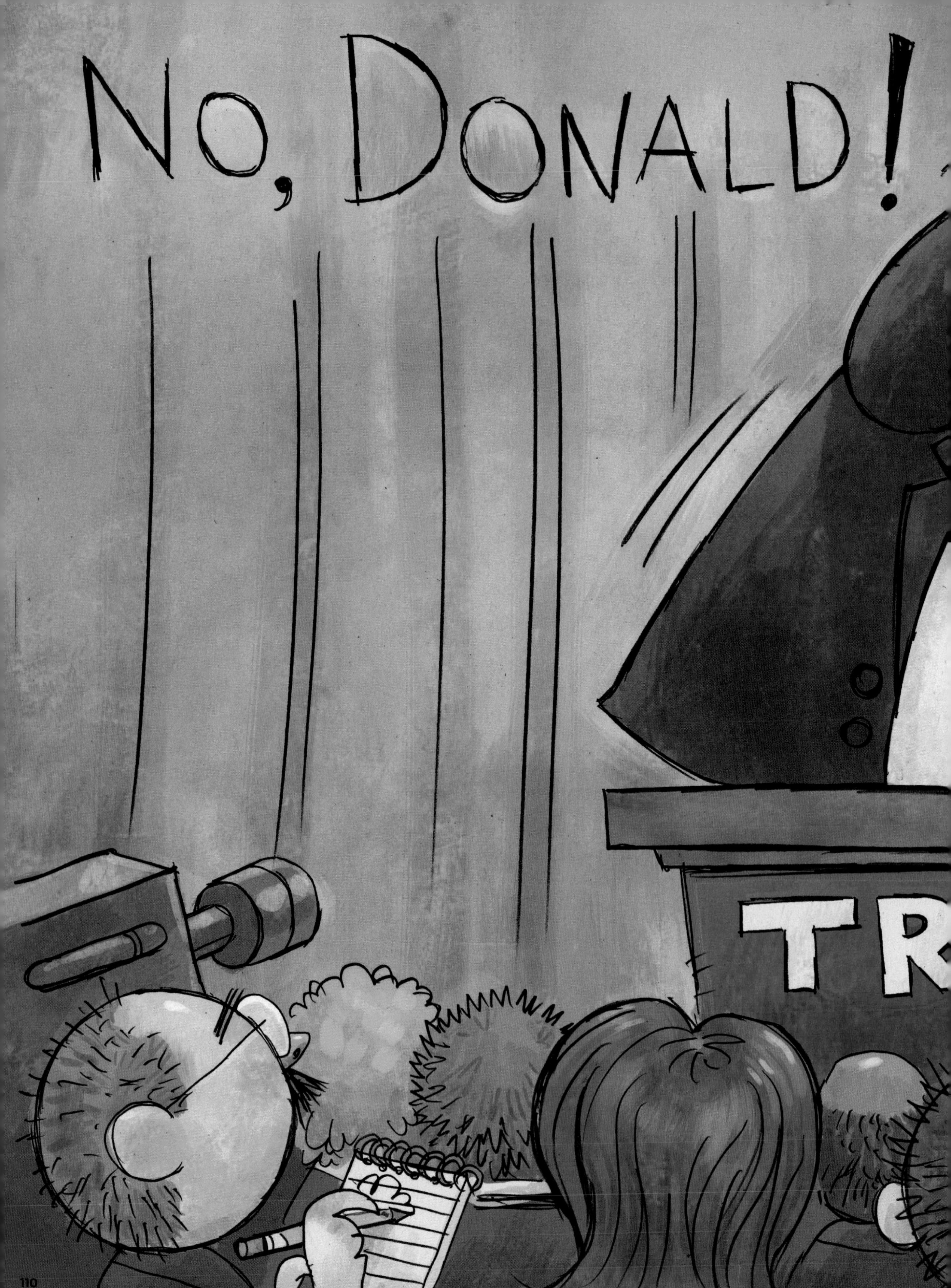
NO, DONALD!
TR

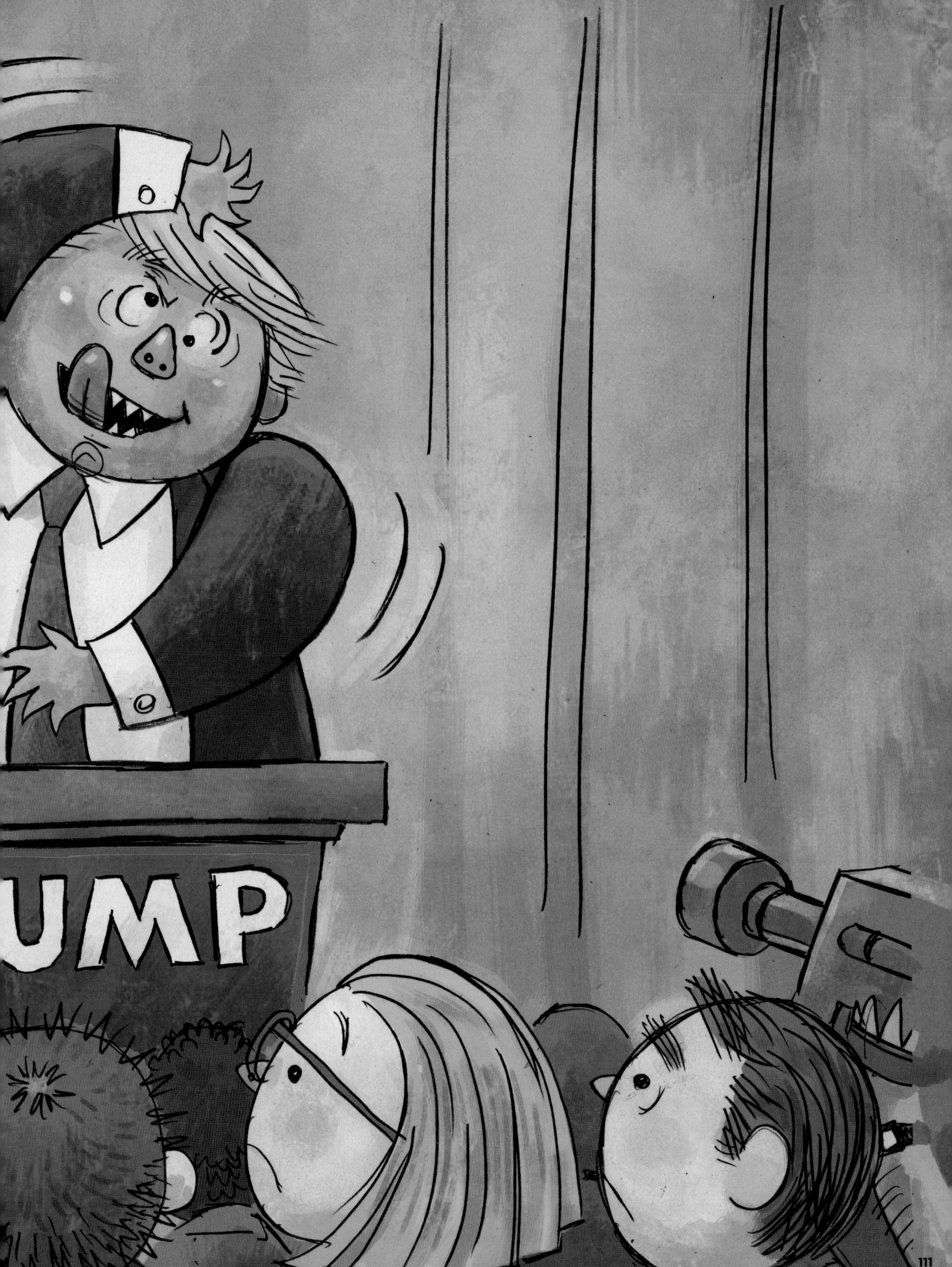
UMP

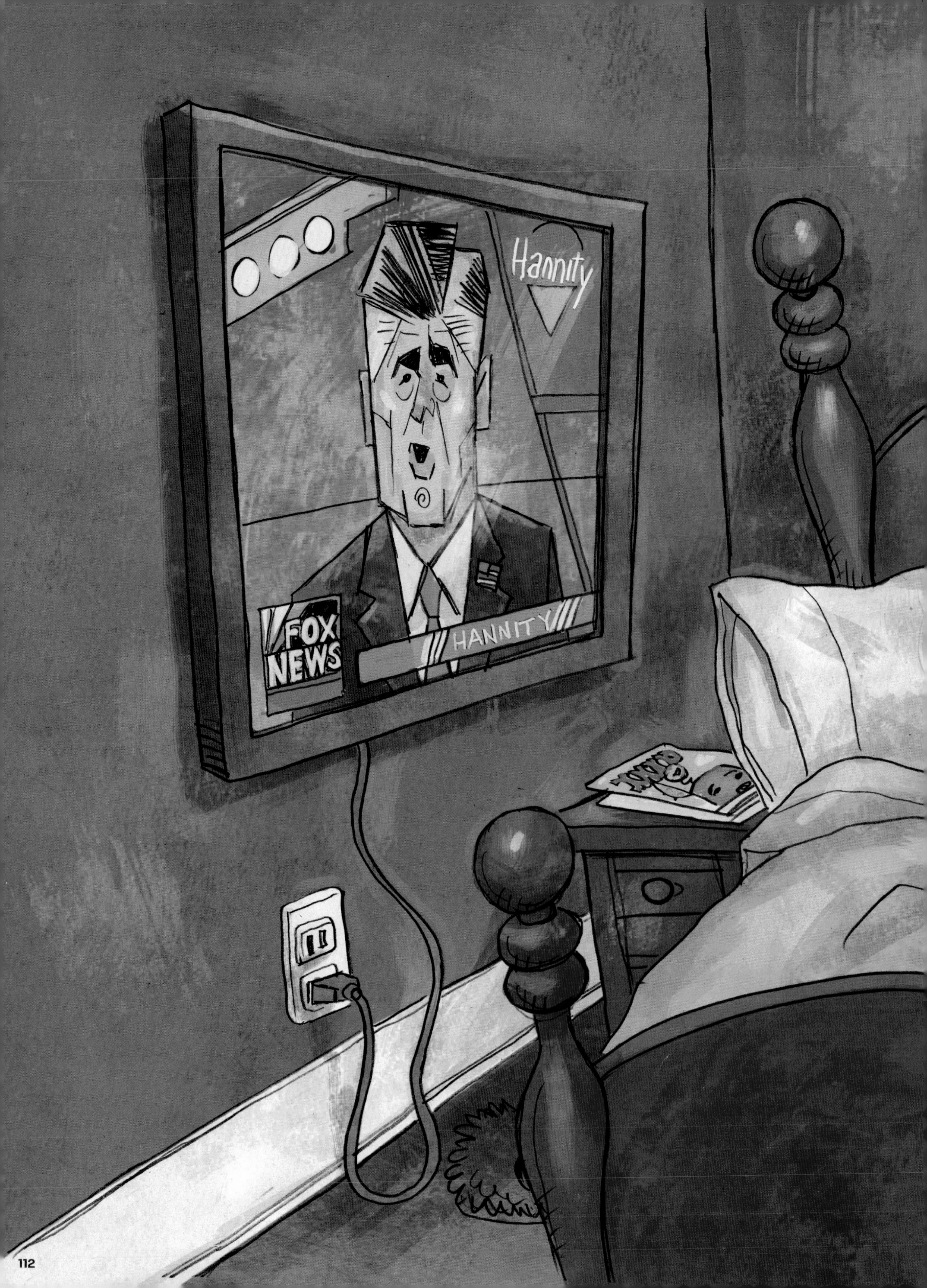
Hannity
FOX NEWS
HANNITY

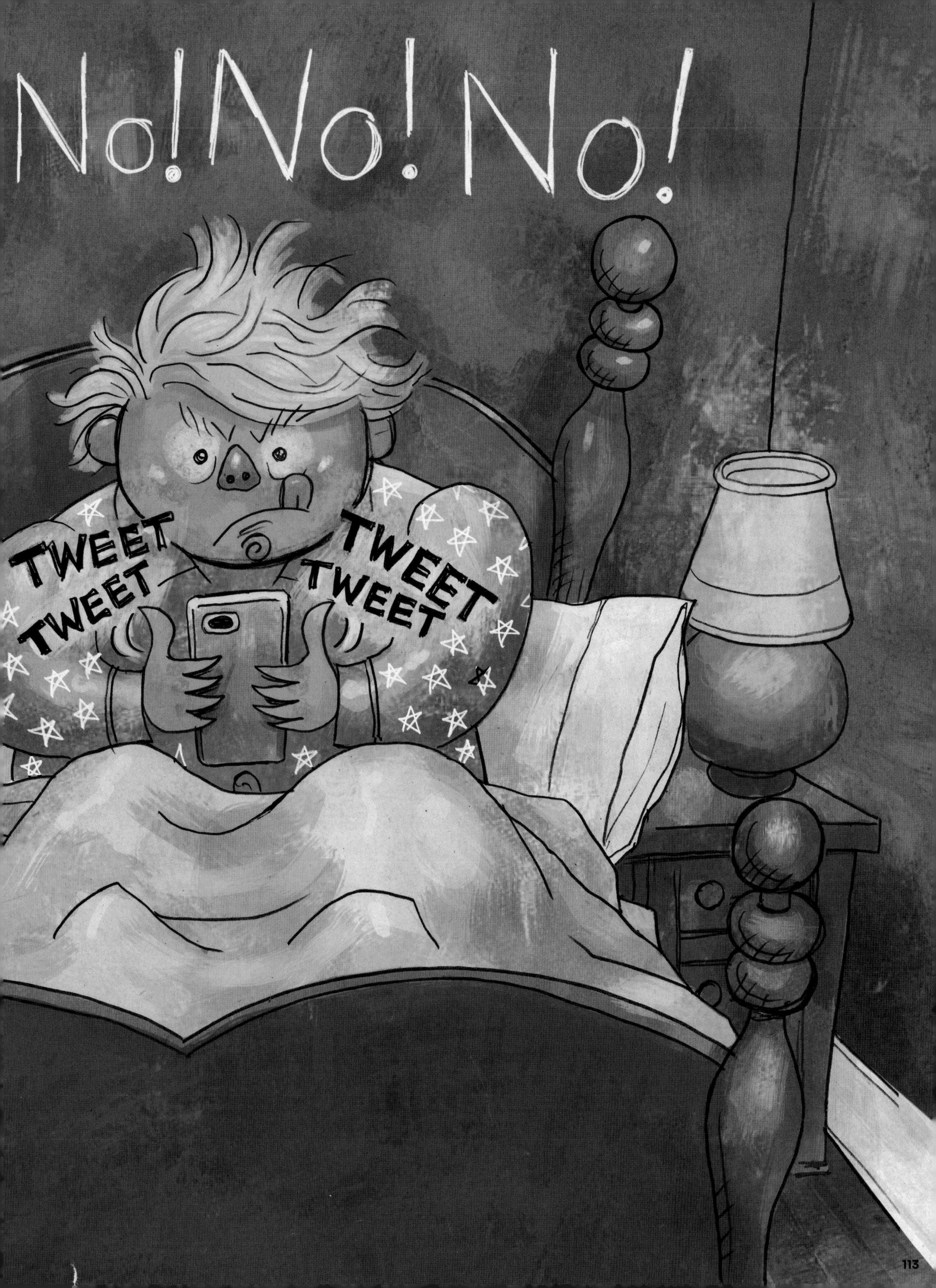
No! No! No!
TWEET
TWEET
TWEET
TWEET

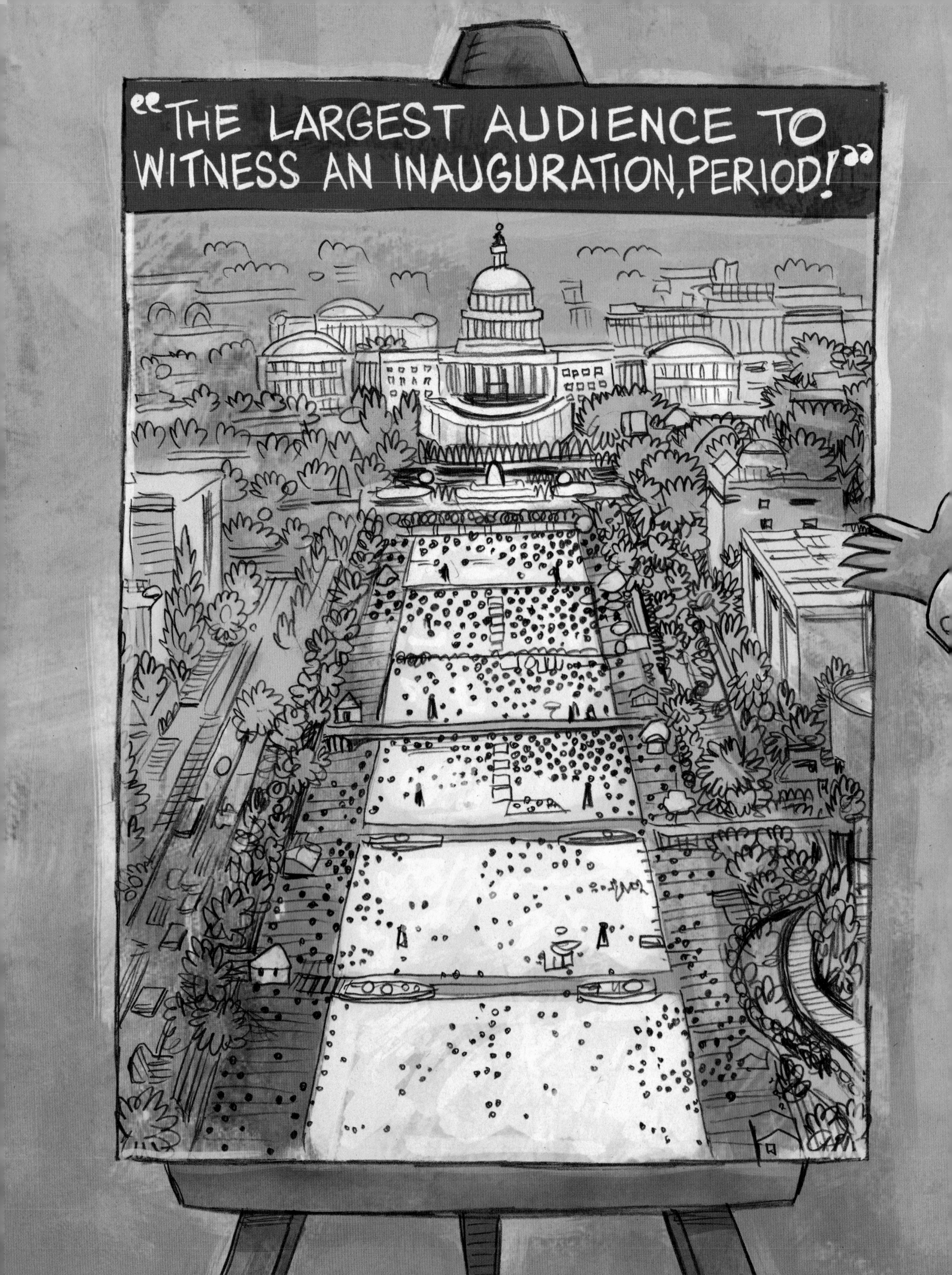
"THE LARGEST AUDIENCE TO WITNESS AN INAUGURATION, PERIOD!"

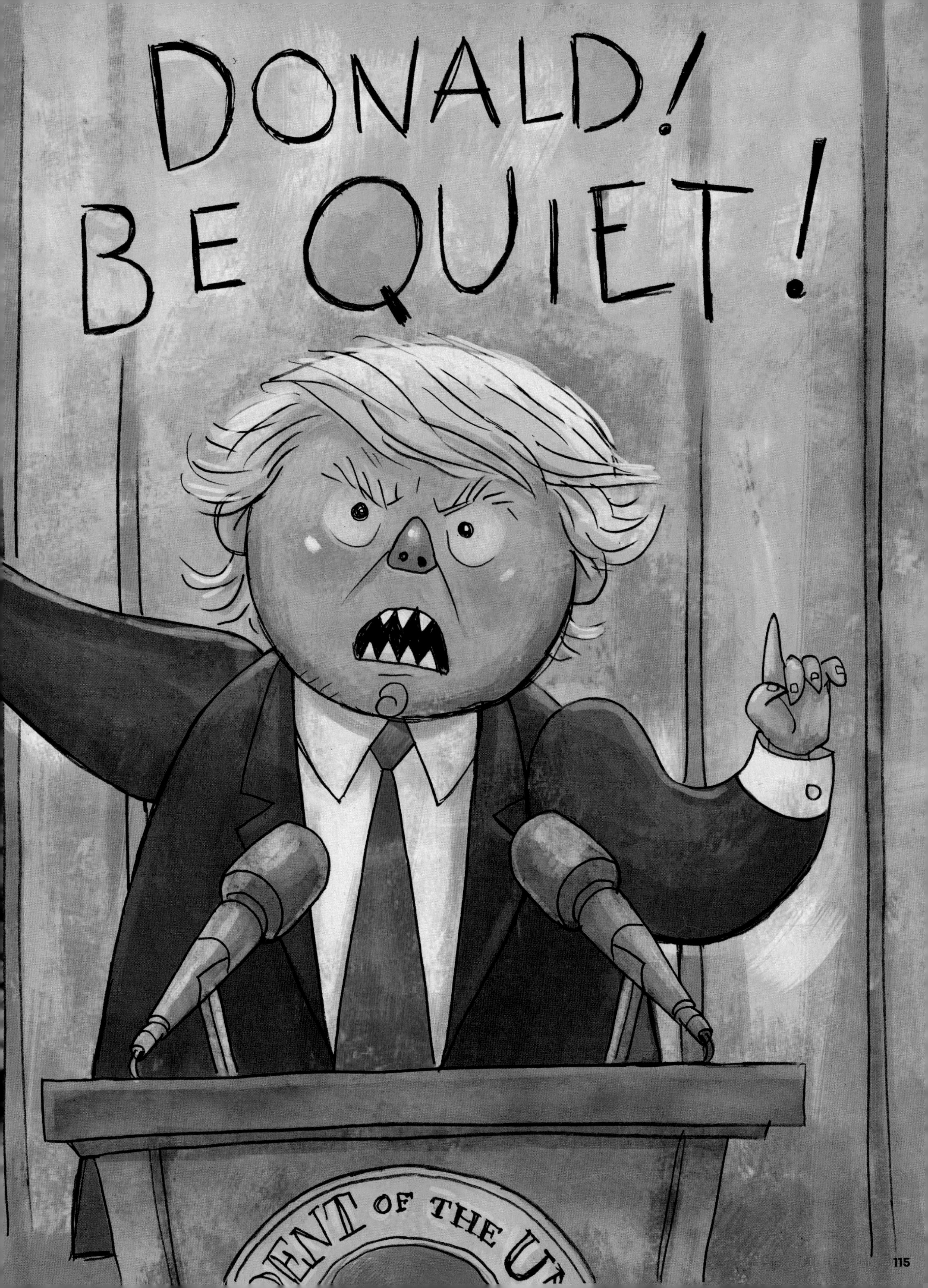
DONALD! BE QUIET!
OF THE

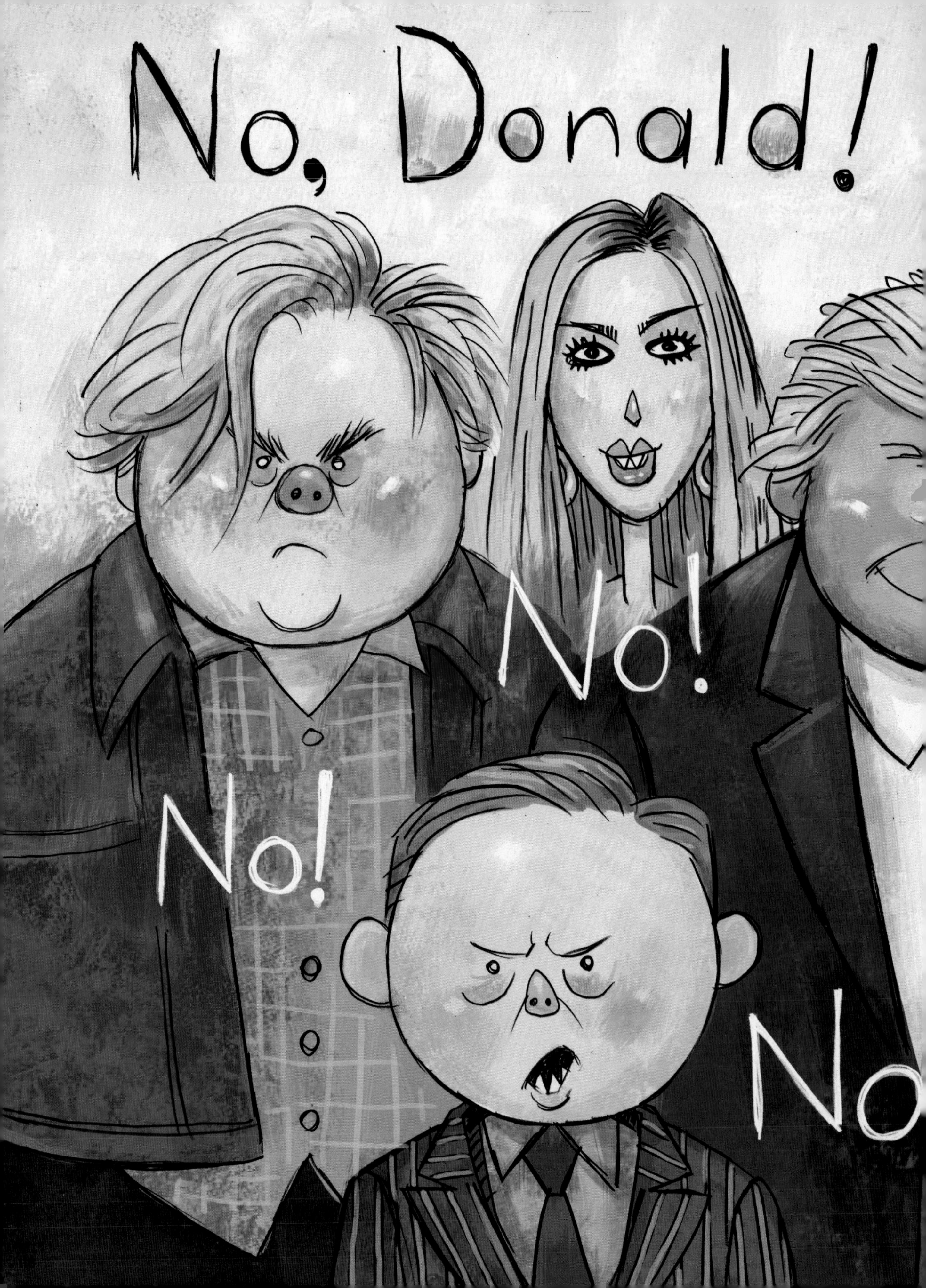
No, Donald!
No!
No!
No

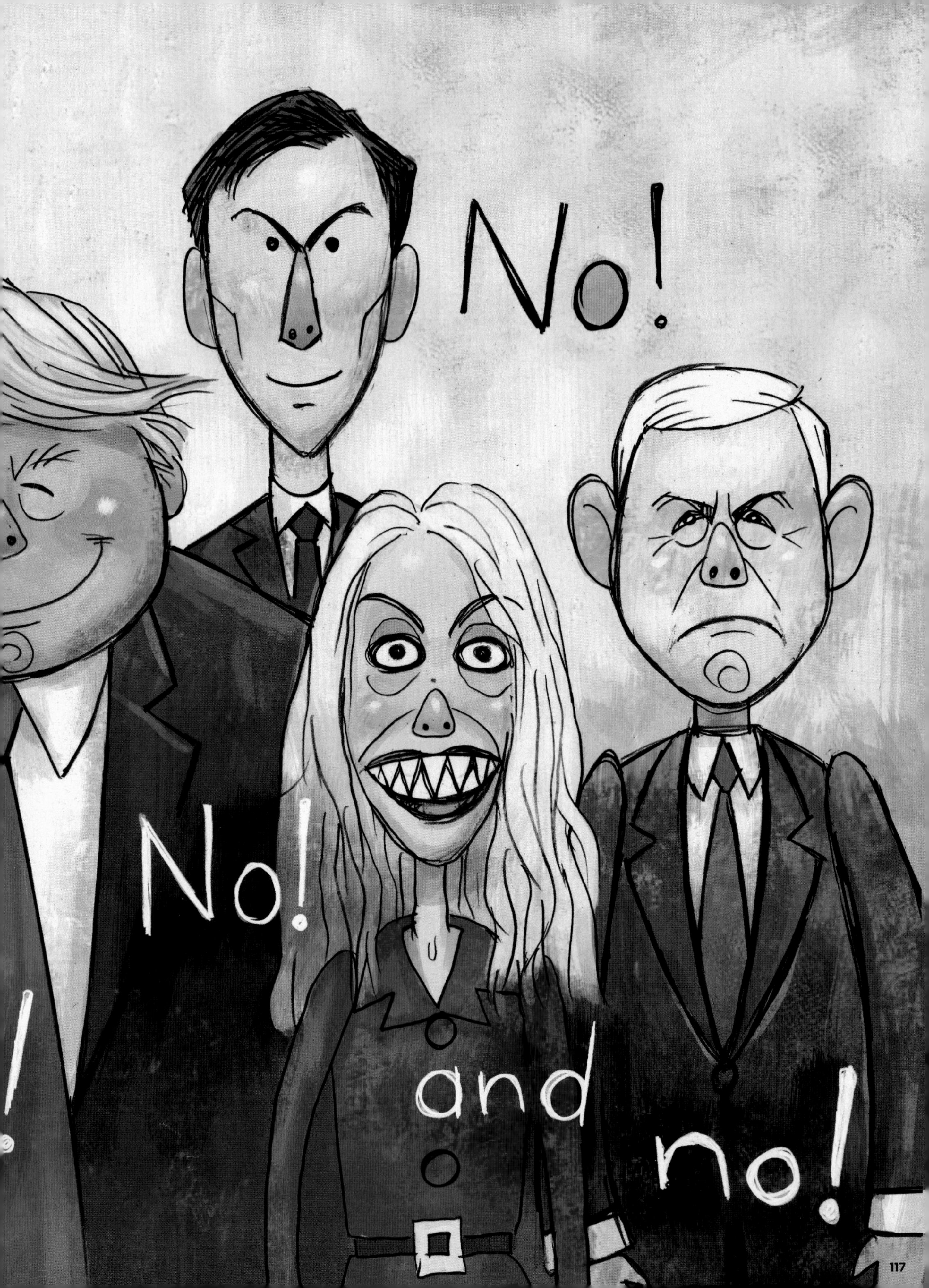
No!
No!
and no!

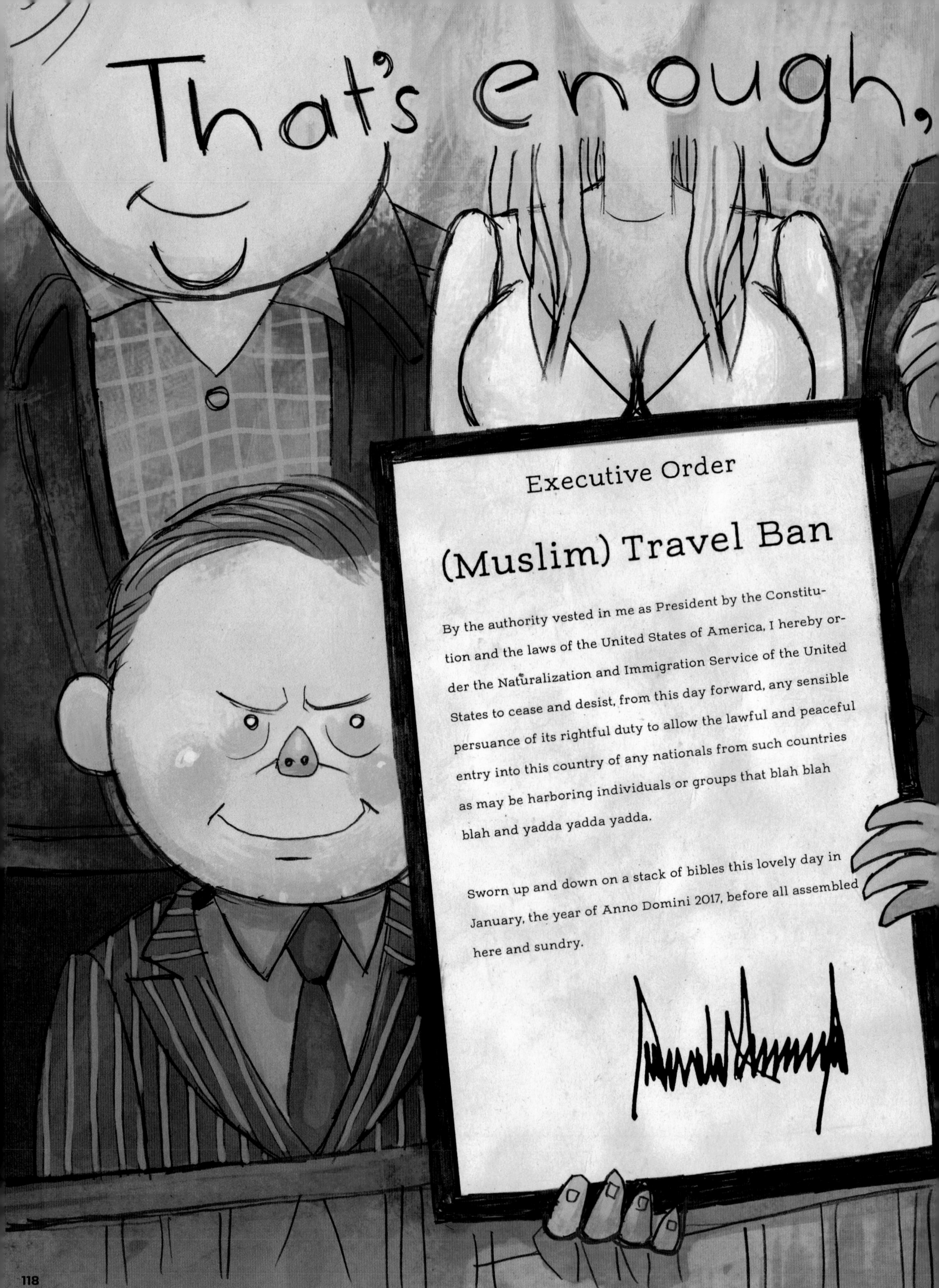
That's enough,
Executive Order
(Muslim) Travel Ban
By the authority vested in me as President by the Constitution and the laws of the United States of America, I hereby order the Naturalization and Immigration Service of the United States to cease and desist, from this day forward, any sensible persuance of its rightful duty to allow the lawful and peaceful entry into this country of any nationals from such countries as may be harboring individuals or groups that blah blah blah and yadda yadda yadda.
Sworn up and down on a stack of bibles this lovely day in January, the year of Anno Domini 2017, before all assembled here and sundry.

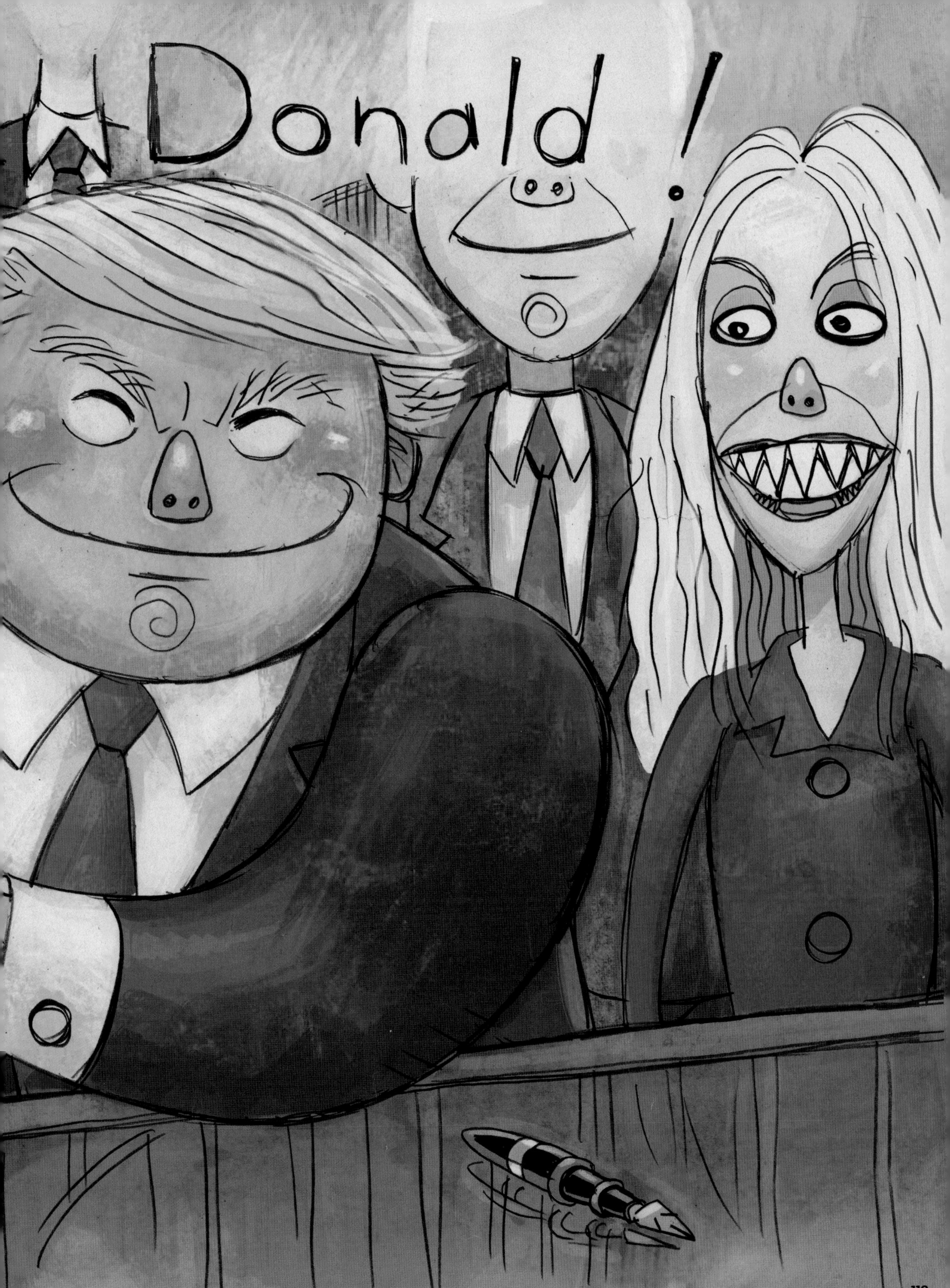
Donald!

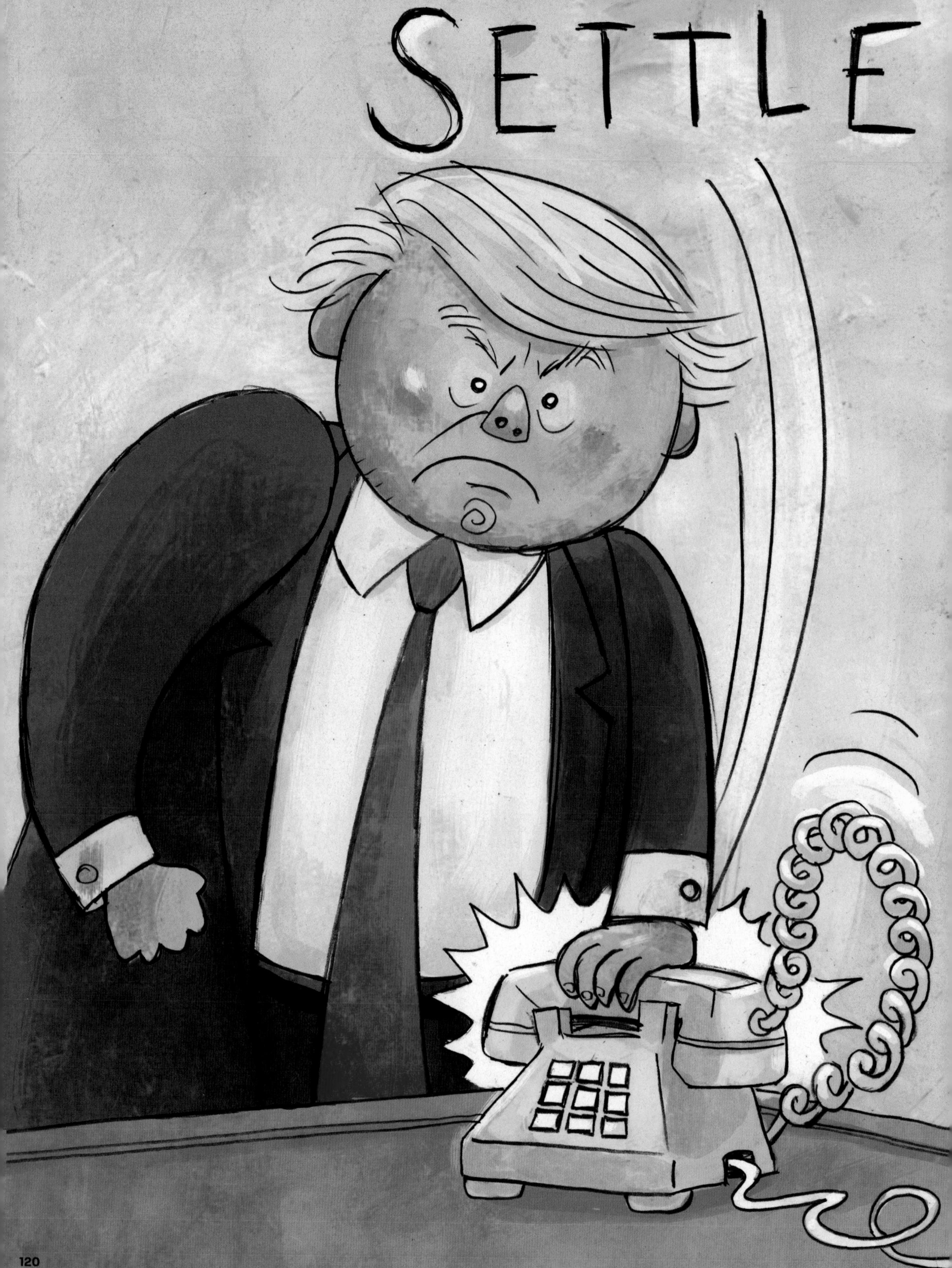
SETTLE

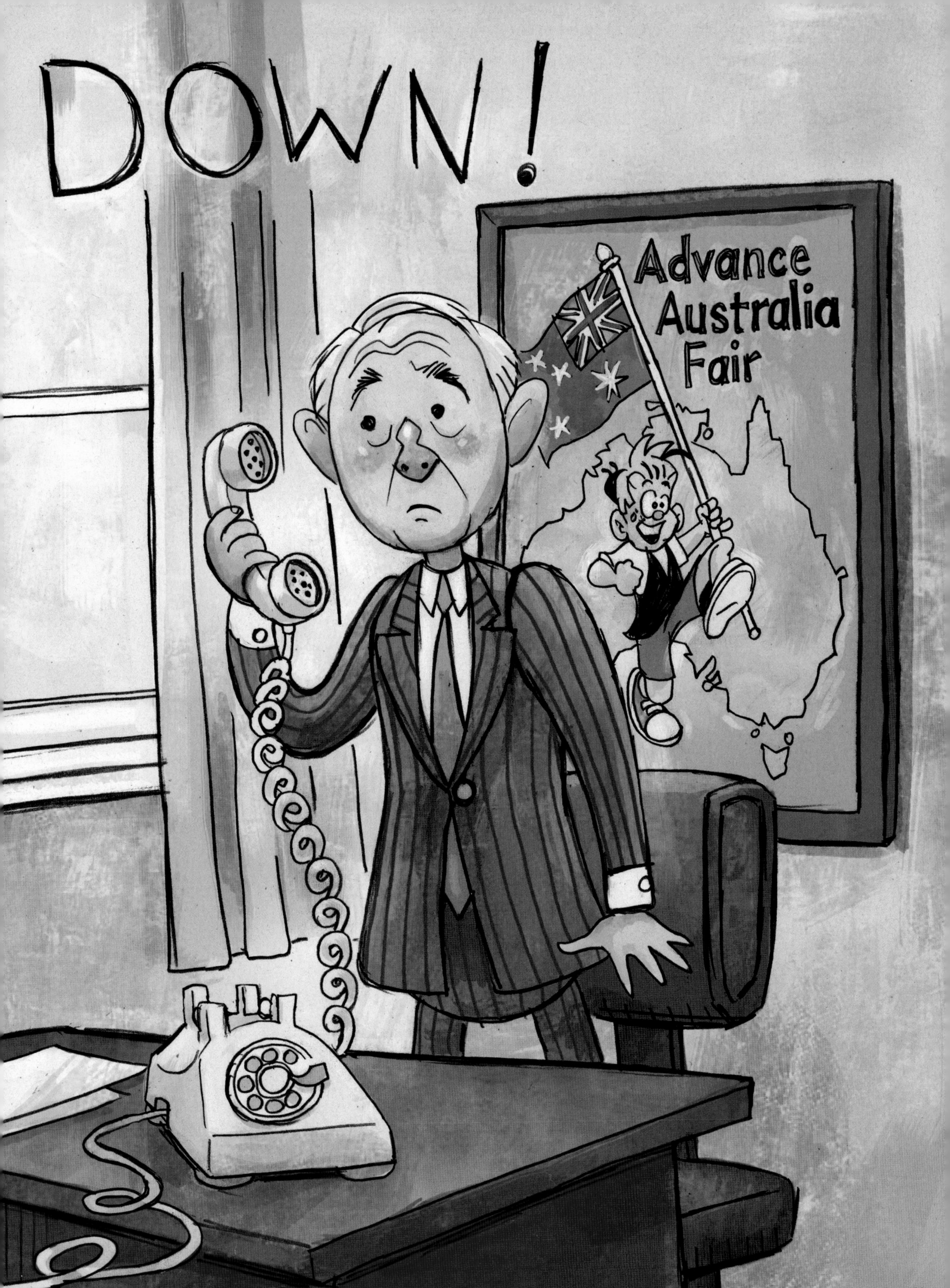
DOWN!
Advance
Australia
Fair

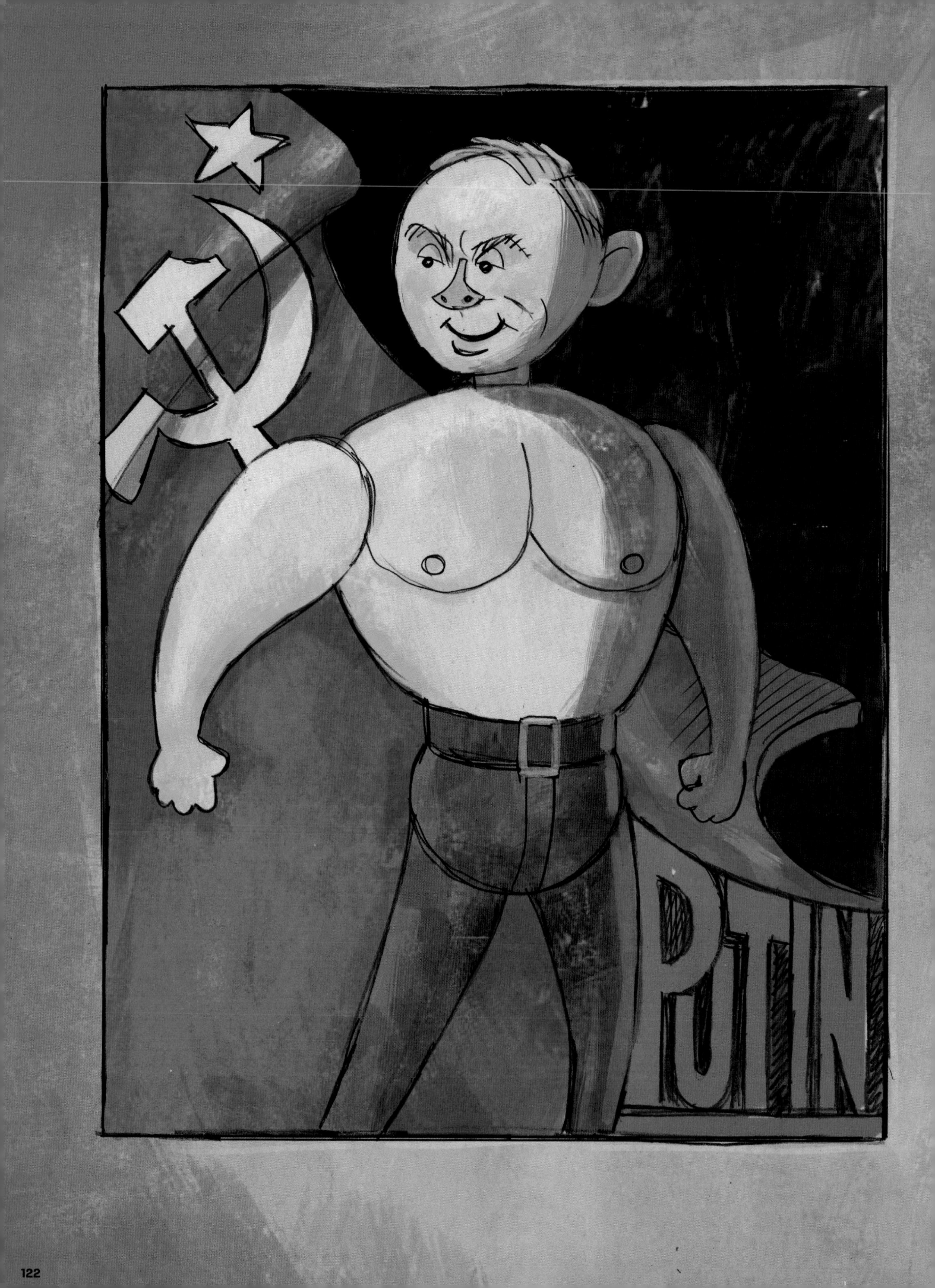
PUTIN

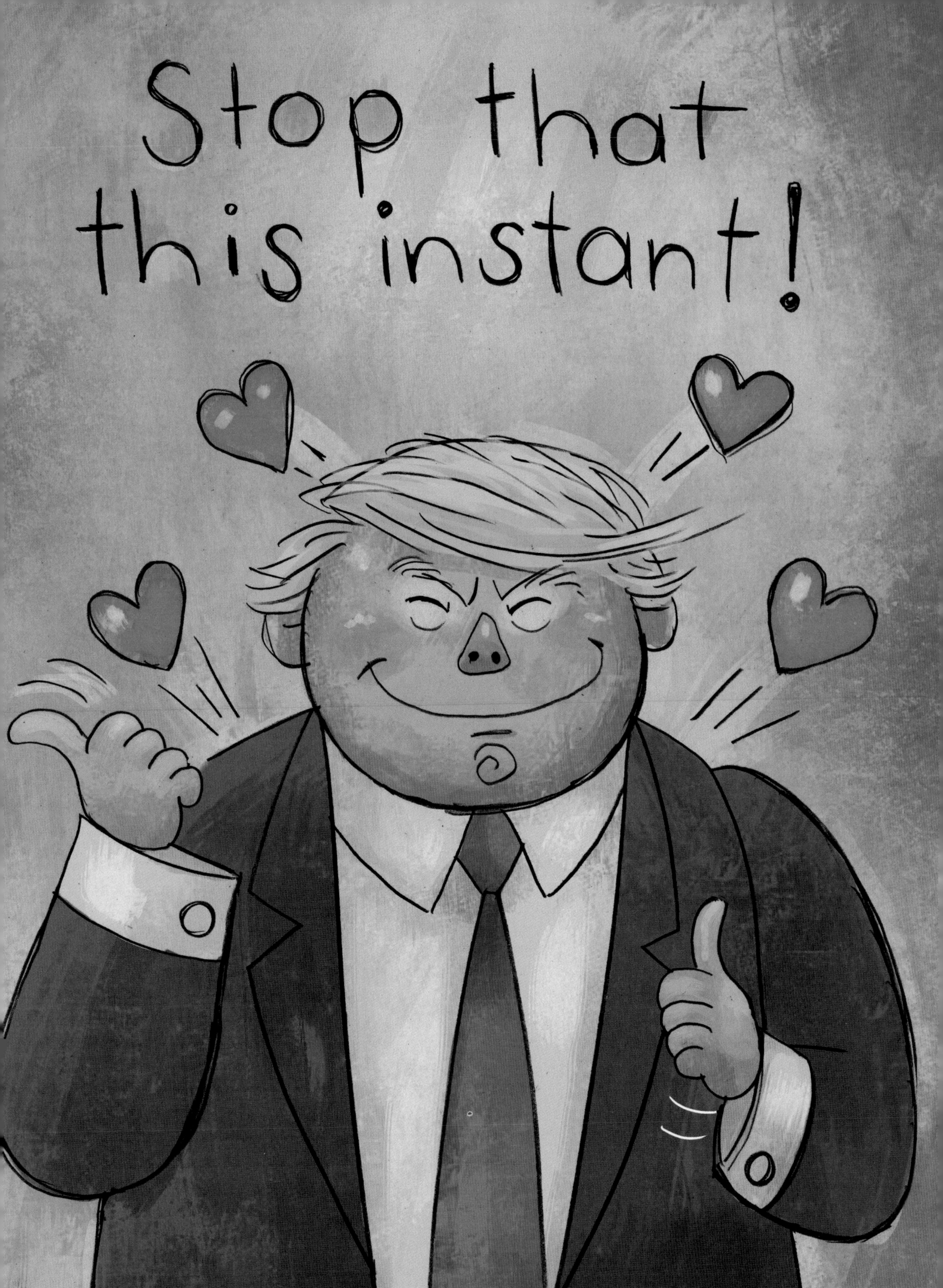
Stop that this instant!

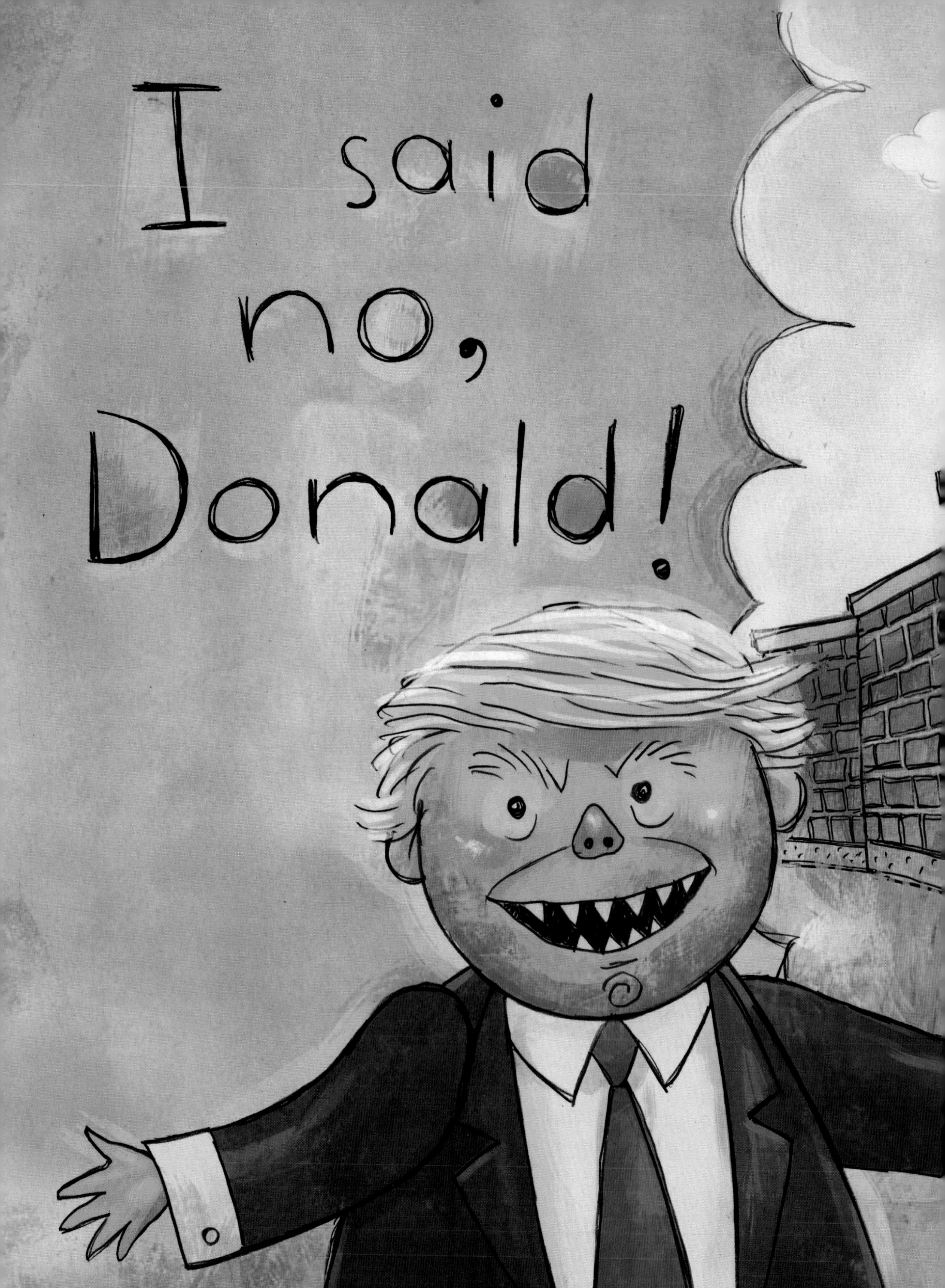
I said no, Donald!

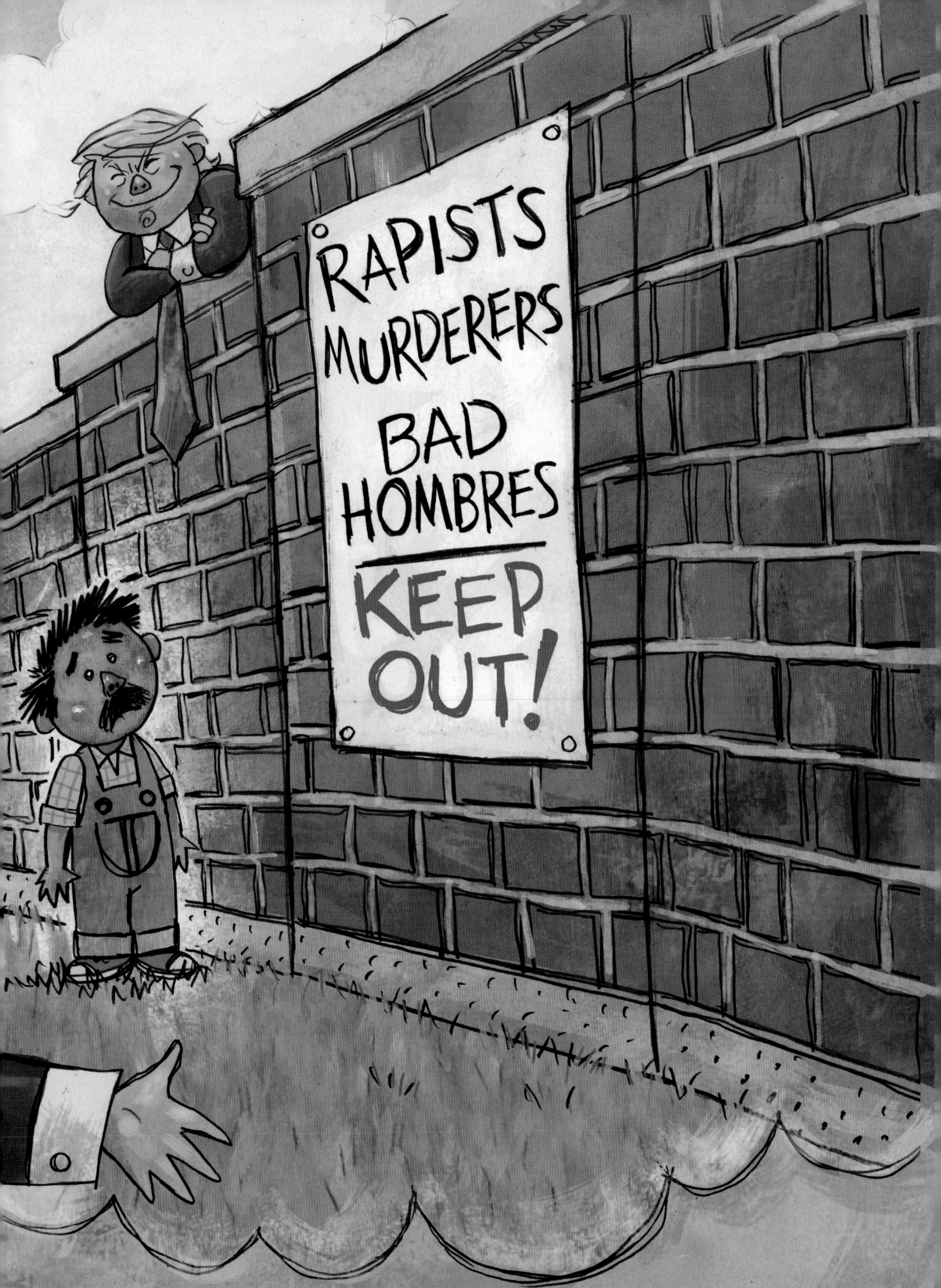
RAPISTS
MURDERERS
BAD
HOMBRES
KEEP
OUT!

Donald,

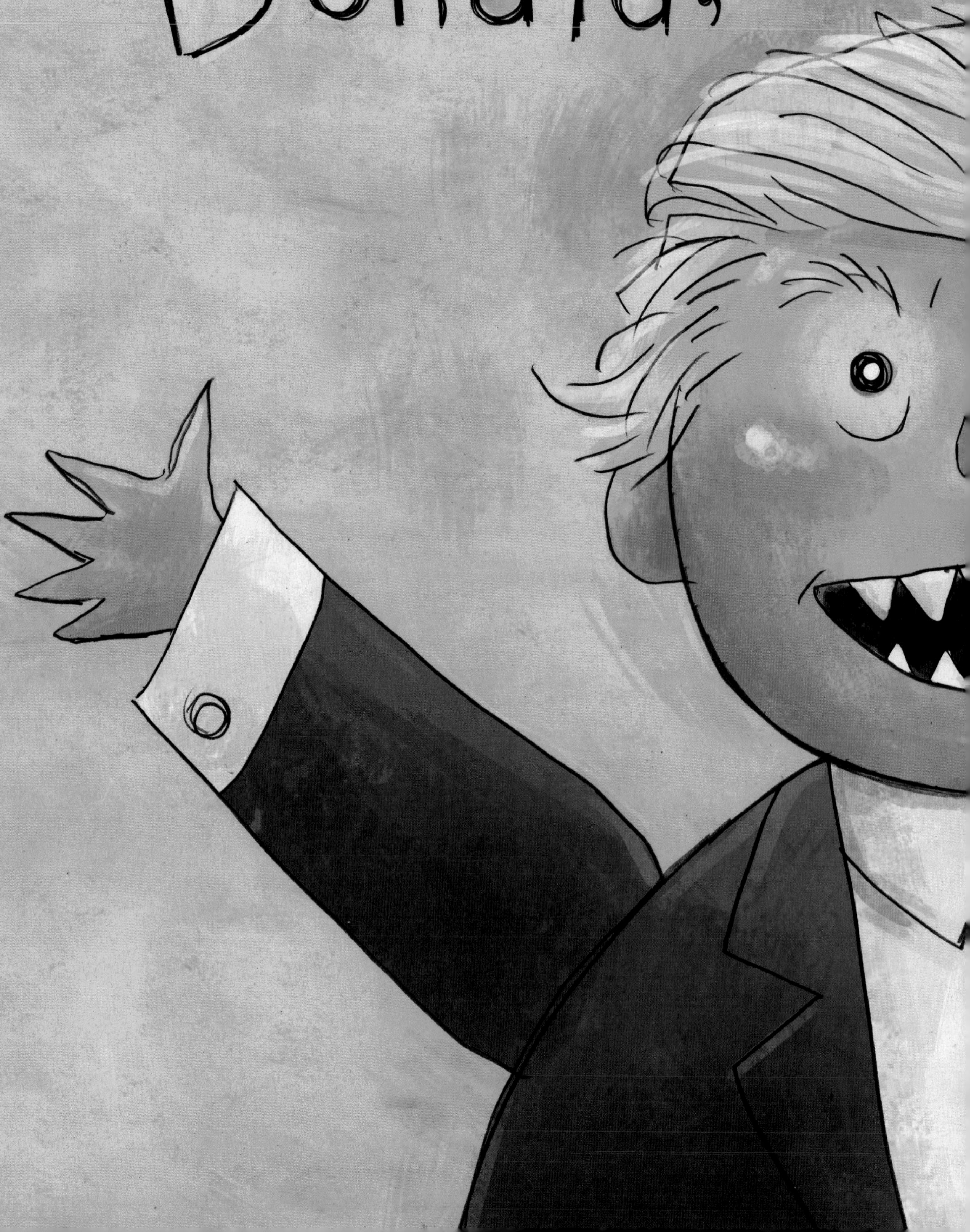

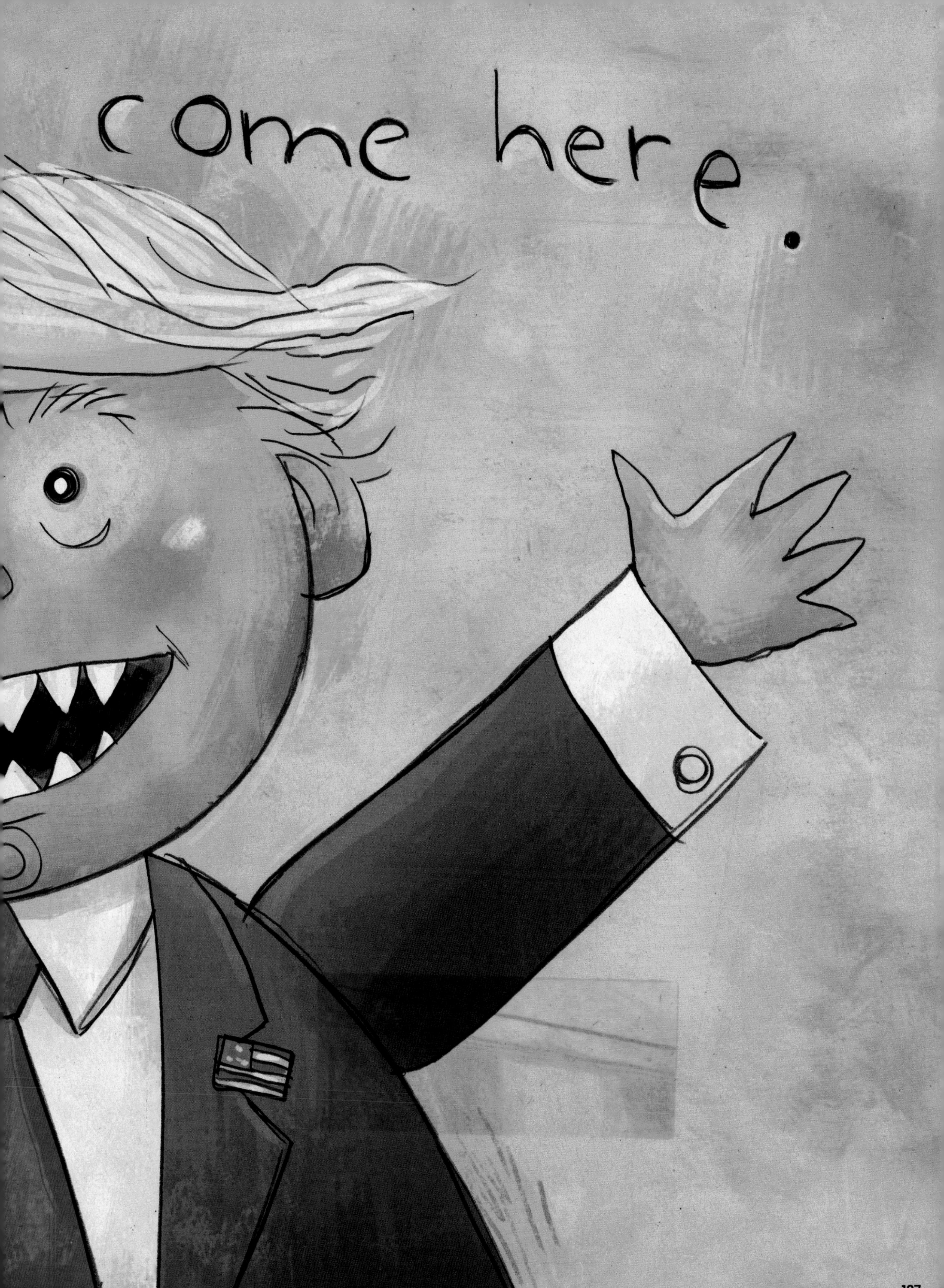
come here.

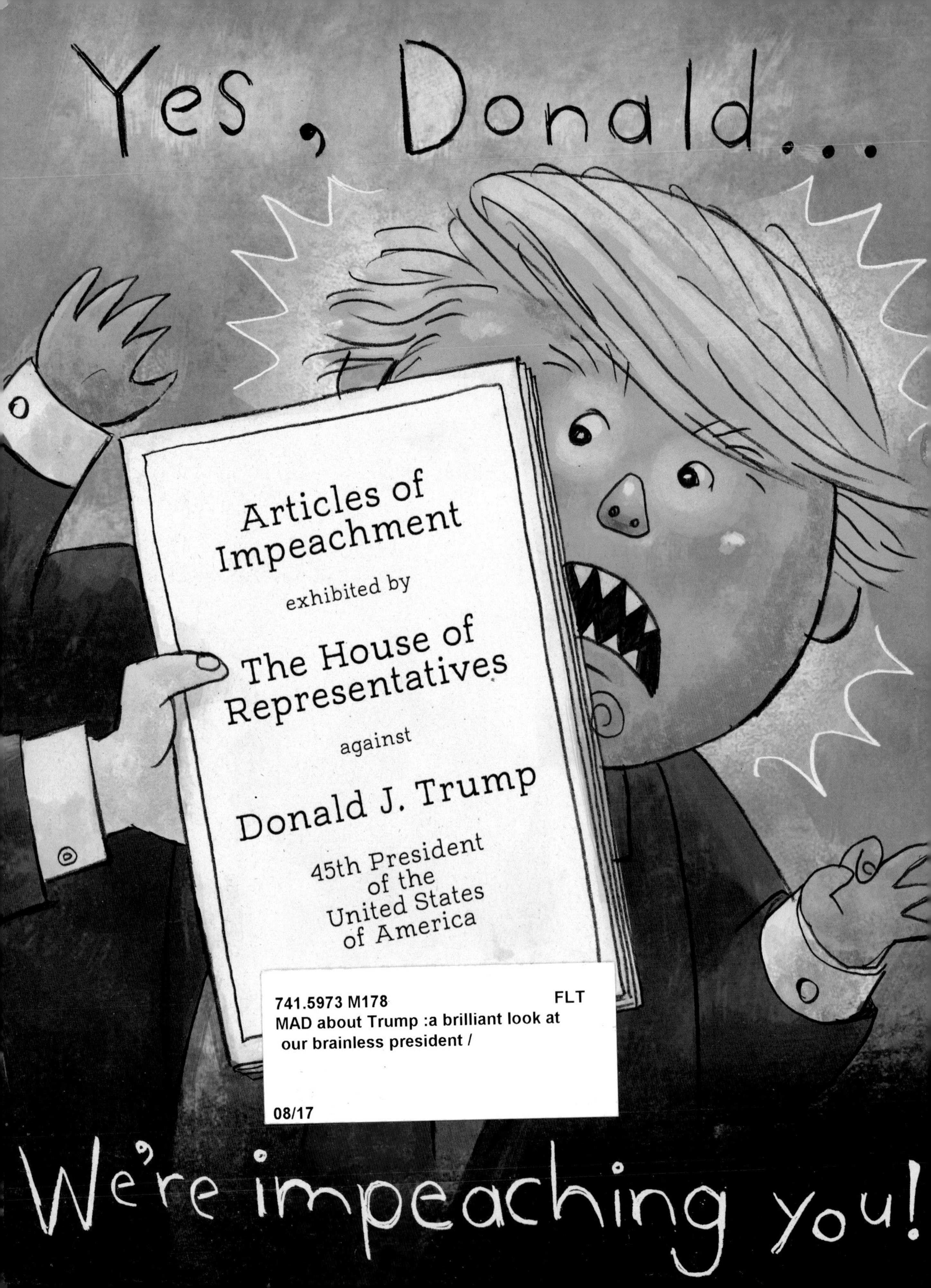
Yes, Donald...
Articles of Impeachment
exhibited by
The House of Representatives
against
Donald J. Trump
45th President of the United States of America
We're impeaching you!